WORDS APART

A DICTIONARY OF NORTHERN IRELAND ENGLISH

WORDS APART

A Dictionary of Northern Ireland English

LORETO TODD

COLIN SMYTHE
Gerrards Cross, 1990

Copyright © 1990 by Loreto Todd

First published in 1990 in Great Britain
by Colin Smythe Ltd., Gerrards Cross, Buckinghamshire

British Library Cataloguing in Publication Data

Todd, Loreto
  Words apart; a dictionary of Northern Ireland English
  1. English language. Northern Irish dialect
  I. Title
  427.9416

ISBN 0–86140–338–X

Produced in Great Britain
Photoset by Textflow Services Ltd., Belfast
and printed and bound by Billing & Sons Ltd., Worcester

CONTENTS

ACKNOWLEDGEMENTS

It would be impossible to list the names of the many people in Northern Ireland who have contributed to this dictionary, because nearly everyone I have ever met there has added something to the items recorded in the following pages. To all of them I owe a debt of gratitude.

The dictionary reflects the linguistic creativity of the Northern Ireland people, their love of language and the fusion of three cultures, the Celtic, the Scottish and the English.

Whilst the dictionary rightly belongs to the Northern Ireland people, I must pay special thanks to my relatives in Armagh, Belfast, Derry and Tyrone, to the Magees, McCauslands, McMillens, McNallys, Morgans, Nolans, Todds and Wallaces. For years they have saved good examples for me and allowed me to interrupt conversations to ask what a certain item meant. I must also thank my informants in Antrim, Down and Fermanagh, and add, in particular, the name of A.N. Seymour who knows the dialect intimately and who revels in its expressiveness.

Since the description which follows is that of my mother tongue, it is perhaps fitting that I should offer most thanks to my mother. She loved her country and her language and was the first living dictionary I ever knew.

SYMBOLS AND ABBREVIATIONS

Pronunciation Guide

Symbols are used sparingly in this book but the following system will give readers an indication of pronunciation. In all Northern Ireland accents *r* is pronounced at the end of words such as *hear* and before consonants in words such as *bird* and *darn*.

Vowels

/i/	the sound of *ee* in *seen*
/ɪ/	the sound of *i* in *sit*
/e/	the sound of *é* in French *thé*
/ɛ/	the sound of *e* in *set*
/a/	the sound of *a* in French *pas*
/a:/	the sound of *aa* in *aah!*
/ɒ/	the sound of *o* in *pot*
/ɔ/	the sound of *aw* in *paw*
/o/	the sound of French *eau*
/u/	the sound of *oo* in *pool*
/ʌ/	the sound of *u* in *but*
/ɜ/	the sound of *ur* in *church*
/ə/	the sound of *e* in unstressed *the*
/ü/	the sound of *oo* in Scots *foot*
/eɪ/	the sound of *ay* in *pay*
/ai/	the sound of *ie* in *pie*
/au/	the sound of *ow* in *how*
/oi/	the sound of *oy* in *joy*

Consonants

/p/	the sound of *p* in *pit*
/b/	the sound of *b* in *bid*

/t/	the sound of *t* in *tot*
/d/	the sound of *d* in *dot*
/k/	the sound of *c* in *card*
/g/	the sound of *g* in *guard*
/f/	the sound of *f* in *fan*
/v/	the sound of *v* in *van*
/θ/	the sound of *th* in *thin*
/ð/	the sound of *th* in *then*
/ᴛ/	a sound intermediate between *t* and *th*. It occurs in the Northern Ireland pronunciation of *tr*, *thr*, and *ter* as in *try*, *through* and *better*.
/ᴅ/	a sound intermediate between *d* and *dh*. It occurs in the Northern Ireland pronunciation of *dr* and *der* as in *dry* and *thunder*.
/s/	the sound of *s* in *Sue*
/z/	the sound of *z* in *zoo*
/x/	the sound of *ch* in Scots *loch*
/ʃ/	the sound of *s* in *sugar*
/ʒ/	the sound of *z* in *azure*
/tʃ/	the sound of *ch* in *chat*
/dʒ/	the sound of *j* in *jot*
/ky/	the sound of *k+y* in *thank you*
/gy/	the sound of *g+y* in *log yet*
/h/	the sound of *h* in *how*
/l/	the sound of *l* in *light* and *full*
/r/	the round of *r* in *row*
/m/	the sound of *m* in *rum*
/n/	the sound of *n* in *run*
/ŋ/	the sound of *ng* in *rung*
/ny/	the sound of *n* in British *news*
/ʍ/	the sound of *wh* distinguishing *which* from *witch*
/w/	the sound of *w* in *wet*
/y/	the sound of *y* in *yet*

Symbols

*	words that are obsolescent
<	derives from

<?   possibly derives from
<<   influenced by

Grammatical Terms

adj.	adjective, adjectival phrase
adv.	adverb, adverbial phrase
conj.	conjunction
exclam.	exclamation
noun	noun, noun phrase
verb	verb, verb phrase

Social Terms

AI	Anglo-Irish, the variety of English spoken by settlers from England.
GAE	General American English, the pronunciation used by US radio and television newsreaders
HE	Hiberno-English, the variety of English spoken by people whose ancestral mother tongue was Irish Gaelic.
NI	Northern Ireland
NHE	Northern Hiberno-English
NIE	Northern Ireland English
SHE	Southern Hiberno-English
RP	Received Pronunciation, the pronunciation used by BBC newsreaders
USc	Ulster Scots, the variety of English spoken by settlers from Scotland.

Languages Cited

AF	Anglo-French
eModE	early Modern English
Du	Dutch
Fr	French
Gael	Irish Gaelic

Lat	Latin
ME	Middle English
ModE	Modern English
OE	Old English
OF	Old French
ON	Old Norse
Sc	Scots
SG/G	Scots Gaelic or Irish Gaelic
unkn	etymology unknown or uncertain

HOW TO USE THIS BOOK

This book is divided into five parts. Section One provides the historical data necessary to a full understanding of the English language in Northern Ireland. The information has been presented simply and, in so far as is humanly possible, objectively. It is not, however, easy to be objective about Northern Ireland because every historical event can be seen from at least two different points of view and even the weather can be a subject of controversy. Perhaps the easiest way to illustrate this point is to quote the lead headlines from two Belfast papers published on the same day, September 19, 1983. Describing the same storm, the *Irish News*, a Catholic paper, proclaimed:

GALE LEAVES WIDE SWATHE OF WRECKAGE

while the *Belfast Telegraph* assured its readers:

ULSTER GETS OFF LIGHTLY AFTER GALES.

This historical section does not try to settle disputes or offer solutions. It merely sets the scene for a fuller understanding of the vocabulary which follows and provides details of the pronunciations found in different areas and different communities.

Section Two is an alphabetically arranged glossary of Northern Ireland dialect words. As in all dialects, many words are dying out and many more have already disappeared. I have recorded as many of these obsolescent words as I could and have indicated their status by means of an asterisk. Each word is followed by an indication of its pronunciation, by its grammatical class (e.g. noun), by an indication of its language of origin (e.g. French) and by a sentence illustrating its use. Most of the sentences are from live speech, recorded in all six counties over a twenty-year period, and those that are from printed sources are marked. The main problems posed by this section related to pronunciation and spelling. Many words have several different

pronunciations. Old people do not pronounce words in
exactly the same way as young ones. Nor can rural speakers
be approximated to people from the cities. In all cases, I
have used the pronunciation of the speaker whose
sentence is quoted or the most widespread pronunciation
for the items from written sources.

The second problem was that some of the words have
written forms while many have not. Where a written form
exists, as with most of the Ulster Scots items, this is the
form selected. Unwritten words are transcribed as simply
and unambiguously as possible. This decision, however,
has resulted in inconsistencies. For example, the word
ending that rhymes with English *rogue* is represented in
three different ways. *Collogue*, meaning 'chat, gossip'
appears in dictionaries with an *ogue* ending; *keerog*,
meaning 'beetle' has not appeared in the written medium;
and *sheeoge*, meaning 'changeling' is given an *oge* ending by
Frances Molloy in her book, *No Mate for the Magpie*.

The glossary provides simple etymologies for words,
where these are known. A thorough etymological dictionary of Northern Ireland English is needed but is a task
in its own right. I have, in addition, provided information
on forms or meanings which may have been reinforced by
words from Irish Gaelic. An example of this may be useful.
In some varieties of NIE, words occur with a different range
of meanings from those found in the standard language.
Cold, for example, means 'cowardly' and 'mean' as well as
'not hot'. Irish Gaelic *fuar* covers these meanings so,
although *cold* (often pronounced *cowl*) comes from English,
its range of meanings has been influenced by Irish Gaelic.

A surprisingly large number of French words occur in the
dialect. Thus we find *ashet* 'plate' from *assiette*, *dishabels*
'night attire, state of undress' from *deshabillé*, *grossarts*
'gooseberries' from *groseilles* and *hogo* 'bad smell' from *haut
goût*.

The third section is an alphabetically arranged glossary of
Standard English words followed by their equivalent(s) in
the dialect. For more precise nuances of meaning and for
exemplary sentences, the reader should refer to Section
Two. An interesting side result of this organisation is the

light it sheds on the condition and the preoccupations of the people. The dialect is rich in synonyms for people, of different size, shape and mental capacity; it allows a speaker to subdivide potatoes in ways that are unknown to users of the standard language; and it reserves its greatest scorn for meanness and lack of hospitality. The people to be avoided are those who are 'as mean as get out' and wouldn't 'give a body daylight'; those to be loved would 'give you the bite out of their mouth' or 'the coat off their back'.

The fourth section is a brief selection of texts from Northern Ireland, some written, some oral. The exemplary sentences in Section Two offer a 'taste' of the dialect and the texts provide extra sustenance. Readers will be able to use them to examine narrative techniques or to attempt an analysis of the grammar of the region. This too warrants a study in its own right.

A short annotated bibliography is provided to allow readers to deepen their knowledge of the culture, history and language of Northern Ireland.

SECTION ONE: BACKGROUND

1.1 NORTHERN IRELAND

Many books and papers have been written about Northern
Ireland, about its people and its current difficulties. Most
have concentrated on political and social matters or commen-
ted on the separate development which has characterised the
two communities for almost four centuries. It is tempting for
anyone with a knowledge of the country to enter the arena
and offer solutions to problems that have been described as
intractable. In this book, however, the temptation has been
resisted. My aim has been to describe aspects of the language
behaviour of the people, all the people, rather than to
prescribe political solutions.

The term 'Northern Ireland' is applied to the six northeas-
terly counties of Ireland, namely Antrim, Armagh, (London-
)Derry, Down, Fermanagh and Tyrone. These counties
remained part of the United Kingdom when the rest of
Ireland gained independence from Britain in 1921. Northern
Ireland is neither a natural nor an historic division of Ireland
but is part of Ulster, a nine-county Province (the other three
counties being Cavan, Donegal and Monaghan).

1.2 HISTORICAL OVERVIEW

No short overview can possibly do justice to the historical
complexity of Northern Ireland or its people. I shall avoid
complexity, therefore, providing only a number of general
points and a list of dates which have been of significance in
the history of the region.

Before the reign of Elizabeth I, most of Northern Ireland
was Gaelic speaking and Catholic. Both Vikings and Anglo-
Normans had settled in the area, but they had been absorbed by the Irish. There had also been a long-standing and
close connection between Northern Ireland and Scotland
but, although some Scots had established themselves as
overlords in parts of Antrim, most of the pre-seventeenth-

century Scottish settlers spoke a variety of Gaelic that was mutually intelligible with the Ulster variety.

During the reigns of Elizabeth (1558–1603) and James I (1603–25), Ulster was seen as the greatest potential danger to English power in Ireland, and so it was singled out to be transformed into a stronghold of English law and authority. The transformation was to be achieved by largescale settlements of Protestants from England and Scotland. Some interaction between the native community and the Planters was inevitable but although English gradually ousted Gaelic as the chief language of the region neither group assimilated the other.

Today, most of the descendants of the Planters regard themselves as British and see their future within the United Kingdom, whereas many in the Catholic community think of themselves as Irish and aspire to some sort of union with Eire. It would be wrong, however, to assume that all Catholics want a United Ireland or that all Protestants refuse to have anything to do with Eire. In a 1984 MORI poll conducted in Northern Ireland, 50% of Catholics claimed that they would be willing to accept a system of government for Northern Ireland within the United Kingdom, provided that there were special guarantees for Catholics. In the same poll, 14% of Protestants were willing to allow the Republic of Ireland some say in constitutional matters in Northern Ireland.

Since the signing of the Anglo-Irish Agreement in November, 1985, both the British Prime Minister and the Irish Taoiseach have repeatedly stated that no change in the constitution of Northern Ireland will occur without the consent of the majority of the people in the province.

The following facts will provide the reader with the significant dates and events in the history of Northern Ireland.

1558	Elizabeth succeeds her Catholic sister, Mary
1561–7	Shane O'Neill's rebellion and death
1570	Elizabeth excommunicated by Rome
1587	Hugh O'Neill becomes Earl of Tyrone
1595	Hugh O'Neill proclaimed traitor by Elizabeth declares war on Elizabeth

1601	Hugh O'Neill defeated at Kinsale
1607	Flight of the Earls
	many find refuge in Europe
1608ff	Major Plantation of Ulster
1641	Catholic rebellion in Ulster
1649–51	Cromwellian campaign
	massacres of Catholics
1689	Siege of Derry
	Protestants withstand James II
1690	Battle of the Boyne
	William of Orange victorious
1695ff	Penal Laws against Dissenters
1795	Formation of the Orange Order
1798	'98 Rebellion of the United Irishmen
1800	Act of Union: Ireland integrated into Britain
1829	Catholic Emancipation
1840s	Young Ireland Movement:
	free Ireland envisaged
1845–47	The Great Hunger: over one million die
	hundreds of thousands emigrate
	Gaelic declines as the majority language
1886	Gladstone's first Home Rule Bill
1893	Gaelic League Movement:
	attempt to revive the language and establish
	an independent Ireland
	Gladstone's second Home Rule Bill
1905	Sinn Fein (Ourselves Alone) Movement
1912	Home Rule Bill
	Ulster Volunteers founded by Edward Carson
	UVF threaten rebellion if Home Rule granted
1914	World War 1: Home Rule Bill suspended
1916	Easter Rising in Dublin: leaders executed
1918	Last all-Ireland elections:
	clear mandate for independent Ireland
1919–21	War between England and Ireland
1921	Anglo-Irish Treaty:
	6 counties to remain British
	26 counties to become 'Irish Free State'
1922–23	Civil War in Ireland because of Treaty
1925	Partition of Ireland confirmed
1948	Republic of Ireland declared

1956–62 IRA Campaign in Northern Ireland
1965   Meeting between Northern Ireland Prime
         Minister, Terence O'Neill, and Irish
         Taoiseach, Sean LeMass
1968   Civil Rights Campaign by Catholics in
         Northern Ireland: leading demand 'One man
         one vote'
1969   British troops deployed in Northern Ireland
1971   Internment without trial
1973   Elections for Assembly at Stormont:
         power-sharing not achieved
1980   Anglo-Irish Intergovernmental Council
1983   New Ireland Forum assembled in Dublin
1984   New Ireland Forum reports
1985   Anglo-Irish Agreement signed by Margaret
         Thatcher and Garret Fitzgerald bitterly
         opposed by most Ulster Protestants
1986   Stormont Assembly disbanded

1.3 THE EMERGENCE OF NORTHERN IRELAND ENGLISHES

By 1611, English speakers from Scotland and England had
settled in all six counties of present-day Northern Ireland.
Braidwood (1964: 6) provides the following estimate for the
middle of the seventeenth century:

County	Planters	Irish	Total
Antrim	7,074	8,965	16,039
Armagh	2,393	4,355	6,748
Cavan	6,485	8,218	14,703
Derry	4,428	5,306	9,734
Donegal	3,412	8,589	12,001
Down	6,540	8,643	15,183
Fermanagh	1,800	5,302	7,102
Monaghan	434	3,649	4,083
Tyrone	8,085	10,245	18,330
Ulster	40,651	63,272	103,923

Estimated Population in Seventeenth Century

These figures are probably an underestimate since, at the time of the 1641 rebellion, it was believed that there were 100,000 Scots and 20,000 English settlers in Ulster (Braidwood: 6). The ratio of approximately two planters to every three native Irish seem reasonable in view of the fact that further settlers were encouraged after 1641 and again after 1690.

The proportions of Planter to native Irish were reversed by 1733 when it was estimated that the Ulster population was made up of 62,624 planter families as against 38,459 native Irish or Catholic families (Braidwood: 7) and, although the population has increased during the intervening centuries, the proportions are roughly the same today.

It is not certain when Gaelic speakers adopted English, but by the time of the 1911 census Gaelic had all but disappeared, being claimed as a mother tongue by only 2.3% of the population of the six counties. It continued to live on in the Glens of Antrim and Rathlin Island as well as in the Sperrin Mountains of Tyrone (where it died out as a mother tongue in the mid 1960s), but for most people in Northern Ireland English was the preferred medium.

The native Irish must have learnt their English originally from Planters and so would have been influenced by English or Scottish norms, depending on the strength of English or Scottish settlers in the area. It seems likely, however, that Gaelic continued to influence their pronunciation, vocabulary and idiom. The influence of Gaelic did not diminish as quickly as might be expected because of the segregated nature of Northern Ireland society. Even today, there are two entirely distinct education systems: a state system (which is almost exclusively Protestant) and an independent Catholic system. 1988 has seen the first government-inspired moves for integrated education but both communities view the experiment with suspicion. There are also two separate systems of teacher training with the result that Catholic children are taught by Catholic teachers who were trained by Catholic lecturers. It is only in Polytechnics and at University level that education can accurately be described as non-denominational.

Nor is the segregation limited to education. Catholics and Protestants tend to consult dentists, doctors and solicitors from their own communities. As Boyle and Hadden (1985: 57) claim:

> *It is perfectly possible, and quite normal, to live a full and varied life in Northern Ireland without having any real contact with people from the other community.*

1.4 NORTHERN IRELAND ENGLISHES

All speech in Northern Ireland is influenced by media norms and all varieties are rhotic, that is, the 'r' is pronounced in words such as 'par' and 'park'. Nevertheless, it is possible to distinguish three main types of English:

1. Anglo-Irish (AI), the English spoken by the descendants of settlers from England
2. Ulster Scots (USc), the English spoken by the descendants of Scots
3. Hiberno-English (HE), the English spoken by people whose ancestral mother tongue was Gaelic.

It must be stressed, however, that these three types overlap and interinfluence each other.

ANGLO-IRISH is a variety of English spoken over most of Ulster. It is descended from English brought to Ireland by seventeenth-century Planters from England, modified by contacts with Gaelic, Ulster Scots and Hiberno-English. Like the other varieties, AI is really a spectrum of Englishes, influenced by the education and the regional origin of its speakers. The 'r' is pronounced in words such as *dark* and *deer* and, in this as in other respects, AI shows certain similarities to General American English (GAE).

Educated AI speakers approximate to network norms whereas uneducated speakers have a markedly different distribution of vowel sounds.

1. Words such as *sea, tea* have the same vowel sound as *day, hay*
2. *old* words are frequently realised as *-owl* so that *hold* and *howl, old* and *owl* are identical in pronunciation.
3. There is a set of commonly occurring words, including *bull, bullet, bush, butcher, could, cushion, foot, full, look, pull, pullet, push, put, shook, took, wood, wool* and *would* which are pronounced with the vowel sound that occurs in *hut*.
4. There is also a tendency for all short vowels (with the exception of the unstressed vowel in words like 'the') to be realised as 'a' in rapid speech, and thus *pat, pit* and *pot* are often almost indistinguishable in sound.

Speakers of AI use many words which are not part of standard British usage. These include:

1. words which are no longer current in the standard language:
   cog (cheat)
   mitch (play truant)
2. words which occur with different meanings:
   backward (shy)
   doubt (strongly believe)
3. words which are restricted now to other dialects:
   akwent (familiar with)
   unbeknownst (unknown)

It should be added that many regionally-marked words are dying out in Northern Ireland as in other parts of Britain.

The grammar of uneducated speakers of AI includes many features which are found in other non-standard varieties:

1. use of *done* and *seen* instead of 'did' and 'see' in affirmative, past tense sentences:
   He done you no favour.
   He seen you coming.
2. use of alternative past tense and past participles:
   clum (climbed)

  took (took, taken)
  wrought (worked)
3. use of 'a + past tense' for 'have + past participle':
   She would a took the foot off you.
   You might a knew.
4. use of *them* as a demonstrative plural adjective and
   pronoun:
   He has them shoes yet.
   Them's the ones I want.
5. use of different forms of the verb 'be'
   John and Mary's (are) tired so they are.
   Mary and me's of an age.
   Yiz is tired.
   We be tired now.

and it is probably true to say that non-standard features are
tolerated higher up the social ladder than in other parts of
Britain.

ULSTER SCOTS (USc) is a variety of Scottish English
spoken mainly in parts of Antrim, Down and the northern
part of (London)Derry. Like the Lowland Scots from which
it comes, it occurs in a variety of forms closely related to the
extent of one's education and social position. It is still
possible to find speakers:

1. who use markedly Scots pronunciations in that they
   rhyme:
   blood with *good*
   cow with *shoe*
   die with *see*
   do with *say*
   ground with *soon*
   home with *came*
   long with *sang*
   more with *share*
   own with *sane*
2. who often omit the 'l' sound in words such as *call* and *fall*
3. who roll the 'r' sound especially in words like *rat* or *red*
4. and who distinguish between 'loch' and 'lock'.

Such speakers, however, tend to be over fifty and rural. Education and media influences have eradicated many of the most distinctively Scottish features from the pronunciation of the young.

A similar point can be made about vocabulary. Young people, especially those in towns, rarely use:

bairn (child)
brae (hill)
burn (stream)
een (eyes)
fash (anger, angry)
gar (make)
gey (very)
greet (cry)

but they would recognise them and would possibly use them as a marker of humour or intimacy.

The grammar of Ulster Scots also varies with the age and education of the speaker. Many older, rural speakers still produce:

Dinna ye ken? (Don't you know?)
where their children prefer:
Do you not know?
but the use of *nae/ny* is still widely found as a negative, especially with *can, could, does, will*:
I canny get it to sit.
He couldny come.
He disnae want for to see her.
She willny tell me.

HIBERNO-ENGLISH (HE) is a variety of English employed mainly by uneducated speakers whose ancestral mother tongue was Gaelic. This variety is strongest in rural areas and in parts of the country such as the Glens of Antrim and the Sperrin Mountains in Tyrone, where pockets of Gaelic speakers survived until the 1960s.

In pronunciation, HE speakers approximate to the AI or USc norms of the area but certain features of Gaelic are preserved. These include the tendency to:

1. use 'cy' and 'gy' in words such as:
   cyart (cart)
   gyarden (garden)
2. call the eighth letter of the alphabet 'haitch' rather than 'aitch'
3. pronounce names like *Hugh/Hughes* as if they began with 'ky':
   Did you see Kyughie Green last night?

The vocabulary of HE contains many words from Gaelic although most of them have been anglicised in that they take English endings:

banshee (fairy woman) *banshees*
bum (boast) *bums, bumming*
moilly (bald) *moillier*

As we might expect, the majority of the Gaelic words that survive in HE relate to cultural beliefs, farming, food and social interaction:

cairn (stone mound associated with the supernatural)
camogie (game)
caulcannon (food)
ceilidhe (get-together)
clabber (mud)
clamp (method of cutting turf)
clannish (cliquish)
cuddy (one's share)

A number of other Irish items occur in translation. They include:

be on the pig's back (be extremely comfortable)
plead a poor mouth (complain about poverty)
walk on hungry grass (be excessively hungry)

And malapropisms are a marked feature of the language of many HE speakers:

And then, God help him, ammonia (pneumonia) *set in.*
Half these people haven't paid their descriptions
(subscriptions).
He was caught thryin till ajax (hijack) *a lorry.*
She was as cool as a concubine (cucumber).
She was furious. Talk about fire and broomsticks (brimstone)!

In grammar, HE speakers again reflect the norms of their English-speaking neighbours but the following tendencies, related to Gaelic, are frequent in their speech.

1. In conversation, questions often begin with 'and', always pronounced 'an':

   An will you go?
   An what did she say?

   Part of the reason for this is that Gaelic questions often began with an unstressed 'an':

   An rabh tú? (Were you?)
   An maith leat é? (Do you like it?)

2. Questions are rarely answered by 'yes/no':
   An will you go? I will, surely.
   An did you tell her? I did not!

   Once again, this is partly a relic of Gaelic, which did not have words for 'yes' and 'no':

   An racaidh tú? (Will you go?)
   Racaidh, cinnte. (I will go, surely.)

3. There is a tendency to use nouns where other speakers of English would prefer verbs:

   Give me the full of it. (Fill it.)
   Put ears on ye. (Listen attentively.)
   Cut that apple into three divides. (Divide that apple in three.)

4. Prepositions + pronouns occur at the end of sentences, sometimes implying non-English meanings:

   My head's always at me. (I always have a headache.)
   or appearing to be redundant:
   You've lost me book on me.

5. We find the use of foregrounding, that is, emphasising part of the sentence by stating it first:

It's John I seen. (I saw John.)
It's themselves they must blame. (They must blame themselves/accept reponsibility.)
Well now, me myself I do it this road. (I do it this way.)

6. The verb 'be' is used differently in such constructions as:

I don't be at myself until dinner-time. (I don't feel right until midday.)
She doesn't be confused all the time.

7. We also find the use of 'after + ing', to indicate a recently performed action:

I'm after doing it. (I have just done it.)
This usage is derived from Gaelic:
Tá mé indhiaidh/tar éis sin a dheanamh. (I'm after doing it = I have just done it.)

8. 'And + pronoun/noun + ing' constructions are used to indicate that two actions occurred at the same time:

He came in and me singing.
She walked out and John talking.

The Gaelic equivalents of these sentences are:

Tháinig sé istigh agus mé ag ceol. (Came he inside and I singing [at music])
Shiubhal sí amuigh agus Seán ag cainnt. (Walked she out and John talking [at talk]).

9. There is a tendency to use the present participle more often than is usual in English:

I'm wondering if you're going into town.
You're asking for a quare lacing, boy. (You deserve a good beating.)

10. HE speakers often use expressions involving 'God':

In the name o' God, what do you think you're at?

I am not, of course, claiming that the above structures could never occur in the speech of a USc or an AI speaker. The communities have, after all, lived in the same country for four centuries and it would be most unusual if the influence was all one-way traffic. Nor am I denying that some of the above structures may occur elsewhere in the English-speaking world. I am, however, suggesting that Gaelic has affected the speech of the original natives of Northern Ireland in much the same way that African languages have influenced the English of creole-speaking West Indians.

1.5 OVERLAPPING VARIANTS

The three varieties of English described above are not, of course, separate or even separable. The sound systems of all three are similar in many respects. The majority of speakers in Northern Ireland when they are speaking to family and friends:

1. use 'in' for 'ing' in almost all contexts
2. say 'an' for 'and'
3. use what sounds like 'th' and 'dh' instead of 't' and 'd' when 't' and 'd' are followed by 'r' and 'er':
   dhry (dry)
   thry (try)
   cotther (poor person)
   ordher (order)
4. tend to delete the 'th' in words containing '-ther':
   fa'er (father)
   wea'er (weather)

   Neither of these rules applies to words where the '-er' is attached to a verb and means 'one who/which + verb'. Thus we have:

   butter (one who butts)
   footer (one who uses a particular foot)

   but:

   butther (butter)
   foother (fidget clumsily, clumsy person)

and:

bather (one who bathes)
but:

la'er (lather).

5. use 'cowl', 'owl, 'towl' pronunciations of 'cold', 'old', 'told'. Among older speakers, especially from rural areas, we also find:

bowl (bold) (more)*bowler* (most)*bowlest*
bowlt (bolt)
cowlt (colt)
howl (hold as in *I howl ye* = I assure you)
howlt (hold as in *ketch a howlt o'* = catch hold of)
jowlt (jolt) *jowlted* (jolted)
mowl (mould, usually in the fixed phrase *torf mowl*)
rowl (roll)
sowl (sold, soul).

6. use /e/ instead of /i/ in such words as:

beak (especially in *'Shut your bake.'*)
beast
beat
cheat
conceity (*'She's consaty of herself.'*)
deal (*'I wouldn't dale with him.'*)
decent
eat
Jesus (as an exclamation, not in prayers)
leave
mean
meat
peace (especially in *'Give me head pace.'*)
seat
speak
steal.

7. use the same 'a' sound for:

gas and *grass*
Sam and *psalm*

8. rhyme *bull* with *dull* and *put* with *cut*.

9. lose 'd' after 'l' and 'n'

    chile (child)
    gol (gold)
    ban (band)
    foun (found)

    The loss does not occur with grammatical endings:

    ailed (ailed)
    filled (filled)
    banned (banned)
    fined (fined).
    'T' is lost after 'p' in *kep* (kept) and *slep* (slept).

10. use a great deal of elision:
    Am tired. (I + am tired)
    monly chile (my + only child)
    thawful man (the + awful man)

11. use a plural form of 'you', usually *yiz* in rapid speech
    and *youz* in slower speech (*youse* in writing). *Yizins* and
    youzins also occur:

    Yiz is stupid!
    Here, youse boys, over here.
    Youzins is not a wantin.

12. frequently use 'you/youse' in imperative structures:
    Go you on home.
    Make you yourself a cup o' tea there.
    Shut you your mouth.
    Don't you bother your barney. I'll do it meself.
    Don't youse let on now.

13. prefer to use the full form 'not' in such sentences as:

    He'll not do. (He won't do.)
    Do you not understand? (Don't you understand?)

14. use several negatives for emphasis:

    She never knows nothin when it comes to the bit.
    I never say nothin to nobody. I always mind what me ma said:
    'A shut mouth makes a wise head.'

Double negatives can also occur in tag questions. I have recorded all of the following:

I didn't do it, didin a not?
He wouldn't go, wouldin he not?
They can't do nothin, can'tin they not?
You won't hit me, won'tin ye not?

15. share with other speakers of non-standard English the use of such structures as:

I done/seen it
I have went/I would a went/clum
them things
He fell from off o' the roof

1.6   EDUCATED SPEECH

In Northern Ireland, as in other parts of the world, educated speakers approximate to Standard English in vocabulary and grammar. In pronunciation, three main models are followed:

1. Received Pronunciation (otherwise known as BBC English). Two very small groups of people have RP accents. The first is made up of men who were educated in England. In the past, they held commissions in the British army and were, like the former Prime Minister, Captain Terence O'Neill, virtually indistinguishable in accent from an RP speaker from England. The second group have modelled their accents on BBC norms and can be found in media work.
2. RU or Received Ulster. Many broadcasters speak Standard English with a Northern Ireland regional accent. Such media people are more influential as models than RP speakers.
3. RI or Received Irish. Many Catholics listen to Radio Eireann and watch RTE (Radio Telefís Eireann) where Southern Hiberno-English is the norm. This variety of English is also popular in the media in England, especially in chat shows.

Educated speakers tend not to reveal their regional or religious affiliations as obviously as uneducated speakers do, but the majority would easily be recognised as coming from Ulster.

SECTION TWO: DICTIONARY

This section is a dictionary of Northern Ireland English and the following conventions are used.

* Words that no longer occur frequently in the dialect are marked with an asterisk. Some of the words, such as *heckle* meaning 'comb', have died out completely. Others occur only in the speech of the elderly and so are likely to disappear from use.

(HE) indicates that the word occurs most frequently in the language of Hiberno-English speakers. These are speakers whose ancestors spoke Irish Gaelic.

(USc) indicates that the word occurs most frequently in the language of Ulster Scots speakers. The ancestors of these speakers came originally from Scotland.

NORTHERN IRELAND ENGLISH – ENGLISH

A

a- /a/, prefix. Often used as an alternative to **be-** as in 'afore/before', 'ahind/behind', 'atween/between'.
    < ME 'a-,an, on' = on, in, by
    Put it ahine the press (cupboard) *there.*
a-...ing /a-...ɪn/, passive verb.
    < eModE 'a-doing' = in the process of doing
    << Gael 'á dheanamh' = being done
    The chile's a-chokin. (The child is being choked.)
    The woman's a-killin. (The woman is being killed.)
    You're a-lookin at home. (The people at home are looking for you.)
*aback /abak/, adv. and prep. behind, to the rear. Now most frequently heard in the phrases 'heavy-aback' (heavy towards the rear) and 'light-aback'.
    < ME 'abak' = to the back of

They're from aback o' beyon.
*Don't put the load so far forrid in the cyart. It's too heavy aback
on the horse.*

abed /abed/, adv. in bed.
   ME 'abedde' = in bed
   You're not still abed an it past ten?

abide /abaid/, verb. almost always used negatively with
'can/could', endure, put up with.
   < ME 'abiden' = abide, wait for
   I cyant abide thon uppity crayther (that vain person).

able /iəbəl/, adj. strong, physically fit, well-to-do.
   < ME 'able' = fit, wealthy
   He's as able as a cyart-horse but he's lazy with it.
   *Half the boyos that diz be on the sick biz able enough to go to
   dances.*
   *They may be able enough now but I mind them when they hadn't
   tuppence.*

*****ablins** /ablɪnz/, adv. perhaps.
   < Sc 'aiblins' = maybe, perhaps
   Ablins ye've heerd o' Mums Chance that was hung for thinkin.

*****aboon** (USc) /abün/, adv. on top of, over and above.
   < ME 'abuven' = above, over
   Ye've wet your shoes an socks an your feet aboon.

abroad /abrɔd/, adv. out, outside.
   < ME 'abrode' = in the open, from home
   Is your mother in? No, she's abroad the day.

ach /ax, ɒx/, conj. and exclam. expression of depression or
impatience.
   < Sc 'och' = exclamation
   << Gael 'ach' = but
   Ach but I'm tired o' rain, rain, rain.
   Ach give me head pace (peace).

acquent /akwɛnt/, verb. introduced, well known.
   < ME 'aqueynt' = acquainted
   They seem to be well acquent now.

aff /af/, adv. and prep. off, from.
   < ME 'of' = of, off
   << ON 'af' = of, off
   Get that wet coat aff now.
   Get aff o' that roof. It's bost (hollow).

afoot /afʌt/, adv. going on.
　< ME 'on fote' = up and about
　There's throuble afoot, a howl ye (I assure you)!
afore /afor/, adv., conj. and prep. before, in front of.
　< ME 'afore' = before
　Ye'll dhrink a wee dhrop o' somethin afore ye go?
　Did John go afore? Aye but Jimmy was there afore him.
agin /agɪn/, prep. against, as a measure of protection
against.
　< ME 'agein' = against
　<< Gael 'in-aghaidh' = against, as a protection against
　Put the chair agin the door there. Th'owl snib's away with it.
　(The old bolt is broken.)
　Ye may get plenty o' firin (fuel) *in agin the winther. By the look*
　o' them berries, it'll be a hardy (tough) *one.*
*agley (USc) /agle/, adj. disordered, not right.
　< ME 'gley' = squint
　Everything's went agley since the wife went intae the hospital.
ail /iəl/, verb. be wrong with.
　< OE 'eglan' = trouble, afflict
　What ails ye, chile? Have ye a sore head (headache)?
aisy /iəzi/, adj. and adv. easy, gently.
　< ME 'aise' = ease
　Don't be thinkin that aisy chair's yours. We all like a go in it.
　Hit it nice an aisy now. Don't be thickwitted (rough) *with it.*
*alane (USc) /alen/, adj. alone.
　< ME 'al' + 'ane' = all + one
　Alane, alane, al' al' alane,
　A thramp ma lanesome way.
　(Traditional ballad, 'The Tramp')
*alanna (HE) /alana/, endearment. darling.
　< Gael 'a leanbh' = child, darling
　You are goin away, alanna,
　Across the rolling sea.
　And never more, alanna,
　O never, asthore mo cree (treasure of my heart)...
　(Traditional ballad, 'Seamus')
amina /aməna/, verb. Am I not?
　< eModE 'am not I' = am I not
　I'm goin till the dance, amina Mommy?

*amplush /amplʌʃ/, noun and verb. nonplus.

   < Lat 'non plus' = nothing further

   << Gaelic 'amplais' = jeopardy, dilemma

   Nothing daunts or dashes him or puts him to an amplush.
(William Carleton (1794–1869), *Denis O'Shaughnessy
Going to Maynooth*)

   *Like I'm not often at a loss for somethin to say but thon boy had
me teetotally amplushed!*

an /an, ən/, conj. and, while at the same time.

   < ME 'and' = and

   << Gael 'agus' = and, while at the same time

   Me an Sam an Cecil's all goin.

   He came in an him singin.

anaisy /aniəzi/, adv. uncaring, indifferent.

   < ME 'un/on' + 'aise' = unease

   *I'm anaisy about him. The day's long gone when he could crack
his finger at me.*

anger /aŋər/, noun and verb. temper, vex.

   < ON 'angra' = grieve, vex

   Th'owl anger got up in her.

   Don't anger me or I'll give you the rounds o' the kitchen (a good
beating).

annoy /anoi/, verb. disturb, upset.

   < ME 'anui/anoy' = vexation

   She's badly annoyed. The chile won't do (live).

apricock /iəprɪkɒk/, noun. apricot.

   < eModE 'abricock' = apricot

   My father sold fish an fruit an maybe at a set time (time of
celebration) *one o' the nobs or big bucks would a ordhered a
crab now or a basket of apricocks, but we wouldn't a touched
them things. They were too dear for an ordinary body.*

Aprile /eprail/, noun. April.

   < Lat 'Aprilis' = April

   Aprile usually sees a torn (turn = change) *in the weather.*

ark /ark/, noun. container for grain or flour.

   < Lat 'arca' = box, chest

   << Gael 'airc' = chest, coffer

   *Did ye hear this one? There was this girl an she had the boyfrien
home for the first time like an she wanted to make a good
impression so she called to the brother:*

'Bring some meal in from the ark.'
An the brother took the meal out o' the bag. Well this went on
about ten times till the wee boy got tired of it. In he land wi' the
bag an says:
'There's ark an all.'

*armory /armǝri/, noun. sideboard.
< Fr 'armoire' = cupboard, sideboard
They done away wi' the big armories when they rightified the
house.

arra (HE) /ara/, interjection implying a polite or friendly
disagreement.
< Gael 'a dhia!' = God!
          'ara' = now, really
Arra they're only young. Don't be too hard on them.

*ashet /aʃǝt/, noun. large plate.
< Fr 'assiette' = plate
Ye needn't put wee fancy plates down till our boys. It's more
like ashets ye'd want.

ashypot /aʃipɒt/, noun. person who always sits close to
the fire.
< Sc 'ashypet' = menial servant
Will ye come out o' the fire, ye ashypot ye! Ye're nivir done
washin the divil's dishes (poking the fire).

ass-about-face /asabautfiǝs/, adv. the wrong way.
< ME 'arse' + 'about' + 'face' = buttocks + about +
face
Educated he may be but he has a rotten habit o' doin everything
ass-about-face.

astray in the mind, head /asтre ɪn ðǝ main, hed/, adj.
terribly worried.
< ME 'astraie' = wandering
I'm asthray in the mine, chile. I don't know where the next bite's
comin from.

*asthore (HE) /asтor/, endearment. darling.
< Gael 'a stór' = treasure
Come in, asthore. Sure ye're more than welcome!

*athra (USc) /aтra/, adv. the wrong way.
< ON 'um thvert' = over in a transverse direction
Can ye not see that ye've got it all athra?

*atomy /atəmi/, noun. an insignificant person.

   < Lat 'atomus/i' = atom/s

   Is it him? Thon atomy? Ye'd see bigger things up a three.

*attercap /atərkyap/, noun. a bad-natured and bad-tempered person.

   < OE 'attorcoppe' = spider (lit. poison cap)

   She's an owl athercap! Ye couldn't put yir foot on her pad but she'd be shoutin: 'Don't you be micking (making) *a footpad o' my property.'*

*ava (USc) /ava/, adv. at all.

   < Sc 'ava' = at all

   It's pain tae meet him whun A walk,

   Or meet him nae ava.

   (G. Savage-Armstrong, 'The Wee Lassie's First Luve')

*avoirdupois /avərdʒupoiz/, adj. imperial weight.

   < ME 'averdepeis' = have weight

   Now would that be averduipoise or throy weight?

a-waitin-on /awetɪnɒn/, adj. close to death, about to die.

   < eModE 'a waiting' = in the process of waiting

   Owl Joe's a-waitin on.

away /awe/, verb. go away.

   < OE 'on wea' = away

   Away you on home! Away an cla moul (claw mould) *on yourself!*

away in the head /awe ɪn ðə hed/, adj. mad, crazy.

   You're away in the head! Who's goin to pay thirty thousand for a dundherin-in?

*axe /aks/, verb. ask.

   < OE 'acsian' = ask

   Will ye come wi' me for till axe for the daughther?

aye /aːi/, adv. always.

   < ME 'ai' = ever

   He was aye thrifty, never peeled two spuds if one would do.

aye /aːi/, affirmative. yes.

   < eModE 'aye' = yes

   Will ye go? Aye, I will.

*azebra /azibra/, noun. zebra.

   < eModE 'zebra' = striped wild ass

   Has an azebra got black sthripes or white?

*azoo /azu/, noun. zoo.
  < ModE 'zoo' = zoological garden
  If yiz is good childher, your father'll take yiz to the azoo in Dublin.

B

ba /ba:/, noun. child, youngest.
  < ME 'baban' = babe
  << Gael 'báb' = babe
  An where's the ba the day?
back /bak/, adj., adv., noun and verb. back, back garden, put money on a horse.
  < OE 'bæk' = back
  Go you home the back road so that nobody'll see ye.
  Will ye lave that back (return that) *for me?*
  The childher's in the back playin.
  I'm backin nahin the day. I'm as poor as Lazarus.
backchat /baktʃat/, noun and verb. cheeky talk.
  < OE 'bæk' + ME 'chatter' = chat
  I'll have none o' your backchat, me girl.
backend /baken/, noun. latter part.
  < OE 'bæk' + 'ende' = end
  I couldn't guarantee to fix it now before the backen' o' the holidays.
backhand /bakhan/, adj. and adv. underhand.
  < OE 'bæk' + 'hand' = hand
  He has a backhan' way o' doin things.
backroads /bakrodz/, noun. byways, shortcuts, the wrong way.
  < OE 'bæk' + 'rad' = ride
  He hasn't been here but a wheen o' weeks an' he knows all the backroads.
backset /baksɛt/, noun. relapse.
  < OE 'bæk' + 'settan' = to set
  She was doin' rightly an' we thought she'd have another wee go (short period of active life) *but she took a backset an' now she's a-waitin on* (expected to die).

*backstone /bakston/, noun. hobstone.

  < OE 'bæk' + 'stan' = stone

  << Gaelic 'bac' = hob (i.e. a level shelf beside an
open fire)

  Ye could set a kettle on the backstone ti' keep the wather warm.

backward /bakwərd/, adj. shy, retiring.

  < eModE 'abackward' = away from

  She biz backward now, doesn't like singin or recitin poethry.

backy /baki/, adj. lame.

  < Gael 'bacach' = lame, defective

  Who done it? Him wi' the backy leg?

bad scran /bad skran/, exclamation. bad luck.

  < ME 'badde' = bad + ON 'skran' = shrivelled

  Bad scran to you! Don't you thrack (come near) *my door again.*

bagle /biəgəl/, noun. noisy, ill-mannered person.

  < OF 'bé-gueule' = open throat

  I'm ashamed ti' say I've rared a houseful o' bagles.

bags /bagz/, noun. stomach.

  < ON 'baggi' = baggage

  Me bags is full.

*bailiff, bumbailie /biəlɪf, bʌmbiəli/, noun. rent
collecter.

  < ME 'baillif' = administrator

  May the divil tick that ugly bailiff!

  (Traditional ballad, 'The Divil an the Bailiff')

baird /bɜrd/, noun. beard.

  < OE 'beard' = beard

  If ye like him that well, ye can kiss him yersel
Wi' his owl grey baird newly shaven.

  (Traditional ballad, 'The Match')

  Don't get your baird in a blaze! (Don't get angry.)

*bairn (USc), /bern, bɜrn, barn/, noun. child.

  < ME 'barn' = child

  An the poor wee bairns is left motherless!

bake /biək/, noun. rude word for mouth.

  < ME 'bec' = beak, bill

  << Gael 'béic' = shout, yell

  Shut you your bake! Your owl gub's nivir closed.

*bannock /banək/, noun. homemade loaf, often with
oats. It is not baked in the oven, does not contain fruit,
is bigger than a 'bap' but smaller than a 'cake o' bread'.

< Gael 'bannóg' = homemade cake
A piece (slice or sandwich) *in their han nivir done our'ns.*
Even the chile could ate a bannock.
banshee /banʃi/, noun. fairy woman who presages a
death.
< Gael 'bean' + 'sí' = woman + fairy
I nivir seen a banshee myself but I know others seen them
(other people who have seen them).
bap /bap/, noun. small, soft roll.
< Sc 'bap' = baker's roll
Baps biz (are usually) *tasty but they don't go far.*
*bardicks /bardɪks/, noun. belongings, few possessions.
< Gael 'barrdóg' = pannier (It is not uncommon in
languages for the word for a container to be applied to the
contents. We see the same change in the shift of meaning
of 'brat' from 'shawl' to the 'child in the shawl'.)
Here's the cowlt can take me in the seddle,
With you an' yir bardhix behin'.
(W.F. Marshall, 'The Runaway')
barge /bardʒ/, noun and verb. cross woman, scold.
< Sc 'bairge' = abuse, upbraid
<< Gael 'bárd' = a scold (often female)
Pay no attention. Sure she's only an owl barge.
I'm anaisy (uncaring) *about you an your bargin!*
barmbrack /barmbrak, barnbrak/, noun. bread with fruit.
For Hallowe'en, the barnbracks often contained such
gifts as a small coin (symbolising wealth for the person
who got it), a ring (marriage), a rag (death).
< Gael 'bairghean' + 'breac' = bread + speckled
Ye don't get good barmbracks now. People has got lazy. They'd
rather buy loafbread than bake.
barney /barni/, noun. 1. self; 2. row, debate.
< unkn
<< Gael 'barn-ghlaodh' = battle-shout
1. *Don't bother your barney doin it! I'll do it myself. You're very*
selfish. You wouldn't turn your heel to your toe for a body.
2. *They had a wee bit of a barney. Och, but sure what's that*
among friends?
barring /barn/, conjunction. except, unless.
< OF 'barre' = rod
They've all ate, barrin the youngsther.

Ye'd never hear a peep (slight sound) *barrin the cow would give a kick.*

baste /biəst/, verb. tack, stitch roughly.

    < OF 'bastir' = sew lightly

Will ye baste that for me, chile. Me owl eyes is not the whack.

baste /biəst/, noun. beast, obnoxious person.

    < ME 'beste' = beast, animal

A baste like that wants puttin down (deserves to be put down).

*bastins /biəstɪnz/, noun. milk from a cow that has recently calved.

    < OE 'bysting' = milk from cow

Give the bastins to the cat. It's lucky.

bat /bat/, noun and verb. hard slap.

    < ME 'batte' = club

    << Gael 'bata' = stick

What that'n is badly in need of is a quare good bat on the mouth!

bat /bat/, verb. close (of eyes).

    < ME 'bate' = flutter eyelids

I didn't bat an eye the whole night I was that worried about the childher flyin till America.

(on the) bat (of) /bat/, adv. approximately.

    < ?ME 'batte' = club > stroke

That clock cost me on the bat of fifty pound.

batter /batər/, noun. road.

    < Gael 'bothar' = road

That'n biz on the batther mornin, noon an night.

*baukie /bɔki/, noun. louse.

    < unkn

    << Sc 'baukie bird' = bat

Thanks be ti' God ye nivir see childher wi' baukies these days.

be /bi/, verb. be. The standard forms are gaining ground but the following forms are still widespread:

Present	Present Continuous	Past
I be	*I do be*	*I was*
you be	*you do be*	*you were*
he biz	*he diz be*	*he was*
she biz	*she diz be*	*she was*

we be	*we do be*	*we were*
yiz be	*yiz do be*	*yiz was*
they be	*they do be*	*they were*
them'ns be	*them'ns diz be*	*them'ns was*

< OE 'beon' = to be
<< Gael 'bí' = be
'Neighbours' doesn't be on until half six here.

be at (HE) /bi at/, verb. give a lot of pain, trouble.
< OE 'beon' + 'at' = be at
<< Gael 'tá a chroidhe ag cur air' = his heart is aching (be his heart putting on+him)
Th'owl chest's at him again. It's as if the spool of his breast has fell.

be at oneself (HE) /bi at wʌnsɛlf/, verb. be in good form.
Is he not at himself the night? He is not. He's not at himself at all. Ach, he doesn't be sick all the time but he biz bad right an regular now.

be to (HE) /bi tə/, verb. have to, must.
<< Gael 'tá sé orm sin a dhéanamh' = I must do that (be it on+me that to do)
It broke me heart to see him headin off, ach but sure he'd be to go if he wants to make anything of himself.

be up to /bi ʌp tə/, verb. fully understand.
You couldn't be up to her. She's as likely to cut you as to give you a civil how-do.

beddies /bediz/, noun. children's game. Shapes are drawn on the ground and children hop to a pre-arranged pattern.
< OE 'bed' + diminutive = small bed
Are we playin ball beddies or slate beddies or just beddies?

bedther /bɛdər/ (HE), noun. poor person, cripple, person who has lost the use of a limb.
< Gael 'lámh bodhar' = hand/arm + dead
Lady Charlemount knocked him down an left him a bedher.

bee's toe /biz to/, noun. in 'neat as a bee's toe'.
< OE 'beo' + 'ta' = bee + toe
I'm tellin' you. You're as nate (neat) as a bee's toe!

*beelie /bili/, noun. cat.

  << Gael 'píle cait' = huge cat

That beelie should be put out at night. It should be out mousin instead o' clockin by the fire.

beetle /bitəl/, noun. potato masher.

  < OE 'betel' = beating implement

They called him 'Juke-the-Beetle' because when he got dhrunk the wife bate him wi' the beetle an he got brave an nifty about jookin (dodging) it. Mind you there's people tell it a different road. They say that a 'juke-the-beetle' is a wee, tiny bit o' potato that never gets mashed.

bellowses /bɛləsəz/, noun. bellows. (cf **gallowses**)

  < ME 'belows' = bellows + plural marker -es

A nivir use bellowses now. A nivir have to. The firin biz all dhry an a firelighter whooshes it all up.

belt /bɛlt/, verb. beat severely.

  < OE 'belt' = girdle

He's a laugh for (he sorely needs) a good beltin.

beroo /bəru/, noun. Unemployment Office, dole.

  < Fr 'bureau' = desk, office

There's many a one on the beroo that's on the double (drawing social security but working at the same time).

*bicylic /baisɪlɪk/, noun. bicycle.

  < Fr 'bicycle' = bicycle

I've come for the len' (loan) o' your bicylic.

bid /bɪd/, verb. say.

  < OE 'biddan' = to ask, pray

Ye may bid them goodnight for you're for your bed, young lady!

biddable /bɪdəbəl/, adj. obedient.

  < OE 'biddan' + ME 'able' = fit

Now, you could do worse. She's civil wi' her tongue an biddable forby.

bidding /bɪdɪn/, noun. command, beck and call.

  < OE 'biddan' = to ask

Sure that wee woman hasn't the livin of a dog. She's at his biddin mornin, noon an night.

bield /bil(d)/, verb. fester.

  < Sc 'beil' = fester

A doubt ye may (I believe you'll have to) go till the docthor. By the look o' thon knee, it's bieldin.

*big /bɪg/, adj. friendly.
  < eModE. 'big' = big
  << Gael 'mór' = big, friendly
  Them'ns was always very big together.
bile /bail/, noun. boil.
  < OE 'byl' = boil
  The best traitment for a bile - an it's sore but - is to put the mouth of a bottle over it to dhraw it.
bite-'n-sup /baitənsʌp/, noun. sustenance.
  < OE 'bitan' = to bite + 'supan' = to sup
  << Gael 'greim agus bolgam' = sustenance (bite and swallow)
  Sure what's his bite-'n-sup? (Very little sustains him.)
bizz /bɪz/, noun and verb. make a hissing or buzzing noise.
  < ME 'busse' = buzz
  My very ears is bizzin' from the time I light the lamp...
  (W.F. Marshall, 'Sarah Ann')
*bizzum /bɪzɪm/, noun. home-made broom.
  < OE 'besma' = broom
  Bizzums was good for liftin the dust but they woren't much good wi' stoor (heavy dust).
black (HE) /blak/, adj. devout Protestant, often one who is a Presbyterian and a member of the Orange Order or the Black Preceptory.
  < OE 'blac' = black
  'Orange' is it? He's as black as your boot! (Is he loyal to the Orange Order? Very much so.)
black /blak/, adj. dark-haired.
  < OE 'blac' = black
  << Gael 'dubh' = black, dark-haired
  We always had two or three Roberts in the family so there'd be Black Robert (dark-haired) and Red Robert (red-haired) and White Robert (fair-haired).
*blackavised /blakavaist/, adj. dark skinned.
  < OE 'blac' + OF 'aviser' = see
  That was the time the tickiemen started ti' come roun. They were swarthy of themselves, blackavised, ye might say.
*blad /blad/, noun. lump of something solid.
  < OE 'blæd' = leaf

< Sc 'blaud' = large fragment
He took the eye out o' me (hit me on the eye) *wi' a blad of earth.*
blade /bliəd/, noun. young girl.
< OE 'blæd' = leaf, sword, carrier of sword
I seen your wee blade down the sthreet.
blaze o' whins /bliəz ə ʍɪnz/, noun phrase. quickly.
< OE 'blase' = blaze + ON 'hvine' = gorse, whin
She came in like a blaze o' whins!
blear(y) /blir(i)/, adj. and noun. sleeper, eye matter.
< ME 'blere' = dim-sighted
If you washed the blears out of your eyes ye might see betther.
blert /blɜrt/, noun and verb. cry, cry-baby.
< Sc 'blirt' = burst out crying
He's worse than a blert. He's an owl clashbag! (telltale)
blether /blɛðər, blɛər/, noun and verb. idle or foolish
talk or talker, talk foolishly.
< ON 'blathra' = talk nonsense
<< Gael 'bladaireach' = idle talk
Would ye give me head pace wi' yir owl blether!
He may look like a ble'er but he's the head o' wit (very
intelligent and capable).
He's as well bletherin there as in bed!
blether(come)skite /blɛər(kʌm)skait/, noun. talkative
person.
< ON 'blathra' + 'skyte' = shoot
*You're worse than mad for listenin to that owl bletherskite. Sure
she was ony* (only) *takin a han' out o' ye* (making a fool of you).
blink /blɪŋk/, verb. curse, give somebody the 'evil eye'.
< eModE 'blink' = glance, peep
*I wouldn't go next or near her! She could blink me. They say it
was hore* (her) *sowed* (planted) *the egg at the gate for ti' give
the cow a lame leg.*
blitter /blɪtər/, noun and verb. pass wind repetitively.
< Sc 'blitter' = rattle
Whisky makes you frisky
An stout makes you shout.
But atin (eating) *well-cooked peas or beans*
Will make you blitther out.
(Children's rhyme)

blootered /bluːtərd/, adj. very drunk indeed.
< ?ON 'blautr' = soaked
The man was teetotally bloothered. He couldn't put a foot in front of him.

blue-eye /blu ai/, noun. favourite, pet.
< ME 'blue' = blue + OE 'eage' = eye
It's not hard to see who's the blue-eye here.

blowhard /blohard/, noun. methylated spirits.
< OE 'blawan' = to blow + 'heard' = hard
His poteen's no betther nor blowhard! It'd kill ye!

board /bord/, noun. bird.
< OE 'brid' = young bird
An tell me, Nora, was it a blackboard or a crow?

boast /bost/, hollow, not strong.
< Sc 'boss' = hollow
The walls is boast. Ye cud poke yir fingers through them.

*bodach /bʌdɒx/, noun. small man.
< Gael 'bodach' = lusty youth
Look what's talkin! A bodach like that wantin people to vote for him!

body /bɒdi/, noun. person, oneself.
< OE 'bodig' = body
A body'd (anyone would) be glad of it now.

bog /bɔg/, noun. bog.
< SG/G 'bog' = soft, penetrable
'bogach' = marsh, swamp
Now 'bog' would be like the polite word, as ye might say. A body roun'about here would say 'munchees', not 'bog'.

bogging /bɔgɪn/, adj. dirty, filthy.
< SG/G 'bog' = soft, marshy
The whole place was boggin. Ye couldn't a got a place for ti' sit even.

boggyman /bɔgiman/, noun. ghost, spirit.
< ME 'bugge' = bugbear + man
<< SG/G 'bog' = bog + man
O, the wind an the rain
Brings me daddy home again
Keep away from the windy (window), boggyman.
(Traditional children's song.)

bogle /bogəl/, noun. poltergeist.

   < Sc 'bogle' = dreaded spirit

Their house was alive wi' bogles. They threw the delph on the floor an broke it an they pulled the pictures off the wall. The McConnimeys had to send for the clergy for to thry an put them in bottles.

boke /bok/, verb. retch, vomit.

   < ?ME 'bolknen' = to retch

   < eModE 'puke' = retch, vomit

That smell would mick (make) ye boke!

bold /bold/, adj. cheeky, impertinent.

   < OE 'bald' = courageous

If you're bold again, you'll not get goin out.

bonnet (USc) /bɒnət/, noun. man's cap.

   < OF 'bonet' = headdress

When ye're buying me a new bonnet, ye'll mind that I tick (take) six an seven eighths.

bonny (USc) /bɒni/, adj. attractive.

   < Sc 'bonny' = beautiful

   << Fr 'bon' = good

She's as bonny a wee blade as you could wish to clap eyes on.

*bonnyclobber /bʌniklɒbər/, noun. thick milk, curds.

   < Gael 'bainne clabar' = curds (milk + thick/sour)

D'ye know what bonnyclobber is? When ye get cruds (curds) on the milk, that's bonnyclobber.

boolie-legged /buli legd/, adj. bandy.

   < Sc 'bowlie-leggit' = bandy-legged

   << eModE 'boule' = curved handle

Golong (go away) ye boolie-legged crayther! You couldn't cyap (stop) much wi' them legs!

boord /burd/, noun. board, plank.

   < OE 'bord' = board, table

Give me head pace about the 'good old days'. There was nahin good about them. Me ma had to get an orange box for a creddle (cradle) an me da had ti' sthrenthen the bottom of it wi' a wee boord. How was them days good?

bore /bor/, noun and verb. make a whirring noise.

   < Sc 'birr' = whir

He has a new-fangled lawn mower that cuts the grass well an' good but the bore of it would deeve ye.

*borgeegle /borgigəl/, noun. mess.
   < Gael 'barrghalach' = refuse, inferior stuff
   *I have ate some dort (rubbish) in my time but nivir in all
   my born days did I sit down till a borgeegle like that!*

borl /borl/, noun and verb. turn round rapidly.
   < Sc 'birl' = whirl round
   Come on, ye girl ye, till I give ye a borl.
   Don't borl me too quick. It gives me a light head.

boron /bərɔn, baurɔn/, noun. hand-held drum.
   < Gael 'bodhrán' = drum
   *Borons and uilleann (elbow) pipes was played regular when
   I was a child an then they died out nearhan' but if you put
   on the television of a night, you can see them now. Sure
   even the foreigners is playin them.*

*bottle /bɒtəl/, noun. small tied section of hay or straw.
   < OF 'botel' = bundle of hay
   << Gael 'batal' = bundle of hay
   *First, ye put the hay in bottles, then in stooks an then in stacks.
   But there's other people has different words for the same thing.*

*bottom /bɒtəm/, noun. spool or length of thread.
   < eModE 'botme of threde' = reel
   *Give us a needleful o' thread there, chile. There's a bottom o'
   thread in the dhrawer.*

(small) bounds /(smɔl) baunz/, noun. (little) space.
   < ME 'bunne' = bound
   *Ye may cruddle up in small bounds for there's three of you'll be in
   that bed the night.*

boxty /bɒksti/, noun. fried potatoes + leftovers, mess.
   < Gael 'bacstaidh' = bread made from leftover
   potatoes
   *I think the English call 'boxty' 'bubble-and-squeak' but I'm not a
   hundhred percent sure o' that.*
   In the name o' God, what's that boxty you're playin with?

boy /boi/, address term and noun. 1. boy, 2. thing, 3.
cold or flu, 4. death.
   < ME 'boie' = male child
   1. *Hear wee boy, will ye run a message for me? That's the boy!*
   (Well done!)
   2. *'Will-ye?' is a bad boy. No matter who says 'will you?', you
   say 'no'.*

3. *Tell your mother not to be comin near me. She brought the boy with her the last time an I haven't overed it yet.*
4. *There's one boy that none of us can juke an that's the boy wi' the peg in his hat!*

*bra /bra/, adj. fine, only in the rhyme.

    < Gael 'breagh' = fine
           'dadamh' = something of no worth, jot
Every day bra makes Sunday a da. (Wearing finery every day means there's nothing special for Sunday.)
(Proverb)

*brach /brax, braθ/, noun. halo round the moon that foretells bad weather.

    < SG/G 'bruth' = halo round the moon
A doubt (strongly believe) *there'll be bad weather. Did you see thon brach roun the moon*?

*brachag (HE) /braxəg/, noun. rag, often red rag.

    < Gael 'bratóg' = rag
A body'd tie a brachag till a cow's leg ti' prevent it bein overluked (blinked or cursed).

*brachan, brochan /braxən, brɒxən/, noun. porridge.

    < Gael 'brachán' = broth, pottage
           'brochán' = porridge
A dhrop o' brachan in the mornin would stick to ye (sustain you for a long time) *now.*
She'd know more about a bad breakfast than about makin a dhrop o' brochan.

*bracky (HE) /braki/, adj. speckled, spotted, used of something living or of bread with fruit in it. A piece of cloth could not be 'bracky'.

    < Gael 'breac' = speckled, spotted
Them bracky hens is quare layers.

bracky /braki/, adj. bad tasting (of water).

    < eModE 'brackish' = salty
That's bracky wather. It has a filairy (musty) *taste.*

brae (USc) /bre/, noun. hill, stony hill.

    < Sc 'brae' = hill
Sit down an get yir breath back now. That brae's purty steep.

brammle /braməl/, noun. bramble, bramble bush.

    < OE 'bræmel' = bramble
There's allus as much brammle roun a house as'll born it. (Everyone has faults if you look for them.)

branknew, spanknew /braŋknyu, spaŋknyu/, adj. brand new.
> < ModE 'brand new'
> *It's not a second-hand boy at all, now. It's a branknew job!*

brash /braʃ/, noun. up and down movement when churning.
> < Gael 'brais' = bout, turn
> *I went in an a gave a couple o' brashes at the chorn (churn), like to show that I meant well.*

brash /braʃ/, noun. illness.
> < Sc 'brash' = illness
> *That owl brash comes over him every couple of hours an he's not just himself.*

brat /brat/, noun. child, usually an ill-mannered child.
> < Gael 'brat' = rag, cast-off clothing
> *One thing I can maintain, thanks be ti' God. A nivir rared a brat nor a byblow (bastard).*

brave (an) /briəv (ən)/, adj. and adv. good, fine, fairly. As an adverb, it parallels 'good an', 'nice an', 'quare an' and 'right an'.
> < F 'brave' = fine
> *A brave day, the day, Pether.*
> *You're brave an quick on it!*

bravely /briəvli/, adj. fairly well.
> < F 'brave' + -'ly'
> *How's the form the day, Mickey?*
> *Thanks be to God, I'm bravely.*

break /brɛk/, verb. embarrass.
> < OE 'brecan' = to break
> *You broke our Bridie wild. She was all broke when you didn't spake till her.*

brightify /braitəfai/, verb. brighten, cheer up.
> < OE 'beorht' = bright + '-ify'
> *She's a great wee worker. When she has the work done inside the house, she's out thrying to brightify the garden.*

brock /brɒk/, noun. refuse, food left over.
> < ME 'broccan' = fragments
> << Gael 'broc' = filth, refuse
> 'brochán' = porridge
> *Did the brockman come yit? The brock'll be kyoch (stale) by the morra.*

brogue /brog/, noun. Irish accent, often stage Irish.
   < Gael 'bróg' = shoe
   Where in the name o' God did he get a brogue like thon? He could
   talk rightly before he went to Dublin to live!
*brosny (HE) /brɒsni/, noun. dry sticks for lighting a
fire.
   < Gael 'brosnaidh' = faggots, kindling
   I like ti have a wee pile o' brosny left past. It's handy if ye haven't
   a torf (piece of peat).
*brownkittlies /braunkɪtliz/, noun. bronchitis.
   < folk etymology of 'bronchitis' from Lat 'bronchi' =
   branches of windpipe
   Th'owl chest nivir laves me! I'm desthroyed with the brownkit-
   tlies!
*bruch (HE) /brux/, noun. furrow, shallow water at the
side of a lazy bed (type of furrow for growing potatoes).
   < OE 'broc' = stream
   << Gael 'bruach' = brink, edge, bank of river
   Then, to themselves may be towl (told), he was dhrownded in
   the bruch.
*brudgy /brʌdʒi/, noun. mashed potatoes mixed with
butter, vegetable or meat.
   < Gael 'brúighte' = pounded, mashed
   'brúightín' = boiled potatoes and butter
   Ach, ye'll tick the full o' yir mouth o' brudgy.
bubbelizer /bʌbəlaizər/, noun. person with stammer,
hesitant speaker.
   < eModE 'bubble' = bubble
   << Gael 'buabhallach' = trumpeter
   God an who elected thon bubbelizer!
buck /bʌk/, adj. and intensifier in the phrase **buck
stupid**; male in such compounds as **big-buck** (important
person), **buckcat** and **buckgoat**.
   < OE 'buc' = male deer
   << Gael 'boc' = a male goat
   He couldn't insense anything into that'n. He's buck stupid.
   What does he look like anyway? An owl buckgoat!
*bucknyay /bʌknye/, noun. term of contempt.
   < 'buck' + Gael 'nia' = hero, champion
   An who does he think he is an him dhrest up like a bucknyay?

bucky wire /bʌki waiər/, noun. barbed wire.
< OE 'wir' = wire
<< Sc 'buckie brier' = wild rose
They had the whole place done round in bucky wire an I nearly tore the leg o' myself climbin over the wee stile.
*buddley /bʌdli/, noun. sausage, fat person.
< unkn
I could go a quare fry - a lump o' bacon an a couple o' buddlies would do rightly!
bully /bʌli/, exclamation of support. Good for you!
< eModE 'bully' = fine fellow
Bully for you, son!
bum /bʌm/, verb. boast.
< Gael 'boman' = boast
She would dhrive ye daft with her bummin an blowin about the childher. No childher ivir done well till hores (hers) by the sound of it.
bum /bʌm/, noun. polite equivalent of 'ass'.
< ME 'bom' = bottom
I fell on the snow an hort me bum.
*bum /bʌm/ , noun. bomb.
< F 'bombe' = bomb
Did ye hear about Nellie? She was arrested for carrying a bum up her clothes.
(Traditional joke)
bumbee /bʌmbi/, noun. bumblebee.
< ME 'bumme' = buzz + OE 'beo' = bee
I'm alive since I was born an a while before it an I've nivir seen as many big bumbees in my life!
bumboozle /bʌmbuzəl/, verb. fool, cheat someone.
< eModE 'bamboozle' = hoax, humbug
Look out for the smart boys. They'd bumboozle their mother.
bunty /bʌnti/, adj. short and thickset.
< eModE 'bunting' = short and thick
Och, ye know him surely. He's the wee bunty man that comes home carryin fish an chips for the childher an him parlatic.
burn (USc) /born/, noun. small river.
< OE 'burna' = stream
They're playin by the burn.

but /bʌt/, adv. and conj. although, however, but.
  < OE 'be-utan' = outside
  She's a brave size but, but she can squeeze herself into very small bounds.
*but 'n ben (USc) /bʌt ən ben/, noun. very small house.
  < Sc 'but 'n ben' = two-roomed house
  'Twas aye a but 'n ben they ca'ed it.
by-blow /baiblo/, noun. bastard.
  eModE 'byblow' = bastard
  Many's an innocent girl was left with a by-blow an there was no harm in the childher.
byre /baiər/, noun. cowshed.
  < OE 'byre' = cowhouse
  A byrefull an a barnfull
  An ye couldn't get an armful. What's that? (Smoke)

C

In speech, it is impossible to differentiate between words which start with 'c' and those which start with 'k'. Here, the following conventions have been used. Words in NIE deriving from an English word begin with the same letter as their English cognate. Gaelic has no 'k' but words which may derive from Gaelic are transcribed with an initial 'k' if they begin with 'ci' or 'ce', phonetically /ky/.

caboodle /kyabudəl/, noun. lot.
  < ModE 'caboodle' = entire lot
  That's the lot, the whole caboodle.
cadge /kyadʒ/, verb. get something for nothing.
  < eModE 'cadge' = carry a pack
  << Gael 'goid' = steal
  That'n would cadge the eye out of your head.
*caillyeach /kyailyax/, noun. old woman, hag.
  < SG/G 'cailleach' = old woman, hag
  Well now, the best way to explain it is to say that a caillyeach is a cyarl, an owl woman, that biz aizy cross (gets angry easily).

cairn /kyɜrn/, noun. pile of stones, usually associated with the supernatural.

< SG/G 'carn' = heap of stones

Do you notice that the M1's not straight just before you get to Dungannon? Well there was a cairn on the sthraight line and the men were afraid to knock it down so the engineer had to go round it.

Wise man, that engineer! He done right to go round the cairn. Isn't he still to the fore an all goin well with him?

cale /kyiəl/, noun. cabbage.

< ME 'cale' = cabbage

<< Gael 'cál' = cabbage

A bit of boiled ham, spuds and cale is as good a meal as I ever got!

call /kɔl/, noun. need, reason; scholarship to higher education.

< OE 'ceallian' = to call

<< Gael 'call' = want, necessity

You'd no call to bring anything, now. Sure you're more than welcome.

Your wee boy must be brave an' smart. I hear he has got a call to Queen's (Queen's University, Belfast).

camogie /kyəmogi/, noun. girl's game, similar to hockey.

< Gael 'camógaí' = lady hurler

She was the captain of the Camogie team when she was at school.

candlesticks /kyɛnəlstɪks/, noun. runny nose.

< OE 'candelsticca' = candlestick

She would be a quare nice wee blade if she didn't have them candlesticks constant.

canker /kyaŋkər/, adj. and noun. twisting weed.

< eModE 'cankerworm' = plant-eating worm

Thon owl canker has grew up all round the rose.

cankersome /kyaŋkərsʌm/, adj. festering, hard to heal.

< OE 'cancer' = gangrene + '-some'

That cut looks cankersome now. You're like myself, hard to cure.

cannae (USc) /kyane, kyani/, verb + neg. cannot.

< Sc 'can + nae' = cannot

A cannae hear his name an' hide

My thought wi' ony art;

A cannae see him come, an' calm

The flitterin' uv my heart;

(G.F. Savage-Armstrong, 1845–1906)

canny (USc) /kyani/, adj. nice, dexterous, careful.
   < Sc 'canny' = adroit, sagacious
   She's a canny wee blade an trig (neat) of herself.
cap /kyap/, verb. stop.
   < Gael 'ceap' = stop
   << OE 'cæppe' = cap
   He built a wee wall for to cap the water.
***care** (HE) /ky3r/, noun. family, people to be provided for.
   < ME 'care' = charge
   << Gaelic 'cara' = beloved
   An how are you an all your care?
case o' pistles /kyiəs ə pɪstɪlz/, noun. rude or jocular term
for bottom.
   < ME 'case' = receptacle + eModE 'pistol' = small gun
   Here, gather yourself together and put your case o' pistles in the
   warmest chair in the house.
***cat** /kyat, kyɛt/, adj. bad, terrible.
   < OE 'catt' = cat
   << Gael 'cat marbh' = calamity (cat + dead)
   That's cat all right. It would be hard for it to be worse.
   Is the pain bad, son? It's cat.
catch -self on /kyɛtʃ sɛlf ɔn/, verb. behave sensibly.
   < ME 'cachen' = catch
   Catch yourself on, will ye! Who do you think you are? Lady
   Muck from Clabber Hill!
catchpenny /kyɛtʃpɛni/, noun. technique likely to make
one lose money.
   < ME 'cachen' + OE 'penig' = penny
   Them raffles is all rigged. They're a bloody owl catchpenny.
caul /kɔl/, noun. covering on a child's head at birth.
   < ME 'calle' = membrane over head
   A child born with a caul is lucky. He'll want for nothing.
caulcannon /kɔlkyanən/, noun. cabbage and butter, often
with mashed potatoes.
   < Gael 'cál' = cabbage + 'ceann-fhionn' = head white
   In the bad days, my mother had no cabbage to put in the
   caulcannon so she put nettles in.
ceili(dhe)/kyiəli/, noun and verb. evening get-together, dance.
   < SG/G 'ceilidhe' = evening visit
   My mother's away on her ceili.

cess /sɛs/, noun. luck, success in the phrase **bad cess**.
  < eModE 'cess' = local Irish tax
  Bad cess to you! May ye never have luck!

champ /tʃamp/, noun. mashed potatoes and butter with leeks or scallions.
  < ME 'champ' = chew
  That champ would stick to you! (You wouldn't feel hungry after that champ!)

chancy /tʃansi/, adj. good-looking, well-endowed.
  < ME 'chaunce' = opportunity, luck
  Jist let him keep his daughther, the hungry-lukin' nur,
  There's jist as chancy weemin, in the countryside as her.
  (W.F. Marshall, 1888–1959)

*chanty (USc), /tʃanti/, noun. chamber-pot.
  < Sc 'chanty' = chamberpot
  Chanties was on the go when people didn't have bathrooms. My mother had a lovely big delph one.

chap /tʃap/, verb. knock loudly on a door.
  < Sc 'chap' = knock, strike
  Who would be chapping at the door at this time of day?

chape /tʃiəp/, adj. and adv. cheap.
  < ME 'chepe' = low priced
  Ach I sell them chape and low
  Buy a box before you go
  From your broken-hearted farmer, Dan O'Hara.
  (Traditional ballad)

chape /tʃiəp/, noun. cheep, slightest sound.
  < Sc 'cheip' = chirp
  He hasn't let a chape out of him all day.

chapel /tʃapəl/, noun. Catholic church.
  < OF 'chapele' = chapel
  << Gael 'séipéal' = chapel
  (This usage goes back to the days of the Penal Laws when severe restrictions were imposed on the building of churches by Catholics or Dissenters.)
  We would a went to the chapel two or three times a day in October. You would a went in the morning for Mass and in the evening for the Rosary.

chapfallen /tʃapfɔlən/, adj. very hungry indeed.
  < eModE 'chap' = jaw + OE 'feallan' = to fall

I'm chapfallen. As the man says: 'I haven't chawed cheese (eaten anything) *the day!'*

charm (HE) /tʃarm/, noun. cure, talisman.

< OF 'charme' = a song

Do you know anybody with the charm for shingles? The stuff the doctors give a body is just useless. They put the charm for my rheumatics in a bit o' wool an I wear that wool on my ankle constant.

chate /tʃiət/, verb. cheat.

< OF 'escheat' = booty

I sometimes think that the ones that chate and rob gets on better than the ones that diz their best.

*chaw /tʃɔ/, verb. chew, especially tobacco.

< OE 'ceowan' = chew

Once upon a time when boards (birds) *shit lime an monkeys chawed tobacco, then little dogs took out their tails an wagged them in the snow.*

(Expression sometimes used as a put down when children want a story.)

check /tʃɛk/, pull someone up about a story.

< OF 'eschec' = sudden stoppage

If I'm living and spared in the mornin I'll check her.

chick /tʃɪk/, noun. cheek.

< OE 'ceace' = cheek

The chick of that blade! God himself only knows what she thinks she has to be consaty about!

*chile /tʃail/, noun. girl.

< OE 'cild' = child

Tell us, is it a chile or a boy?

chile, childer /tʃail, tʃɪlDər/, noun and affectionate term of address. child, children.

< OE 'cild/ cildru' = child/children

<< Gael 'a leanbh' = child, darling

Here chile, buy yourself a wee cup of tea.

Them that reared you was fond of childer! (Traditional insult, akin to: *Them that reared you would drown nothing!*)

chim(b)ley /tʃɪm(b)li/, noun. chimney.

< OF 'cheminée' = fireplace, flue

Chimley, chimley, chimley sweeper

Married a wife and he could not keep her.

(Children's skipping rhyme)

*chitterling /tʃɪtərlɪn/, noun. weakling.
   < ME 'cheterlingis' = intestines of small animals used for food
   The poor chitterlin'll not do. He's as thin as a sleigh hook.
*chookther /tʃükτər/, noun. highlander, one who wears a kilt, kiltie.
   < Sc 'teuchter' = Highlander
   Ma, ma the chookther's (kiltie's) comin
   Ma, ma, he's none at all.
   Ma, ma, the chookther's comin
   Comin from the Dornyen Ball.
   Some o' them have shoes an stockins
   Some of them have none at all.
   Some o' them have big bare asses
   Comin from the Dornyen Ball.
   (Children's song)
chorch /tʃortʃ/, noun. Protestant church.
   < OE 'circe' = church
   They get out of the chapel at half twelve and meet the people coming out of the chorch at the same time.
chullers /tʃʌlərz/, noun. jowls, chins.
   < ME 'cholle' = dewlap
   He has a quare pair of chullers on him, that boy!
chunter /tʃʌntər/, verb. nag.
   < eModE 'chunter' = grumble
   My head's astray with his chunterin constant. In the name o' God, does that man's tongue nivir rest!
clabber,clobber /klabər, klɒbər/, noun. mud.
   < SG/G 'clabár' = filth mire, mud
   I'm dying in Drumlister, in clobber to the knee.
   (W.F. Marshall, 1888–1959)
*clachan /klaxən/, noun. strip of land.
   < SG/G 'clachán' = village, townland
   They used to divide the land into clachans, each son with his own wee strip, but that's all done away with.
clag /klag/, noun. big fly.
   < ON 'kleggi' = horsefly
   << Gael 'cuileog' = fly
   It's the clags that spoil picnics.
clamp /klamp/, noun and verb. method of cutting and stooking turf. 'Peat' is never used in colloquial NIE.

< Gael 'clampa' = fixture for turf
<< OE 'clympre' = lump
They're not in at the minute. They're out clampin torf.
clannish /klanɪʃ/, adj. cliquish, likely to favour their own family.
< SG/G 'clann' = family + '-ish'
They're very clannish now. They might fight among themselves but they'd turn on you if you insulted breed, seed or generation of them.
clap /klap/, noun and verb. cow pat.
< OF 'clap' = heap of stones
<< OE 'clæppan' = beat, slap
Why did the horse laugh?
Because the cow clapped.
clapped-in /klaptɪn/, adj. sunken, shrunken.
< OE 'clæppan' + 'in'
A doubt she'll not do. She's like a gation with the jaws all clapped-in.
clart /klart/, noun. dirt, woman who keeps a dirty house.
< Sc 'clart' = sticky mud
Now, I'll not say she's an out 'n out clart but she could be a bit tidy of herself. The house biz boggin even at eleven in the mornin!
clash /klaʃ/, verb. tell tales.
< Sc 'clash' = gossip
<< ME 'clash' = loud noise
Away you on, you clash-bag you! You'll not clash on me the morrow.
clash-bag /klaʃ bag/, noun. tell-tale.
See **clash**.
clat /klat/, verb. wash badly.
< Sc 'clatty' = slimy, muddy
<< Gael 'cladach' = dirty, untidy
It's only clatting they biz doing, not washing at all.
clatter /klaтər/, noun. lot.
<< Gael 'cladrán' = heap of stones
There's a whole clatter of childher, a big threvally of them.
clatty /klati/, adj. dirty.
< Sc 'clatty' = slimy, muddy
<< Gael 'cladach' = dirty, untidy

An' if me shirt's a clatty shirt
The man to blame's me da.
(W.F. Marshall, 1888–1959)
claw mould /kla maul/, verb. dismissive expression, similar to 'drop dead'.
    < OE 'clawu' = claw + 'molde' = mould
    Away an cla mowl on yourself. Just you poke your nose out o' my business.
clever /klɛvər, klɪvər/, adj. big, capable of holding a lot.
    < ME 'cliver' = adroit
    That's a quare clever pocket you have!
cleave/clove /kliv, klʌv/, verb. cut severely.
    < OE 'cleofan' = to hollow out
    God you should a seen him and the head clove open.
*cleugh /klüx/, noun. steep, stony hill.
    < OE 'cloh' = ravine
    << Gael 'cloch = stone
    Many's the cleugh we clum thegither.
click /klɪk/, noun and verb. attract a boy/girlfriend.
    < Fr 'cliquer' = to click
    I clicked with a lovely Scotch boy, goin over till Ardhrossan.
clift /klɪft/, noun. fool, unintelligent person.
    < unkn
    He's not just stupid. He's the two ends of a clift (a complete fool).
clink /klɪŋk/, verb. stub one's toe.
    < ME 'clink' = sharp sound
    I've every right ti' complain. A clinked toe may be very little to you because you haven't it but it's very sore indeed.
clinker /klɪŋkər/, noun. unburnt remains of poor-quality coal.
    < Du 'klinckaerd' = fused cinders
    That owl Scotch coal isn't worth a-buyin. D'ye see the big clinkers it laves (leaves) *in the grate?*
clinking /klɪŋkɪn/, adj. excellent.
    < ME 'clink' + '-ing'
    That's a clinkin day for ye! The sun's splittin the threes (trees).
clipe /klaip/, noun. large piece of something.
    < ON 'klippe' = to cut
    He cut off a big clipe of beef.

clocher /klɒxər/, noun and verb. clear the throat, death rattle.
  < Gael 'clochar' = wheezing, death rattle
  He was sitting there, clocherin and spittin for all he was worth.
clock /klɒk/, noun. beetle.
  < eModE 'clokk' = beetle
  It's the weather for clocks. They like the rain.
clock /klɒk/, noun. dandelion in seed.
  < Lat 'clocca' = clock, bell
  The childer tells the time by blowin away the clocks.
clock /klɒk/, verb. sit on eggs; sit idly.
  < Sc 'clock' = sit on eggs
  << Gael 'cloch' = stone, lump
  Me ma's away to Ardboe to see about borrowin a clockin hen.
  I've fothered all the kettle, an' there's nothin' afther that
  But clockin' roun' the ashes wi' an oul Tom cat;
  (W.F. Marshall, 1888–1959)
clock /klɒk/, verb. beat severely.
  < ME 'clout' = blow with hand
  < Gaelic 'cloch' = stone, lump
  Thon kittherdy would clock you as soon as bid you the time o' day.
clod /klɔd/, noun and verb. piece of earth, stone, throw a piece of earth.
  < OE 'clod' = lump of earth
  A got clodded in the eye. Thon'n lifted a stone an clodded me.
clootie /klüti/, adj. and noun. awkward, left-hander.
  < Sc 'cloot' = hoof
  You're not clootie-handed are ye? Your whole breed is clooties.
cloots /klüts/, noun. hooves, feet
  < Sc 'cloot' = hoof
  Get your dorty big cloots down o' the sofy (sofa).
*clouster /klausтər/, noun and verb. rough woman, ragged headdress.
  < Gael 'clamhstar' = awkward person, mess
  She's a big clouster of a woman.
  She could see nothing with thon clouster pulled round her eyes.
clout /klaut/, noun and verb. heavy blow, hit hard.
  < ME 'clout' = blow with hand
  The big hallion gave me a clout and I thought I'd never see daylight after it.

cod /kɔd/, noun and verb. fool, play tricks on.
    < eModE 'cod' = fool
    Would you quit your coddin. Take a hand out o' (make a fool of) *somebody else.*

cog /kɔg/, noun and verb. cheat, copy someone else's homework.
    < eModE 'cog' = cheat at dice
    << Gael 'caog' = wink
    We always cogged other's (one another's) *exercise* (homework).

*coggly /kʌgli/, adj. unsteady.
    < Sc 'coggly' = shaky, unsteady
    I doubt he has a dhrop on him. He's a bit coggly on his pins.

cold-rifed /kaulraift/, adj. invariably cold.
    < eModE 'cauldrife' = cold
    He's cowl-rifed good enough. He could wear a top-coat on the warmest day an he's not like another body. He never sweats.

*colleen /kɒlin, kɒlyin/, noun. poetic word for girl.
    < Gael 'cailín' = girl, maiden
    I married a wee blade, her age was sixteen.
    She was the fairest wee colleen my eyes ever seen.
    Her eyes were like diamonds and her skin like the pearl (often /poil/)
    She was the pride of lovely Derry on the banks of the Foyle (Traditional folksong)

collogue /kəlog/, verb. gossip, chat privately.
    < OF 'colliguer' = to conspire
    Women like to be colloguing.

colloguin-match /kəlogin matʃ/, noun. a long, friendly chat.
    < OF 'colliguer' + OE 'gemacca' = mate
    It's only at a wake that a body has time for a good colloguin-match.

collop /kɒləp/, noun and verb. large piece, cut roughly.
    < ME 'coloppe' = piece of meat
    << Gael 'colpa' = something thick
    << French 'escalope' = cut of meat
    Cut you a decent bit of beef. Don't collop it.

colour(ing) /kʌlər(ɪn)/, noun and verb. very little milk in tea.
    < OF 'color' = colour
    Very little milk, please. Just a wee colour there.

come-all-ye /kʌmɔlyə/, noun. boring song often beginning 'Come all you lads and lasses', rigmarole.

   < eModE 'come all ye' = come

Her an her owl come-all-yes! They've neither tops, bottoms nor sides to them.

comestibles /kəmestəbəlz/, noun. polite word for food.

   < Lat 'comestibilis' = eatable

Don't you worry your head. We'll see to the comestibles for the wake.

commit -self /kʌmɪt sɛlf/, euphemism for 'soiling pants'.

   < ME 'commit' = entrust

I doubt the chile has committed himself. He has left a wee message (second euphemism) *on the floor.*

compliment /kɒmplɪmənt/, noun. obligation.

   < Fr 'compliment' = tribute of courtesy

I wouldn't want to be under a compliment to that boy! He only talks from the teeth out (i.e. he's not to be trusted).

coney /koni/, noun. rabbit.

   < OF 'conil' = rabbit

   << Gael 'coinín' = rabbit

I haven't warmed to eating coneys since they took myxamatosis.

consaty /kɒnsiəti/, adj. proud, conceited.

   < eModE 'conceit' = fanciful opinion

The McConnimy's was that consaty of themselves that the name 'McConnimy' wasn't good enough for them so they changed it to 'Conway'.

contrary /kɒnтrəri/, adj. argumentative.

   < OF 'contraire = antagonistic

That'n is as conthrary as a bag o' wheezles.

coolie /kuli/, noun. water dog, retriever.

   < Sc 'coll' = coalblack (applied to a dog)

That chile took ti' the wather like a coolie dog.

*coolygullen /kuligʌlən/, noun. earwig.

   < Gael 'cuileog an lín' = earwig

'Coolygullens' is eariwigs, if a body would call them right.

corly cale /korli kyiəl/, noun. type of cabbage with curly leaves.

   < OE 'crul' = curl + ME 'cale' = cabbage

Corly cale is tasty now if you boil it with a wee pickle (grain) *of baking soda.*

corn /korn/, noun. currant.

   < Fr 'raisin de Corinthe' = currant

   Have ye no corn bread?

   I'm that full. I couldn't eat another corn.

corp /kɔrp/, noun. body, corpse, the deceased.

   < Lat 'corpus' = body

   An why wouldn't he be at the wake an him a full cousin of the corp?

corrie-fisted /kɒri fɪstəd/, adj. clumsy, left-handed.

   < Gael 'cearr' = wrong, crooked, left-handed + OE 'fyst' clenched hand

   They say that Catholics biz more apt to be corrie-fisted but that could be just a story but.

cotter /kɒtər/, noun. penniless outcast.

   < Sc 'cottar' = cottager

   << Gael 'cothuightheóir' = one in need of support

   Mind you, I'm no cotter! I've a bob or two (a few pence) *between my fingers yet.*

cowl /kaul/, adj. cold, cowardly.

   < OE 'ceald' = cold

   << Gael 'fuar' = cold, unadventurous

   He's cowl now! Wouldn't spend Christmas! He's the type of boy would want you to go havvies (half-shares) *on a horse.*

*cow's clash /kauz klaʃ/, noun. cow's udder, swollen with milk.

   < OE 'cu' = cow + Gael 'clais' = quarter, as of beast

   There's no two ways about it, when God made her, He made her both coorse (coarse) *an ugly. Look at the hans on her, thick as a cow's clash.*

cow's lick /kauz lɪk/, noun. 'widow's peak', point of hair in the centre of the forehead.

   < OE 'cu' + 'liccian' = to lick

   A cow's lick is a sign o' beauty an if a man has a cow's lick there's a good chance he won't go baldy.

cowstails /kauztiəlz/, noun. pigtails.

   < OE 'cu' + 'tægel' = tail

   Cowstails takes the corl (curl) *out o' childher's hair but it's cool for them when they're runnin about an' enjoyin themselves.*

cowp /kaup/, verb. overturn, throw.

   < eModE 'coup' = overturn

<< Gael 'cúb' = bend, stoop
I didn't fall at all. I was cowped.
crab /krab/, noun. unripened apple.
< ME 'crab' = crab apple
<< Gael 'crapadh' = shrinking, stunting
She never learned that you have to throw a crab to catch an apple.
crab /krab/, noun. bad-tempered person.
< OE 'crabba' = crustacean
Thon owl crab! He'd ate ye without salt.
crabbit /krabɪt/, adj. bad-tempered.
< Sc 'crabbit' = bad-tempered
A crooked, crabbit crathur that bees neither well nor sick,
Girnin' in the chimley corner, or goan happin' on a stick.
(W.F. Marshall, 1888–1959)
crabby /krabi/, adj. bad-tempered.
< OE 'crabba' + '-y'
Don't be so crabby! I didn't mean no harm.
crack /krak/, noun and verb. chat, joke, enjoyment.
< OE 'cracian' = to crack
<< Gael 'crac' = talk, gossip
Come on in an give us a while of your crack.
crack /krak/, noun. beginning of dawn, day or doom.
< OE 'cracian' = crack, break
I've been up since the crack o' dawn.
She's hardly in bed by the crack o' day.
I'll mind (remember) *that till the crack o' doom.*
crafty /krafti/, adj. smart, capable.
< OE 'cræftig' = skilful
Well done, child! You're as crafty as a bee.
crake /kriək/, noun and verb. creak, complain.
< ME 'crake' = shrill noise, croak
They say a crakin gate hangs long. (A person who complains a lot does not die young.)
cran /kran/, noun. quantity of herring.
< ModE 'cran' = 37.5 gallons of herring
<< Gael 'crann' = 37.5 gallons of herring
He would buy about a cran of fresh herns (herrings) *of a Thursday an if they weren't all sold on Friday, we'd salt them.*

cran (HE) /kran/, noun. crane.
  < OE 'cran' = crane
  << Gael 'crann' = tree, crane
  She had a neck on her like a cran. (Her neck was long and thin.)

cranky /kraŋki/, adj. cross, cantankerous.
  < OE 'cranc' = bent axis + '-y'
  He biz cranky when the leg biz at him.

crayther /kriəᴛər/, noun. creature, person; poteen.
  < OF 'creatour' = created thing
  << Gael 'créatúir' = creature, person to be pitied
  Och the poor owl crayther hasn't a shoe till his foot.
  Ye wouldn't have a dhrop o' the crayther about the house? I've a very sore head (headache).

craw /krɔ/, noun. throat.
  < ME 'craw' = gullet in bird
  I couldn't be nice to that'n. A civil word'd stick in my craw.

creddle /krɛdəl/, noun and verb. cradle.
  < ME 'credel' = cradle
  Ye know what they say: The hand that rocks the creddle rules the world.

creel /kril/, noun. basket for fish or turf.
  < SG/G 'críol' = basket
  God be with the days that my Da used to carry the turf home in a creel!

*creepie /kripi/, noun. hand-made stool, usually with three legs.
  < Sc 'creepie-stuil' = three-legged stool
  You couldn't buy a creepie now for love or money.

creeping-Jesus (HE) /kripɪn dʒezɪz/, noun. hypocrite, religious fanatic.
  < OE 'creopan' = to creep + ME 'Jesus'
  You wouldn't mind if he practised what he preached but he's no better than a creepin-Jasus.

crickety-croytell /krɪkɪti kroitəl/, noun. endearment.
  < OF 'criquet' = grasshopper + '-y' + unkn
  My wee crickety-croytell! My wee cock above water!

crig /krɪg/, verb. stub one's toe.
  < Gael 'críog' = crush
  I crigged my wee toe against the corner of the door an, by God, it's giving me jip.

*croilly /kroili/, adj. weak, small
   < Gaelic 'cróilighe' = weak, infirm
   Och the wee croilly crayther! Sure it was better dead.
crock /krɒk/, noun. earthenware pot.
   < OE 'crocca' = earthenware vessel
   Butter was kept in crocks and the small ones was called meskins.
*croobeen (HE) /krubin/, noun. pig's trotters.
   < Gael 'crúibín' = hoof, trotter
   *I can put away two or three croobeens when I'm in good eatin
   heart* (good form for eating = hungry).
*croodle /krudəl/, verb. cradle in the arms.
   < Sc 'croodle' = nestle close
   He's the best wee boy goin! I love croodlin him.
*croodlin-doo (USc)/krüdəlɪn dü/, noun. pet.
   < Sc 'croodling doo' = wood pigeon
   Och ma wee croodlin-doo! My wee pigeon-pie!
crooked /krukɪd/, adj. perverse.
   < ON 'krokottr' = crooked
   << Gael 'crosta' = crooked, perverse
   He's a crooked, crabbit crayther!
cropping /krɒpɪn/, noun. fowl's crop.
   < OE 'crop' = bird's craw
   *Mind ye clean the croppin well out an d'ye see that yellow stuff?
   That's bile an if ye don't get it all out, ye'll desthroy the taste o'
   the board* (bird).
crow /kro/, noun and unflattering term of address or
reference. crow, unattractive person; special way of sliding
on ice.
   < OE 'crawe' = black carrion bird
   That owl crow! An who does he think he is?
   The curse of the crows on you. (Curse, assumed to be a
   variant of 'The curse of Cromwell on you!')
   *'Shoot the crow' was going down the slide on your hunkers but
   with one foot stuck out in front of you.*
cruds /krʌdz/, noun. curds.
   < eModE 'cruddes' = curds
   When you've give a few brashes (When you've churned for a
   while) *you get cruds in the milk.*
cruddle /krʌdəl/, verb. curdle.
   < eModE 'cruddle' = curdle

Don't be drinking so much. Your dinner could cruddle in your guts.

crummle /krʌməl/, noun and verb. crumb, make crumbs.
  < OE 'cruma' = crumb + '-le'
  Eat that or leave it but quit crummlin your meat (food).

cub /kʌb/, noun. boy.
  < eModE 'cub' = young animal
  I'll take the girls in the car for it's rainin but the cub can walk.

cuddle /kʌdəl/, verb. bake an apple in an oven.
  < eModE 'codle' = roast
  A cuddled apple cuts the fat now if you're eating pork.

cuddy /kʌdi/, noun. spoon, opinion.
  < Sc 'cutty' = short-handled spoon
  Don't put your cuddy in among spoons (Know your limitations). (Proverb)

*cuddy /kʌdi/, noun. share, what one deserves.
  < Gael 'cuid oidhche' = share for night. This word occurs as 'cuidich' in Edmund Spenser, *A View of the State of Ireland*, 1596: 623
  He got his cuddy right enough and if anybody asked for it, he did.

*cugger (HE) /kʌgər/, verb. whisper.
  < Gael 'cogair' = whisper, rumour
  They were cuggerin and colloguin in the corner.

culchie (HE) /kʌltʃi/, noun. person from the back of beyond.
  <? Lat 'cultor dei' becoming 'culdee' = member of Scots-Irish religious order
  << Gael 'coillteach' = a wooded area
  He started to roar an' laugh an said te the driver, we've got a right culchie here, Mick. A toul him what he could do way hes number nineteen bus an' gat aff.
  (Frances Molloy, *No Mate for the Magpie*, 1985: 140)

cut /kʌt/, adj. and verb. 1. embarrass(ed), 2. slap hard, 3. very drunk (in phrases 'half cut' and 'well cut'), 4. reduce the effects of.
  < OE 'cyttan' = to cut
  << Gael 'bain' = cut, surprise
  1. *I was cut to the very bone when she didn't ask me if I had a mouth on me* (if I'd like a cup of tea).

2. *She cut the jaw o' me with her big heavy hand.*
3. *He's away to bed for an hour to sober himself. He came in half cut.*
4. *Now you'd want* (i.e. need) *to eat something that would cut the grease. Pork's very fatty of itself.*

cut cat /kʌt kyɛt/, fixed phrase. very lucky.
 < OE 'catt' = cat
 << Gaelic 'cat' = cat
You're as lucky as a cut cat. If you fell intil the wather you'd come up dhry. Aye, an with a fish in your mouth!

cutty /kʌti/, noun. girl.
 < Sc 'cutty' = girl, hare
Och, she's a quare wee cutty, always thryin to help about the house.

cyarkidge /kyarkədʒ/, noun. carcase.
 < Fr 'carcasse' = dead body
He may be a good enough butcher but, mind you, I don't like lookin at all them cyarkidges he has hanging from hooks.

*cyarl /kyarl/, noun. old person, often an old woman.
 < ON 'karl' = man
 < ON 'karling' = old woman
Now take Carlingford Lough. The Vikings settled there and the story goes that they called the lough after an old hermit of a woman, a cyarl, that lived there.

cyarnaptious /kyərnapʃəs/, adj. unhelpful and bad-tempered.
 < Sc 'carnaptious' = irritable
 << Gael 'cearnaighe' = grumbling
He's a cyarnaptious owl divil! You'd think he had forgot how till laugh.

cyast /kyast/, verb. shed hairs.
 < ON 'kasta' = cast, heap, pile
You must be castin. There's a dale (lot) o' hairs in the jarbox (sink).

cyast /kyast/, noun. squint.
 < eModE 'cast' = twist, turn
She has a bad cyast in the right eye. That's why they say she has four o'clock eyes.

cyast the creels /kyas ðə krilz/, verb. quarrel.
 < ME 'cast' = throw + SG/G 'críol' = basket
 << Gael 'caith' = throw

*They cast the creels years ago about an owl bit o' land an they've
nivir spoke since.*

cyast up /kyast ʌp/, verb. go over a person's misdeeds.
  < ON 'kasta' + OE 'upp' = up
  *I was red up from the time o' my granfather. She cyast up
  everything she could think of!*

cyavvie /kyavi/, noun. coward.
  < Lat 'cave' = be alert
  *Get you on out there and fight your corner. I'm damned if
  I'll rare a cyavvie.*

cyermudgeon /kyərmʌdʒən/, noun. unhelpful,
untutored person.
  < eModE 'curmuggion' = churlish fellow
  << Gael 'cearramansaidheacht' = contrariness
  *Sure you're worse than mad bothering with an owl cyermudg-
  eon like that. All he knows is what the spoon put in him.*

D

dabhand /dabhan/, noun. expert.
  < Sc 'dabhaun' = expert
  *My son's a dabhan at dhrawin. He can dhraw anybody and the
  pictures are that good ye'd think they could talk to you.*
*dae (USc) /de/, verb. do
  < Sc 'dae' = do
  I dinnae ken what I'll dae.
daft /daft/, adj. foolish, foolishly in love.
  < ME 'daffte' = mild, meek, foolish
  *You're daft in the head. I'm not payin good money to go an watch
  ballet! Sure that's not dancin!*
  Thon blade's daft in the mind about your boy.
dag /dag/, noun. unflattering term for a man.
  < ?Gael 'deaig' = blow, slap
  *Thon dhrunken dag! There'll be a day at the catchin o' thon boy
  yet* (one day he'll get what he deserves).
daicent /diəsənt/, adj. and adv. generous, very.
  < Fr 'décent' = becoming
  *You couldn't a got a daicenter man. There's one thing you can
  say about him, he hadn't his heart in a sixpence. He's as daicent
  a man as ever faced the clay* (died).

Daicent an well (Very well) *you're lookin.*
dainty /diənti/, noun. titbit.
  < OF 'daintié' = dignity
  I'm lookin for a wee dainty for the child. She's not too well an I
  want something to taste her mouth.
dale /diəl/, noun and verb. deal.
  < OE 'dæl' = part, amount
  An inch is a dale in a man's nose. (Proverb, roughly
  equivalent to 'A miss is as good as a mile.' It means that
  an inch is not always a small amount.)
dale /diəl/, noun (used as an emphatic positive). devil.
  < Sc 'deil' = devil.
  Dale a one was rared cleaner. (No-one was brought up
  better.)
***dale-clock** /diəlklɒk/, noun. cockroach, clock.
  < Gael 'daol' = beetle + eModE 'clokk' = beetle
  Dale-clocks is black an very dorty. They say ye should always
  put your foot on one if ye see them because they bethrayed
  Christ. On Spy Wednesday, when the soldiers were lookin for
  Christ an they couldn't find him, the dale-clocks called out:
  'That's the way he went.' (The dislike of dale-clocks is
  probably Irish in origin. There is an Irish proverb:
  'Is fearr daol a losgad ná aoine trosgadh.'
  Better to scald a dale-clock than fast on Friday.)
dam /dam/, noun and verb. wide part of river, part of river
near mill; block running water.
  < ME 'demme' = dam
  They're playin football in the dam field (the field with the
  wide part of the river).
  If you dammed that wather, ye'd flood the yard.
damage /damədʒ/, noun. cost.
  < OF 'damage' = loss
  Well, what would the damage be if I had an extension built as well?
damnedable /damdəbəl/, adj. strange, utterly
unacceptable.
  It's damnedable the way people has lost all the owl ways. There's
  bodies would pass ye now an no come-along (friendly
  exchanges) *at all with them.*
dander /danɒər/, noun and verb. stroll; temper.
  < Sc 'dander' = stroll; anger

Come on for a wee dandher. Sure a body'd be mad to stay in on a day like this.
It didn't take much to get his dandher up. One word an he lost the head completely.

(well) dare you /(wel dar yə/, exclam. Just you try!
< OE 'durran' = to have boldness
'I'll walk where I like,' says he. 'Well dar ye,' says I. 'If you as much as put your foot on my property I'll piss (set) the dogs on ye.'

darkavised /darkəvaist/, adj. dark-skinned.
< OE 'deorc' = dark + Fr 'aviser' = heed, see
The Quinns were all darkavised of themselves with jet black hair and lovely big black eyes.

*day'l-agaun (USc) /deləgɔn/, noun. twilight.
< OE 'dæg' + 'leoht' + 'gan' = day + light + to go
It's near eneuch (enough) day'l-agaun.

daylight /delait/, noun. the bare necessities of life.
< OE 'dæg' + 'leoht' = day + light
Give ye somethin to hansel your house! For God's sake have you no wit? Thon'n wouldn't give ye daylight.

dead /ded/, adv. completely, very.
< OE 'dead' = no longer alive
Och, I'm dead bate (extremely tired) laughin. Thon boy's dead funny.

deadbell /dedbel/, noun. ringing in the ears.
< OE 'dead' + 'belle' = dead + bell
When ye get that deadbell in your ears, you should always say a prayer for anybody that's dyin.

*deadman's fingers /dedmanz fiŋərz/, noun. foxglove (also called 'fairy fingers').
< OE 'dead' + 'man' + 'finger' = dead + man + finger
I don't like the childhren playin wi' deadman's fingers. That owl blue comes off on their hands an then they put their hands in their mouth.

dead spit /ded spɪt/, noun. exact reproduction.
< OE 'dead' + 'spætan' = dead + to spit
Thon wee blade o' yours is the dead spit o' your mother. She'll never be dead as long as that chile's on the sod!

dear /dir/, noun. alternative to 'God'.
< OE 'deore' = noble

I know where I'm going and I know who's going with me.
I know who I love, but the dear knows who I'll marry.
(Traditional ballad)
Dear knows but she took an awful toss (fell heavily).
*dee (USc) /di/, verb. die.
  < Sc 'dee' = die
  I think I could jus' lee doon an dee.
deeve /div/, verb. deafen.
  < Sc 'deave' = deafen
  I can't hear my ears with all the noise. The childher has me deeved.
delph /dɛlf/, noun. crockery.
  < Du 'Delft' = place
  You like to have a nice bit o' delph if a sthranger comes in for a dhrop o' tea.
deserve /dəzɜrv/, verb. serve.
  < OF 'deservir' = serve zealously
  It deserved you right. What did you want to be pokin your nose in another body's business.
desperate /desprɪt/, adj. very bad.
  < Lat 'desperatus' = despaired of
  The weather's just desperate, so it is.
destroyed /dəsтroid/, verb. damaged, adversely affected.
  < ME 'destroie' = put an end to
  << Gael 'mill' = ruin, destroy, spoil
  I'm desthroyed with me chest (I've bronchitis).
diddle, dowdle /dɪdəl, didəl, daudəl/ hum a tune for someone to dance to.
  < ? eModE 'diddle' = jerk an object up and down
  << Gael 'díodán' = humming
  In them days, you might a found somebody with a fiddle or somebody else with a mouth organ, but most times ye'd only have a comb with tishie paper or spoons or if ye were down an out ye would a had to dowdle to help the dancers keep time.
diddly /dɪdli, tɪdli/, adj. small but with overtones of affection.
  < unkn
  He's a diddly wee man.
  Aye, diddly but daicent.
  She's only a wee tiddly thing.

diddy /dɪdi/, noun. female breast.
  < Gael 'did' = teat
  << OE 'tit' = teat
  The youngest was on the diddy till he was two.
*didgeen /dɪdʒin/, noun. clay pipe.
  < Gael 'dúidín' = short tobacco pipe
  The didgeens was a quare smoke. You could get a quare good dhraw out o' one. But the shank was always a-breakin an you were left with the cuddy (bowl + short piece of stem).
die /dai/, noun. singular of dice.
  < ME 'de' = one dice
  She's a decent body an as sthraight as a die! (It is not absolutely clear why dice should be straight but perhaps their sides had to be straight if they were to be 'unloaded'.)
dig /dɪg/, noun and verb. blow, hit; cutting remark.
  < ME 'digge' = dig
  He gave me a right dig in the ribs.
  Thon was a brave dig she gave you about Rita's man.
dilsy /dɪlsi/, noun. foolish person, usually female.
  < Gael 'dílse' = fidelity, loyalty
       'diúlach' = busybody
  They kept her a chile that long they made a dilsy out of her.
dinge /dɪndʒ/, noun and verb. dent.
  < ON 'dengya' = hammer
  Would ye look at me new car an it all dinged!
*dishabels /dɪʃabəlz/, noun. in a state of undress.
  < Fr 'déshabiller' = to undress
  In her dishabels yet an it afther eleven!
dip /dɪp/, noun and verb. hot gravy or an egg to dip in.
  < OE 'dyppan' = let down into liquid
  They might only a had one egg for everybody so the pan was set in the middle o' the table so that everybody could get a dip. Och, the dip was tasty now. There's many's a one runnin round in big motors that was rared (reared) *on dip.*
ditch /dɪtʃ/, noun. mud rampart, dyke.
  < OE 'dic' = embankment
  I stood on top o' the ditch to get a good view.
  It's as safe as a hedge tied till a ditch.

divide /dɪvaid/, noun. share.
   < Lat 'dividere' = to divide
   Cut that apple into three divides.

divil /dɪvɪl/, adv. and noun. the sort of devil who would give you a sporting chance.
   < OE 'deofol' = spirit of evil
   Did you hear about how Paddy Irishman bate the divil? Well…
   so when the divil had took Paddy Englishman an Paddy Scotchman to hell, he turned to Paddy Irishman an said: 'Now can you think of something I can't do?' An Paddy Irishman said: 'I want you to let a fart, catch it in a bottle an paint it red, white an blue.' An the divil couldn't do that so Paddy got aff.
   Divil the bit o' throuble that is. (That's no trouble at all.)

divilment /dɪvɪlmənt/, noun. mischief.
   < OE 'deofol' + '-ment'
   They meant no harm when they progged his orchard. Sure it was only a wee bit o' divilment.

divil's needle /dɪvɪlz nidəl/, noun. dragonfly.
   < OE 'deofol' + 'nædl' = devil + needle
   << Gael 'snathad an diabhail' = needle of the devil, dragonfly
   Is the divil's needle the same as a daddy longlegs?

do your own do /du yər on du/, phrase. have it your way.
   < OE 'don' = to do
   Do your own do, chile, but don't come cryin to me when it goes wrong.

***dob** /dɔb/, verb. to play truant (usually boys).
   < unkn
   Boys is always dobbin but girls only mitch sometimes.

docken /dɒkən/, noun. a plant whose leaf is reputed to counteract a nettle sting.
   < OE 'doccan' = weeds
   Docken in an docken out,
   Please docken take the sting of the nettle out.

doddle /dɒdəl/, noun and verb. walk slowly and pleasurably.
   < eModE 'doddle' = dawdle
   Now go you sthraight an don't be doddlin.

dodder(y) /dɒpəri/, adj. and verb. totter(y).
   < eModE 'dooder' = tremble + '-y'
   She was dodderin all day. The owl legs is away with it.
dogstool /dɔgstul/, noun. toadstool.
   < OE 'docga' = dog + ME 'stole' = stool
   *The wee Mallin girl's in hospital. They went out looking for
   mushrooms but she got dogstools instead an they nearhand
   killed her.*
*doits (USc) /doits/, verb. stupefies.
   < Sc 'doit' = foolish person
   Tha' doits me senseless.
dolly /dɒli/, verb. walk slowly and for pleasure.
   < eModE 'doddle' = dawdle
   Come on an I'll dolly up the road with you.
dortboard /dortbord/, noun. person not to be trusted.
   < ME 'drit' = dirt + OE 'brid' = bird
   That owl dortboard. She'd argue a hole in the wall! (She'd try
   to convince you that you couldn't trust your own eyes.)
downdrop /daunɒrɒp/, noun. leak, runny nose.
   < OE 'dune' + 'dropa' = down + drop
   *I'd need to get the roof seen till. When it's rainin now, there's a
   wee bit of a downdrop near the chimley.*
*downy /dauni/, adj. and noun. weak, small person.
   < Gael 'donaidhe' = miserable, in poor health
   << OE 'dune' = down
   He was the youngest of a big family an them'ns is often downies.
dote /dot/, noun and verb. pet, darling; lose control of one's
mind.
   < ME 'dotie' = silly
   What did you say, my wee dote?
   She's just havin a wee dote. She'll be as right as rain in a minute.
doubt /daut/, verb. firmly believe.
   < OF 'duter' = to waver, hesitate
   I doubt you're a playboy. (I strongly suspect you're not
   serious.)
   I wouldn't misdoubt it. (I'm sure what you say is true.)
(no) dozer /(no) dozər/, noun. alert in one's own
interests.
   < ON 'dusa' = doze + '-r'

No matther what ye say, Maggie's no dozer. She sowl (sold) *the lan just before the prices went down an when everybody else was howlin* (holding) *out for more.*

*drachy /ᴅraxi/, adj. deceptively long.
  < Sc 'dreich' = dull, monotonous
  << Gael 'draoidheacht' = magic
  God but thon was the dhrachy road!

draw /ᴅrɔ/, verb. brew.
  < OE 'dragan' = to draw. pull
  Will ye let the tay dhraw, chile. It's tay we want not scalded wather.

dreech /ᴅrix/, adj. miserable
  < Sc 'dreich' = dull, monotonous
  << Gael 'drioch' = grimace
  He does be dhreech when he biz his lone (alone).

dreep /ᴅrip/, verb. dry by dripping.
  < ME 'drepe' = drip
  I've left your coat over the bath to dhreep.

dribble /ᴅribəl/, noun. small amount.
  < ME 'drib' = small quantity + '-le'
  Would ye have a wee dhribble o' sugar? I don't take much but the tay's not the same without it.

dribs and drabs /ᴅribz ən ᴅrabz/, noun. small amounts.
  < ME 'drib' + ?Du 'drab' = dregs
  I lent him the money an he's payin it back good enough but I'm getin it in dhribs an dhrabs instead of in a lump.

drill /ᴅril/, noun. potato bed.
  < ModE 'drill' = small furrow
  O you're a rascal, Terry Flynn,
  You're writin poethry instead o' diggin dhrills.
  (Traditional song)

*drookit (USc) /ᴅrükit/, adj. soaked to the skin.
  < Sc 'droukit' = soaked
  I'm aye dhrookit! It's pourin out o' the heavens!

drop (on you/taken) /ᴅrɒp/, phrase. be intoxicated.
  < OE 'dropa' = small quantity of liquid
  He has a wee dhrop taken so he's a bit sleepy.
  You have a quare dhrop on ye the night, boy.

drop o' tea /ᴅrɒp ə te/, phrase. light refreshments.
  < OE 'dropa' + eModE 'tay' = tea

Och sit yourself down and take the weight off your feet. You're not leavin this house without a dhrop o' tay. I'm goin to no bother at all. It's just a wee dhrop in your hand.

drowned /draundəd/, adj. drenched, soaked to the skin.
< ME 'drun' = drown
<< Gael 'báidhte' = drowned, drenched
Och, ye're dhrownded, chile, dhrownded. Take all off ye or ye'll get your death.

drunk as a monkey /drʌŋk əz ə mʌŋki/, adj. happily drunk.
< OE 'druncen' = drunk
He's dead to the world (fast asleep) *now, for he was as dhrunk as a monkey when he come in.*

druth /druθ/, noun. dryness; one who is overly fond of alcohol.
< OE 'drugath' = dryness
Have you anything to dhrink? I ate salt herrin's an I'm dyin o' the dhruth.
I'm afraid Tommy's goin the same way as the father. He's gettin to be a druth.

dry /drai/, adj. thirsty; lacking in news.
< OE 'dryge' = dry
I'm that dhry! I could dhrink the Jordan dhry.
I'm very dhry, the day, no news at all. Sure people must walk away when they see me comin!

duchill /dʌxəl/, noun. dunghill, disparaging term.
< OE 'dung' + 'hyll' = dung + hill
<< Gael 'doicheall' = inhospitable
Thon big duchill! She'll neither work nor want.

*dullice /dʌləs/, noun. edible seaweed.
< SG/G 'duileasc' = edible seaweed
Did ye threat your Mary Anne
To some dullice an yella man (sweet)
At the owl Lammas Fair in Ballycastle O?
(Traditional song)

dumfounder /dʌmfaundər/, verb. amaze, flabbergast.
< Sc 'dumfouner' = amaze, stun
Some of the things ye see on the television would dumfoundher ye. They'd make ye think.

dummy tit /dʌmi tit/, noun. baby's soother.
< ModE 'dummy' = counterfeit + OE 'tit' = teat

*Don't be usin a dummy tit on the child. You'll leave him all
out-mouthed* (with protruding teeth).

*duncher /dʌntʃər/, noun. cloth cap.
  < unkn
  Hand us (give me) *my duncher, there. It's a hardy one, the day*
  (it's cold today).

dunder /dʌnɒər/, noun and verb. loud noise caused by
heavy blow.
  < Sc 'dunner' = clatter
  Will ye quit your dundherin or ye'll have the door in on me
  (knock my door down).

dunderin-in /dʌnɒərɪn ɪn/, noun. place that is falling apart.
  < Sc 'dunner' + 'in'
  *The place was like a dundherin-in. It hadn't seen a lick o' paint
  the whole time they were in it.*

dunt /dʌnt/, noun and verb. thump.
  < OE 'dynt' = blow
  You gave me a right dunt with that owl bag o' yours.

dwam /dwam/, noun. slight turn, dizziness, short
trance.
  < Sc 'dwam' = faint
  He doesn't be at himself when he has one of his wee dwams.

E

eariwig /iriwɪg/, noun. earwig, insect.
  < OE 'earwicga' = earwig
  *If an eariwig got intil a child's ear, it would desthroy their
  hearing. I knew a woman that could hear the grass growin an she
  got an eariwig in her ear an she's totally deeved.*

egg on /eg ɔn/, verb. encourage, lead on.
  < OE 'ge-eggedon' = incited
  *Could ye not see that he was makin the balls for you to fire?
  You're aisy* (easy) *egged on.*

*ee, een (USc) /i, in/, noun. eye, eyes.
  < OE 'eage/eagan' = eye/eyes
  *For you'll pull out his gowden hair
  An I'll pick out his bonny blue een.*
  (Traditional ballad)

eejit /idʒɪt/, noun. person lacking seriousness.
  < OF 'idiot' = ignorant person
  Ye did what? In the name of God what sort of an eejit are you? I never thought I'd rare (rear) a kittherdy.
eerie /iri/, adj. surprising, strange.
  < OE 'earg' = cowardly + '-y'
  << Sc 'eri' = timid
  That was an eerie thing to say! I wondher what she meant now.
*eeroch /irɒx/, noun. pains thought to be caused by the east wind in winter.
  < Gael 'oighreach' = chafing caused by ice
  << OE 'eare' = ear + 'acan' = to ache
  Is it any wondher ye have the eeroch an you out on a day that would take lumps out o' ye (that is bitingly cold).
ejaculation (HE) /ɛdʒakyuliəʃən/, noun. short prayer, usually said in times of stress.
  < eModE 'ejaculation' = uttering
  Turbulence, he called it, but if you ask me, that man couldn't a passed his test. The plane went up an down like a yoyo. There was an Englishman beside me dhrinkin whiskey. I think he wanted to talk but I never said 'yes', 'no', 'kiss my heel' or nothing. I just said one ejaculation afther another until we got down an I made one promise that night. I'll never get intil a plane again, not while pussy's a cat.
*elbuck /ɛlbʌk/, noun. elbow.
  < OE 'elboga' = elbow
  Och you know people in them days couldn't talk right. They had different words for things. They called your elbow your elbuck an your armpit was your oxther an your chin was a smig an then the spool o' your breast was your breastbone an the back o' your leg was your hough.
*elder /ɛlɒər/, noun. udder.
  < OE 'uder' = udder
  It's that cowl (cold) there's hacks on the cow's eldher.
electric /ɛlɛktrɪk/, noun. electricity.
  < Lat 'electricus' = electricity
  The electric was cut off for two days an we were back to boilin kettles on the fire.
embrocation /ɛmbrokiəʃən/, noun. ointment.
  < Lat 'embrocare' = to apply a linament

The stuff the docthor gives you is useless but you can buy a box of embrocation off a stall near Nutt's Corner and I'm tellin you one good rub on the bad leg an you wouldn't know you have a leg!

(no) empty skite /(no) ɛmpi skyait/, adj. very full.

< OE 'æmtig' = vacant + Sc 'skite' = shoot, splash

Well, you're no empy skite, boy. You've ate enough to keep a battalion goin.

end /en/, noun. death; end, in various compounds.

< OE 'ende' = end, final limit

He got his en (caught something that killed him) watchin the Blues (Linfield Soccer Club).

I doubt we'll not get a delivery now before the back-en o' next week.

I thought you said her hair was corly (curly)? It's as sthraight as wax-en.

He's the two ens (a complete) of a liar!

enterfere /ɛnTərfɜr/, verb. interfere.

< OF 's'entreferir' = strike each other

Thon'n doesn't know how to mind her own business. She'd entherfere in the crib if they'd let her.

entermeddle /ɛnTərmɛdəl/, verb. meddle or interfere in.

< ME 'entremedle' = interfere in

He could pick raisins out of a pie with his nose, thon boy, an him enthermeddlin constant in another body's business.

entitlement /ɛntaitəlmɛnt/, noun. right.

< OF 'entiteler' = to give a title to + '-ment'

Claim surely. You've every entitlement to the money.

entry /ɛnTri/, noun. alleyway.

< ME 'entre' = entrance, alley between houses

There's an enthry between Irish Street an Scotch Street. It cuts off the corner if you're in a hurry but there's dhrunk men in it sometimes.

(one) errand /wɔn ɜrnd, arn/, noun. for the sole purpose.

< OE 'ærend' = message, mission

She come from Belfast one errand to tell me about Davy's mother.

evening (HE) /ivnɪn/, noun. afternoon, evening.

< OE 'æfnung' = close of day

Come round this evening, any time afther two.

exercise /ɛksərsaiz/, noun. homework.
  < OF 'exercice' = keeping busy
  Get you upstairs an do your exercise. When you have it done we'll see can you go to the pictures.
*eye /ai/, noun and verb. ear of corn.
  < OE 'eage' = eye
  << Gael 'súil' = eye, eye-like object, e.g. 'mí na súil buidhe' = July (month of+the eye yellow)
  People would eat manure if ye give it a fancy name! Ye see people now eatin corn an them eyes used to be give to the pigs, ye know.
eye of the ass /ai ə ði as/, noun. anus.
  < OE 'eage' + 'arse' = buttocks
  << Gael 'súil ribe' = mouth of a channel
  Would ye get up an tidy yourself. You do nothin but sit on the eye of your ass day in an day out.
*eye of the thumb /ai ə ðə θʌm/, noun. central point of swirl on thumb.
  < OE 'eage' + 'thuma' = thumb
  << Gael 'súil na h-órdóige' = central point of the ball of the thumb (eye of+the thumb)
  The middle bit on the ball o' your thumb is what childher used to call 'the eye o' your thumb'.
heavy eye /hɛvi ai/, phrase. evil eye, power to 'blink'.
  < OE 'hefig' = heavy + 'eage'
  << Gael 'súil throm' = evil eye (eye heavy)
  Thon blade could blink you! She has the quare heavy eye on her!
eyes at tinkers' time /aiz at tɪŋkərz taim/, noun. severe squint.
  < OE 'eage' + ME 'tinkler' = tinker + OE 'tima' = time
  Things like that run in the breed. The chile had an operation on her eye an the cousin has eyes at tinkers' time. Mind you, she's a brave civil wee thing for all that.
(get) eyes together /gɛt aiz təgeər/, verb. rest, have a little nap.
  < OE 'eage' + 'togædere' = into one
  << Gael 'súil a chur le chéile' = putting eyes together, taking a nap
  I wasn't sleepin! I didn't get sleepin! I was jus' gettin me eyes together when that bagle started roarin.

F

faddom /fadəm/, verb. understand, get to the bottom of.
  < OE 'fæthm' = fathom, 6 feet
  I can't faddom that wee man. He doesn't open his bake (beak)
  till a Christian.

fadge /fadʒ/, noun. rich bread with lots of fruit.
  < Sc 'fadge' = rich loaf
  Now fadge is supposed to be a luxury but for me it's like Barney
  Kughes's bread. It'd stick to your belly like lead.

faggot /fagət/, noun. unflattering term for a child.
  < OF 'fagot' = bundle (of sticks)
  That wee faggot biz up to mischief mornin', noon an night.

failed /fiəld/, adjective. lost weight, in poor health.
  < OF 'faillir' = be wanting
  She's terrible failed. She's away to scrapins an a terrible colour.
  I doubt it's what my mother called 'the quare fake'
  (cancer).

fair /fɜr/, adj. and verb. (become) dry and fine.
  < OE 'fæger' = beautiful, pleasing
  It was dhreary enough lookin a while back but it's faired up
  lovely now.

fair doos /fɜr duz/, noun. justice, equality.
  < OE 'fæger' + 'don' = to do
  Och fair doos now, she thries her best an it's not easy with that
  cross man of hers.

fair enough /fɜr ənʌf/, affirmative. okay.
  < OE 'fæger' + 'genog' = enough
  That's fair enough, then. I'll deliver the carpet on Friday.

fairly /fɜrli/, adv. excellently.
  < OE 'fæger' + '-ly'
  You can fairly make dhresses, Mona. They're just great.

*fake (HE) /fiək/, noun. cancer.
  < Gael 'féach' = look
  << ModE 'fake' = counterfeit
  See **failed**.

falairy /fəlɜri/, adj. unpleasant taste.
  < ME 'flour' = flour + '-y'
  It has a falairy taste now. I doubt it has set (has been allowed
  to sit) *too long.*

falls /fɔlz/, noun. opening at the front of trousers.
  < eModE 'fall' = falling item of dress
  Your falls is open, boy. Them zips is the ruination o' the counthry.

fankle /faŋkəl/, verb. ravel, tangle.
  < Sc 'fankle' = entangle
  Look at my wool, would ye! Ye have it all fankled.

farl /farl/, noun. type of bread.
  < Sc 'farl' = flour scone
  << Gael 'faráil' = offering
  Well, there's soda farls and titty (potato) *farls but soda farls is fillin.*

*farntickles /farntɪkəlz/, noun. freckles.
  < eModE 'ferntykylle' = freckle (fern tickle)
  Farntickles sware an oath but wan:
  They'd never light (rest) *on a yella swan.*
  (People with sallow complexions don't get freckles.)

far out /far aut/, adj. distant.
  < OE 'feor' = far + 'ut' = out
  We're far out friends (distantly related).

fasting-spittle /fastɪn spɪtəl/, noun. saliva of one who
hasn't eaten, thought to have certain powers
  < eModE 'fasting-spittle'
  Now them warts is catchin but ye can get red o' them quick enough if ye just touch them on a Sunday with a fastin spittle.

fat in the forehead /fat ɪn ðə fɒrəd/, adj. stupid.
  < OE 'fæt' = fat + 'forheafod' = forehead
  He's as fat in the forrid as a hen!

*fash /faʃ/, verb. worry.
  < Fr 'fâcher' = to be angry
  Don't you fash yourself about a blade like that wi' a face that could turn milk!

faze /fiəz/, verb. annoy, disturb.
  < OE 'fesian' = drive away
  It would take more than a blatther o' thundher to faze thon boy!

*feasant /fɛzənt/, adj. decent, reliable.
  < OF 'faisible' = capable of being dealt with
  She's a feasant enough crayther an diz (does) *what she's bid.*

feckless /fɛkləs/, adj. feeble-minded.
  < Sc 'feckless' = futile, weak

Och God help them all! It's a terrible cross to carry when your one (only) *child is, as you might say, feckless.*

*feedogue (HE) /fɪᴅog/, noun. jocular word for spider.
< Gael 'fígheadóir' = weaver, spider
<< Gael 'fideog' = flute
Did you ever hear the like? Afraid o' spidhers! Sure what harm could a wee feedogue do ye?'

Fenian /finyɪn/, adj. and noun. Catholic.
< Gael 'fianna' = warriors
They call us Fenians an Tagues an we call them Willies (< William of Orange) *an Dicks (from the rhyme Prodison Dick went up a stick an nivir come down till Monday wick* (week)).

*fenster (USc) /fɛnsᴛər/, noun. window.
< Lat 'fenestra' = window.
The cat give one yelp an was out through the fensther, glass an all, before you could say Jack Robinson.

fey /fe/, adj. with second sight.
< OE 'fæge' = fated to die
She's fey all right but you'd be wise not to enthermeddle wi' that sort o' thing. Mrs M. went one errand (for the sole purpose) *to have her cup read an says Mrs S., says she: 'You be very careful goin home for I see an accident in your cup.' God an she'd hardly put her foot outside the gate when a big lorry knocked her spinnin. She wasn't killed like but thon dunt done her no good.*

fidge /fɪdʒ/, noun. jump.
< eModE 'fidge' = fidget
It wouldn't take a fidge out o' me to take things back to a shop. The way I look at it is this: they should be able to stand over all their merchandise.

(in one's) figure /(ɪn wʌnz) fɪgər/, adv. without a coat or cardigan.
< OF 'figure' = mark, symbol
Is it any wondher she's not well an her out in her figure the cowlest night that ever blew (on the coldest night imaginable)!

*fillybeg /fɪlibeg/, noun. kilt.
< SG/G 'filleadh beag' = a kilt
We were bad baists (beasts). *We would folly the bands an thry*

to look up the men's fillybegs for ti' see if they had any dhrawers
(underpants) *on.*

finnagle /fɪniəgəl/, verb. hustle, scrounge.

< ModE 'finagle' = wangle

He was right an good at finnaglin so they lived brave an high on the hog.

finnickity /fɪnɪkɪti/, adj. overly precise.

< ModE 'finicky' = particular + 'pernickity' = precise

They get a wee bit finnickity about how you do things when they first retire but they're as right as rain in a couple o' months.

firnenst /fərnɛnst/, against, in front of.

< Sc 'fornenst' = facing

An there firnenst the gable was your man (the one we have been discussing).

fissle /fɪsəl/, verb. rustle paper.

< Sc 'fissle' = rustle

Sure they're doin no harm. They're only fisslin paper.

fits /fɪtz/, noun. matches.

< OE 'fitt' = match

Fits finds other (Birds of a feather…).

flannen /flanən/, noun. flannel, face cloth.

< ME 'flannen' = open woollen stuff

That child could be doin wi' a flannen roller to keep her stomach in.

flabbergast /flabərgyast/, verb. amaze.

< ModE 'flabbergast' = confound

Begod 'n that would flabbergast ye! I'm not worth tuppence! I was like a chile. I hadn't a word for ti' say for meself.

flahool (HE) /flahul/, adj. generous.

< Gael 'fleadhamhail' = hospitable, open-handed.

You should be a wee bit careful with the people round here. They're not as flahool as at home.

flay /fle/, noun. flea.

< OE 'fleah' = flea

There was a rhyme we used to say for Keaton's Powdher, I think it was:

'Little flays has smaller flays upon their backs to bite 'em.

Smaller flays has lesser flays so on ad infinitum.'

*flesh /fleʃ/, noun. beef.

< OE 'flæsc' = animal meat

You can't make fish of one an flesh of another. (You shouldn't make a difference between children. They should be treated equally.)

*fleshmeat /fleʃmit/, noun. beef.

< OE 'flæsc + 'mete' = food

You never eat fleshmeat on a fast day (a day when one is instructed to abstain from meat).

flibbertygibbet /flɪbərtidʒɪbət/, noun. silly person.

< eModE 'flibbertigibbet' = flighty woman

It's bad enough wantin to get married an him little more than a chile but to suggest bringin in a flibbertygibbet that has danced the counthry, well now that just bate the band altogether!

flinch /flɪntʃ/, noun and verb. startled movement, upset.

< OF 'flenchir' = to turn aside

That'n has a neck on her for anything. Takin a message back till a shop wouldn't take a flinch out of her.

flit /flɪt/, noun and verb. move house.

< ON 'flytja' = go to another place

You're not thinkin o' flittin on a Sathurday? Don't you know what they say:

A Sathurday's flit's a short sit.

flock /flɒk/, noun. type of dust.

Now, a body didn't talk about 'dust' in the facthory. Like that would a been for for what ye got in the house. Naw, it was flock that ye got from the weavin, flock an pouse an stoor.

flure /flur/, noun. floor.

< OE 'flor' = floor

That wee woman hasn't tuppence but the childher's as nate as ninepence an ye could ate your mate (eat your food) *aff her flure.*

flute /flut/, exclam. of annoyance or surprise.

< OF 'flahute' = flute

Aw flute! This thing's away with it (ruined, of no further use).

fluter /fluтər/, noun and verb. awkward person, behave in an awkward way.

< unkn

<< Sc 'flaughter' = flutter

Watch yourselves. If there's any more flutherin about, it's the stick for the whole o' yiz.

fly /flai/, adj. cunning.

  < ModE 'fly' = sharp, wide-awake

  She seen ye comin! She's too fly for you any day o' the week.

*fog /fɔg/, noun. moss.

  < ME 'fog' = grass, moss

  There's people likes that owl fog growin on their houses but I think it brings damp but.

*folderdol /fɒlɒərdɒl/, noun. trimmings, grace notes.

  < Sc 'folderol' = finery

  You never seen such'n a woman for foldherdols! She even has a wee doily on the television set an the gardhen's full o' them wee gnomes. Mind you, it would take your eye (attract you).

  I can't be doin with singin like thon. Sure they can sing none! It's all squealin and foldherdols.

*folkie /fɒlki/, adj. and noun. interested; welcome.

  < Gael 'fáilte' = welcome

  I wasn't that folkie for the fish anyway.

  Folkie! Folkie! We got chased! He come afther us with a pitchfork an towl (told) *us nivir again to take the light out of his dure. Thon man's too mane* (mean) *to live!*

foot /fʌt/, verb. walk.

  < OE 'fot' = foot

  Ye'll get no bus the night. Ye may foot it (you'll have to walk).

footer /fʌtər/, noun. member of a group, usually 'left-footer' or 'right-footer'. (The only explanation I can find for this usage is that left-handedness and left-footedness are more commonly found among Catholics.)

  < Sc 'fouter' = term of contempt

  << Fr 'foutrer' = to mock

  I doubt he's a left footer (I suspect he belongs to a different religious denomination).

footer /futər/, noun. clumsy person.

  < Sc 'fouter' = clumsy person

  << Gael 'fustaire' = fussy or fidgety person

  Ye nivir seen such a foother in all your born days! He'd break all the delph in the house.

footless /fʌtləs/, adj. the opposite of agile, drunk.

  < OE 'fot' = foot + 'leas' = devoid

  Ye haven't fell again! God chile but you're footless. Dhrunk? He was footless!

foot-the-gutter /fʌt ðə gʌtər/, noun. nickname for untidy walker.

< OE 'fot' + OF 'goutiere' = gutter

Would ye walk right? Ye're hirplin about like a foot-the-gutther!

forby /fərbai/, adv. as well as, as well.

< Sc 'forby' = beside(s)

There was lashins (plenty to drink) an lavins (plenty to eat). There was all kinds o' shop dhrink forby a quare good dhrop o' the crayther (poteen).

Here's a luckpenny in your hand forby.

(to the) fore /for/, noun. alive.

< ME 'fore' = in front

Ye don't mean to tell me that Belfast Biddie's still to the fore? Sure she was an owl woman when I was a child an I'm wantin a year off seventy (I'm sixty-nine)!

foreign /fɔrn/, adv. abroad, overseas.

< OF 'forein' = not in one's own land

You're the daughther that was out foreign?

fortunate /fɔrtʃənət/, adj. unlucky, unfortunate.

< Lat 'forunatus' = lucky

God chile an you're fortunate! Every other wee blade was gettin money an you missed it.

fother, fodder /fɒər, fɒDər/, verb. feed farm animals.

< OE 'fodor' = fodder

<< ON 'fothr' = fodder

I've baists (beasts) ti' fo'er before I can go.

founder /faunDər/, noun and verb. bad flu; make one extremely cold.

< OF 'fondrer' = submerge, send to bottom

He's had the foundther the last eight days. It's not as bad as the shakin aygies (ague) but it's worse than the flu.

I'm foundthered. My feet's like stones.

four o'clock eyes /for əklɒk aiz/, noun. squint.

< OE 'feower' = four + ME 'of/a' = of

'Four o'clock eyes' wouldn't be in it even a wee bit (a sufficient description)! I'd say thon boy could see roun' corners.

four prices /for praisəz/, adj. very expensive.

< OE 'feower' + ME 'pris' = price

Sure a body would be mad to go near her shop – a byutique (sic 'boutique'), I believe she calls it! Everything she has is four prices.

*fozie /fozi/ adj. not good, spongy, applied to turnips.
< ?Du 'voos' = spongy
*The tornips is all fozie in the middle. They must a got a touch o'
frost.*

*fraun /frɔn/, noun. wild blue berry.
< Gael 'fraochán' = whortleberry
*The childher doesn't know to the difference. They're as ap
(likely) till ate poison as frauns.*

freets /frits/, noun. superstitions.
< Sc 'freit' = superstition, whim
They say it's bad luck to pass (go past without killing) *a
dale-clock* (beetle) *but who'd believe them owl freets?*

fret /frɛt/, verb. mourn.
< OE 'fretan' = chafe, irritate
*She used to be as fat as a wee ball o' butther but she's fretted that
much since the man* (her husband) *died that she's away to
scrapins.*

friend /fren/, noun. relative.
< OE 'freond' = relative, kinsman
We're near friends. Him an' me ma's full cousins.

full /fʌl/, adj. drunk, replete.
< OE 'full' = complete
Dhrunk? He was full, as full as a shuch.
I'm as full as a throut! I couldn't eat another corn (currant)!

full cousin /fʌl kʌzən/, noun. first cousin.
< OE 'full' + OF 'cosin' = relative
See **friend**.

fums /fʌmz/, noun. brown turf, intermediate in quality
between 'sthringy sods' and 'black torf, which lasts as long
as a woman's tongue'.
< unkn
<< Gael 'fód móna' = a sod of turf
With the winther comin on, a body would be glad of a load o' fums.
They'd do rightly for throwin a hate (heat) *about the place* (house).

*fyuggy /fyʌgi/, adj. left-handed, awkward.
< unkn
<< Sc 'fyachle' = loaf about
<< Gaelic 'fágtha' = backward.
*He's nearhand bein an out and out fyuggy! He can't do a hate
wi' the right hand.*

G

gab,geb /gyab, gyeb/ noun and verb. talk.

< SG/G 'gob' = beak, animal mouth

Did ye see him an him all guts an gab (stomach and mouth)? *Did ye hear him gabbin away like all that? Thon boy nivir learnt the wisdom of the owl sayin: 'Whatever ye say, say nothin'.*

gaberlunzie (USc) /gyabərlʌnzi/, noun. beggarman.

< Sc 'gaberlunzie' = beggar's purse

The auld gaberlunzie sae reggit an' spare

That used tae gang leppin alang,

Wi' a skep, an' a twerl, an' a boon' in the air,

An' a 'whoop!', an' a bedlamite sang, -

(G.F. Savage-Armstrong, 1845–1906)

gadderman /gyaɒərman/, noun. villain (can be affectionate).

< Gael 'geadaidhe' = thief + OE 'man' = man

<< ON 'gaddr' = goad, sting

Thon owl gaddherman, always on the batther (go)!

gag, geg /gyag, gyeg/, noun. joker.

< ON 'gaghals' = with neck thrown back

He's a right geg, always tellin that one about 'I'm goin as quack as I can'.

***gailin** (HE) /giələn/, noun. brood of chickens.

< Gael 'deilín' = brood of chickens

She went broody on me an then she come home with a gailin.

gallimuffry /gyalimʌfri/, noun. mess, hotchpotch.

< OF 'calimafrée' = ragout, hash

What are the young people comin till? They're not thryin to dhress a wee bit tasty. Hech naw. They're out in a gallimuffry o' clouts that you wouldn't have the cheek till offer till a beggar!

gallisses /gyaləsəs, gyaləsəz/, noun. braces.

< ME 'galwes' = gallows + '-es'

You'll do great! Go on, chile, ye'll do it at the slack of your gallisses (with consummate ease).

gallivant /gyaləvant/, noun and verb. travel about for pleasure.

< Sc 'gallivant' = gad about

You mark my words. You'll see the end of all your gallivantin. Can ye not settle down like another body?

galoot /gyəlut/, noun. rough person, usually male.
< unkn
<< Gael 'gealt' = madman, lunatic
What was that big galoot lookin (looking for)? *Dear knows but he was badly brought up!*

galore /gyəlor, gəlor/, adj. lots of, plenty.
< SG/G 'go leór' = plenty
They had money galore in them days an to the best o' my recollection they never wanted (lacked) *one or two servant girls.*

*galseed /gyalsid/, noun. poppy seed, bad seed, tares.
< Gael 'geal' = white, bright + OE 'sæd' = seed
The field must a been alive wi' galseed for the good seed was teetotally desthroyed.

gam /gyam/, noun. nitwit, fool.
< Sc 'gamf' = buffoon
<< Gael 'gam' = foolish person
Wasn't Silly Jack the right gam to put butther on his head on a sunny day?

game /giəm/, adj. brave.
< OE 'gamen' = diversion, sport
He's a game wee laddie, game as a pheasant!

gammy /gyami/, adj. lame, twisted.
< Fr 'gambi' = bent, crooked
<< Gael 'cam' = crooked
Gammy legs run in their breed.

gamut /gyamət/, noun. knack, special ability.
< eModE 'gamut' = range, compass
You may get that plug in, Mary, for you've got the gamut of it. I'm standin there pullin an pushin an I can make no headway whatsoever.

ganch /gantʃ/, noun. stupid person.
< Sc 'gansh' = snap, stammer
<< Gael 'gaimse' = simpleton
Ye stupid ganch ye! Can ye not stand up an fight your corner?

*gang (USc) /gyaŋ/, verb. go.
< Sc 'gang' = go
Where'll ye gang?

gansey, gensey /gyanzi, gyenzi/, noun. woollen sweater.
< Guernsey = Channel island
<< Gael 'geansaí' = woollen sweater

I know it's not warm but ye can't wear that gansey another day. It'll be walkin to work on its own if it doesn't get a wash.

gation /gyiəʃən/, noun. very thin person.

  < unkn

  << Sc 'gatty' = failing in body

  << Gael 'geataire' = man of slight build

Och chile but you're a gation! Did they not feed you? You're away to scrapins.

*gaun (USc) /gɔn/, adj. busy.

  < Sc 'gaun' = busy

He weaved himsel' an' keepit twathree gaun.

(James Orr, 1770–1816)

gavle-end /gyiəvəl en/, noun. gable-end.

  < ME 'gavel' = gable + OE 'ende' = end

Them childher has took off playin ball agin the gavle-en. You'd think the mother would learn them manners.

gawk /gɔk/, noun and verb. one who looks foolish, stare at.

  < eModE 'gawk' = stare vacantly

That big gawk's still standin there for all the world like a big gazebo.

Will ye quit your gawkin. Thry to look as if you're half in it (as if you have half your wits about you).

gawp /gɔp/, noun and verb. person who stares, stare vacantly.

  < ON 'gapa' = stare with open mouth

I hate anybody gawpin at me. That's why I give up singin.

gazebo /gyəzebo/, noun. useless structure or person.

  < ModE 'gazebo' = tower, look-out

Ye rared a lazy man, no harm to you! He's kind enough but he's like thon other gazebo up the road, fit for nothin but makin feet for childher's stockins.

geek /gyik/, noun and verb. peep.

  < Sc 'keek' = peep

  << Gael 'caoch' = peep

Would ye take a wee geek an see if your father's in the snug (private room in a pub).

get /gyɛt/, noun. bastard.

  < ON 'geta' = beget, obtain

He couldn't a thraited (treated) *her worse if she'd been a beggar's get.*

get /gyɛt/, verb. be allowed.
  < ON 'geta' = obtain, get
  Will you get goin? I'll only get goin if you're goin.
*gey (USc) /gye/, adv. very.
  < Sc 'gey' = very
  It's gey fu' (very full).
 giddy /gyɪdi/, adj. not serious.
  < OE 'gidig' = dizzy, easily distracted
  She's giddy when it comes till her books.
girn /gyɜrn/, noun and verb. twisted smile, complain.
  < OE 'grennian' = to show teeth in smile or anger
  A crooked, crabbit, crathur that bees neither well nor sick,
  Girnin' in the chimley corner, or goan happin' on a stick.
  (Marshall, 1888–1959)
glam /glam/, noun. (make) a grab for.
  < Gael 'glám' = grasp, clutch
  << Sc 'glamour' = catch in magic spell
  Boys ye niver seen sichen (such) *a han'lin',*
  I wos thunnersthruck watchin' the birl (commotion),
  The oul' da limpin' out wi' the pitchfork,
  An' the frens (relatives) *makin' glam for the girl.*
  (Marshall, 1888–1959)
glar, glaur /glar, glaur/, noun. thick, heavy mud.
  < Sc 'glaur' = mud, slime
  The low meadow's nivir the whack. One dhrop o' rain at all
  an you're up to the shoe-mouth in glar.
glassy /glasi/, noun. glass marble.
  < OE 'glæs' = glass + '-y'
  He has as much wit as the childher out playin taws wi' a hand
  full o' glassies.
gleek /glik/, noun and verb. glance, peep.
  < ?OF 'glic' = card game
  'Bo-Peep', they called her for she was keekin and gleekin from
  mornin to night.
glen /glen/, noun. glen.
  < SG/G 'gleann' = glen
  She's one of the Herons o' the Glen. They're a hardy breed
  an well-liked. Owl Lizzie would a give ye the coat off her
  back.
glit /glɪt/, noun. scum, slime.
  < OF 'glette' = slime, filth

You couldn't make soup with a bone now. All ye'd have in the pot is glit.

glory-hole /gloəri hol/, noun. hidden storage cupboard.
    < ModE 'gloryhole' = cell, receptacle for goods
    There's that much owl junk in the glory-hole undher the stairs that I'm damned if I can find a hate (thing). *I'll have to have a quare good redd out one o' these fine days.*

*glow (HE) /glo/, noun. commotion.
    < Gael 'gleo' = strife, battle
    I couldn't hear me ears in all thon glow but God an it was quare crack watchin the pullin an thrahin!

glug /glʌg/, noun and verb. gurgling noise, gurgle.
    < Gael 'gliogar' = rattle, empty noise
    << ModE 'glug' = onomatopoeic
    There's a gluggin in me guts. A bite hasn't passed my lips since mornin.

goat's toe /gots to/, noun. fool (in 'no goat's toe').
    < OE 'gat' + 'ta' = female goat + toe
    I'm tellin ye, Joe's no goat's toe. He could larn (teach) *the whole of us.*

gob, gub /gɔb, gʌb/, noun. impolite word for mouth.
    < SG/G 'gob' = beak, snout
    Look at the girn (twisted smile) *on the owl gob of him* (on his old mouth).

gobberlooney /gɒbərluni/, noun. stupid fool, sometimes humorous.
    < unkn
    << Gael 'cabairlín' = saucy-mouthed person
            'gabhlánaidhe' = bandy-legged person
    << Sc 'gaberlunzie' = beggar's purse
    He's the two ends of a gobberlooney!

going strong /goɪn strɔŋ/, phrase. dating steadily with the likelihood of getting married.
    < OE 'gan' + 'strong' = to go + strong
    They're goin sthrong a brave wee while. I'd say the big day won't be far off.

golong /gəlɔŋ/, exclam. dismissal.
    < OE 'gan' + 'lang' = to go + long
    Golong ye donkey!

gollop /gɒlɒp/, noun and verb. gulp food.
    < eModE 'golpe' = swallow hastily

It cost a fortune to put the belly on thon boy! Did ye see the way he gollops his mate (food)? *A body couldn't wheel it till him.*

*gombeen (HE) /gɒmbin/, noun. a conniving skinflint.

< Gael 'gaimbín' = usury, interest

There'll be a day at the catchin o' thon owl gombeen yet! He's as mane (mean) *as get out so he is.*

*gomeril /gɒmərəl/, noun. fool.

< unkn

<< Gael 'gamal' = stupid looking man

He's no innocent gomeril. Ye could have sympathy with a gomeril but thon boy is full o' badness. He doesn't know what to be up to for to be bad enough.

gooseflesh /gusfleʃ/, noun. gooseflesh, frisson.

< OE 'gos' + 'flæsc' = goose + flesh

I'm covered in gooseflesh. A goose must a walked on my grave.

goosegab, goosegog /gusgab, gusgɔg/, noun. gooseberry.

< ? OE 'gos' + SG/G 'gob' = goose + mouth

It's the red goosegogs I like best. The green ones is apt to be sour.

goosegreen /gusgrin/, adj. yellowish-green.

< OE 'gos' + 'grene' = goose + green

Ye're not goin to wear a dhress made out o' that, are ye? Sure ye know green's fortunate (unlucky) *an that's the worst green there is. It's goosegreen, the colour o' spring skitther.*

gorb /gɔrb/, noun. glutton.

< ?ME 'grubbe' = food

You dorty atin gorb, ye brute!
When I get at ye wi' me boot.

gorbitch /gɔrbitʃ/, noun. garbage.

< eModE 'garbage' = refuse, filth

Ye know what childher's like. They'd ate gorbitch from mornin till night an then not ate their dinner.

gormless /gɔrmləs/, adj. silly, lacking in sense.

< ON 'gaumr' = heed + OE 'leas' = devoid of

He's a gormless crayther. Anybody could take a han' out of him (make a fool of him).

*gortweed /gɔrtwid/, noun. field weeds.

< Gael 'gort' = field + OE 'weod' = weed

Gortweeds is stronger than the ones ye'd find in the garden.

gowl /gaul/, noun and verb. low growling noise in throat, roar.

< ME 'gurle' = growl, grumble
*As soon as you nap (rap) the door, you can hear the gowls o'
their owl dog.*

granny greybaird /granigrebɜrd/, noun. catterpillar of any
colour.
< eModE 'grandam/granny' = grandmother + OE
'græg' + 'beard' = grey + beard
<< Gael 'greannach' = hairy, furry
Grannygreybairds only come out in the good weather.

grape /griəp/, noun and verb. pitchfork.
< OF 'graper' = gather with hook
*Could you give us the len' o' your grape to thry an gather up
some o' this grass?*

***grass** /gras/ noun. grazing land.
< OE 'græs' = grass
<< Gael 'féar' = grass, grazing land
*And me father has forty white shillins
And the grass of a goat and a cow.*
(Traditional ballad)

grating /griətın/, noun. grate.
< OF 'grate' = grille + '-ing'
I dhropped a pound an it rolled down the owl gratin!

gravyring /griəvirıŋ/, noun. doughnut.
< ME 'grauey' = gravy + OE 'hring' = ring
Two coffees an two gravyrings, pet.

graw (HE) /grɔ, gra/, noun. love, affection, 'notion'.
< Gael 'grá' = love, affection
*I'd say there's a wee bit of a graw there yet. They were more than
great a couple o' years back.*

great /griət/, adj. close, very friendly.
< OE 'great' = large
<< Gael 'go mór' = great, friendly
Them'ns has always been very great.

greet (USc) /grit/, verb. cry.
< OE 'gretan' = to cry out
Stop greetin, hen. Your ma didn't mean it.

***greeshy, greeshoch** /griʃi, griʃɒx/, noun. ashes.
< SG/G 'gríosach' = ashes, embers
*Nothin I like betther than sittin at the hearth wi' the greeshy at
me feet.*

grew /gru/, noun. greyhound, term of abuse.

  < unkn

  << Sc 'grew' = shudder

  Alsation, how are ye! It's no more of an alsation than I am. It's nothin betther than a grew!

*grossart /grɒsərt/, noun. gooseberry.

  < Fr 'groseilles' = gooseberries

  Three pounds o' grossarts have I picked this day an me hands is desthroyed on me.

groundshels /graunʃəlz/, noun. dregs, tea leaves.

  < OE 'grundesylige' = plant

  << Gael 'gráinseail' = refuse of corn

  Ye couldn't touch tay (have a cup of tea) *in their house. It's only hot wather on top o' the grounshels.*

*grouse /graus/, noun. a long, miserable face, a 'puss'.

  < ?OF 'groucier' = grumble

  << Gael 'gramhas' = snout, mouth, frown

  Joe was never the one ti' have a grouse on him.

guff /gʌf/, noun. cheek.

  < Sc 'guff' = give off smell

  << Gael 'giofacht' = officiousness

  Any more o' your owl guff, me girl, an I'll leave the thrack o' my hand across your mouth.

gugglingrey /gʌglɪn gre/, noun. grey, used as a put down.

  < Gael 'gogarim' = grey + OE 'græg' = grey

  What colour is it? Gugglingrey, the colour of a mouse's diddy.

guggy (HE) /gʌgi/, noun. child's word for boiled egg.

  < Gael 'gogaí' = egg

  Who's for a guggy this mornin?

*guider /gyaidər/, noun. cart.

  < ?Sc 'guider' = director

  In the name o' God, what'll they turn up in next. Sure that's no motor car. It's more like an owl guider we done away wi' years ago.

gulder /gʌlDər/ noun and verb. loud shout, roar.

  < unkn

  << Gael 'callóid' = uproar

  He let a guldher out of him that was no miss. You could a heard it in Cushendall.

gullyknife /gʌlinaif/, noun. big, sharp knife.
  < Sc 'gully' = large knife
  You couldn't be up to her (predict her behaviour). *She could give me the house out with me or she could chase me with a gullyknife!*

gulpin /gʌlpɪn/, noun. heavy, awkward person, usually male.
  < eModE 'golpe' = swallow
  << SG/G 'giolla' = servant boy
  That big gulpin! Sure what does he know but what the spoon put in him. (He has no intelligence, refinement or polish. He absorbed nothing but food.)

gumption /gʌmʃən/, noun. self confidence, intelligence.
  < Sc 'gumption' = intelligence
  That wee lad o' yours'll go far. He's a good chile an full to the ears o' gumption.

gunk /gʌŋk/, noun and verb. shock, let down, deceive.
  < unkn
  << Gaelic 'geangadh' = mauling, beating
  I got the quare gunk when nobody took me undher their notice (when everyone ignored me).
  She gunked the whole of us! Day after day in the chapel and now she's away livin with a fancy man!

guttersnipe /gʌTərsnaip/, noun. term of abuse.
  < ModE 'guttersnipe' = street urchin
  Well, one word borrowed another. I lost my rag but I wasn't goin to let thon owl gutthersnipe away wi' castin up at me.

guttery /gʌTəri/, adj. muddy.
  < OF 'gotiere' = gutter + '-y'
  As I went over a gutthery gap
  I met a wee fella wi' a red cap.
  A stick in his ass, a stone in his belly.
  Come riddle me that an I'll give you a penny.
  (Children's riddle for 'cherry')

gutties /gʌtiz/, noun. tennis shoes.
  < ModE 'gutta percha' = rubber
  I'm not sure what you call them (what they are called). *Me ma calls them gutties an me da calls them mutton dummies.*

gutty /gʌti/, noun. rubber, bladder.
  < ModE 'gutta percha'

There was good gutty in my day. I can go from mornin to night without ever goin to the lavatory.

*gwall /gwal/, noun. as much as can be carried in both arms (I have only heard the term applied to turf.)

   < Gael 'gabhal' = fork, space enclosed

Go on chile. Bring us (me) in a gwall o' torf, jist as much as you can carry in your two hands.

H

hack /hak/, noun and verb. sore, cause sores; cut in chunks.

   < OE 'haccian' = to cut in pieces

Weather like this would take lumps out o' ye. I've hacks all over my hands.

Don't hack the bread, chile. Use a sharp knife an cut it nice.

haddie /hadi/, noun. in 'finnan haddie', smoked haddock.

   < OF 'hadot' = haddock

   < Sc 'finnan haddie' = smoked haddock

To be honest, I don't think people knowed many names for fish. There was 'herrin' that a body would ask for, especially 'salt herrin' an there was 'pollock' an afther that it was just 'white' fish or 'brown'. Mind you, ye did get some people that called brown fish 'finnan haddie' but mostly it was just 'a half a poun' o' white an a half a poun' o' brown'.

hae (USc) /he/, verb. have.

   < Sc 'hae' = have

Hae ye no manners?

hag /hag/, noun. coward.

   < ME 'hegge' = female evil spirit

He's a hag ti' the backbone. Afraid ti' go up the stairs on his own. He's afraid somebody might ate him!

*haggard /hagyard/, noun. hay-yard.

   < ?OE 'heg' + 'geard' = hay + yard

Wi' people buyin in fother an vetch, there's not so much call for the haggards that people used to have.

hagginblock /haginblɒk/, noun. wooded area.

   < ? OE 'haccian' = to cut + OF 'bloc' = solid piece

Many's a match was made in the hagginblock. That's where everybody went ti' coort (court).

halfers/halvies /hafərz, haviz/ noun. equal shares.
  < OE 'healf' = half + '-ers'
  I believe they went halvies in the farm with the understandin
  that Joe can buy the brother out.
half'n /hafən/ noun. small glass of whiskey.
  < OE 'healf' + 'an' = half + one
  << Gael 'leath cheann' = half one, small whiskey
  I'll have a half'n an a bottle (a small whiskey and a bottle
  of stout).
half-cut, -tore /haf kʌt, tor/, adj. drunk but not fully intoxi-
cated.
  < OE 'healf' + ME 'cutte' = cut, OE 'teran' = to tear
  He was cryin like a child. Some men biz like that when they're
  half-tore.
hallion /halyən/, noun. clumsy person, often female.
  < Sc 'hallion' = buffoon
  << Gael 'eala-bhean' = swan-like woman
  Thon big hallion has broke the leg o' me stool.
  (It was not unusual to compare a woman and a swan as
  we see from the following ballad:
  With her shawl round her shoulders
  He took her for a swan
  And that was the end of his own Molly Bawn.
hames /hiəmz/, noun. mess.
  < unkn
  Would ye cut that hedge right an not be makin a hames of it?
hammer(in) /hamər(ɪn)/, noun and verb. beat severely.
  < OE 'hamor' = hammer
  He was a fair man but a hard man. He'd never listen till a story
  (piece of gossip) *an if he got ye doin somethin wrong, he'd*
  hammer ye. I mind one night I give him his porridge in the goat's
  bowl an he mordhered me. I'm tellin you there was a loodherin
  match that night. Och but sure what does youngsters care about
  a batin? I was just as bad or worse the next day.
hand /han/, noun. hand, in various constructions.
  < OE 'hand' = hand
  That'n would take a han out of (mock) *his own mother.*
  He has hans on him for anythin. (He's very good with his hands.)
  He has quare hans on him. (He's good with his hands.)
  He has a quare pair o' hans on him. (His hands are big.)

handling /hanlın/, noun. big undertaking.

  < OE 'handlian' = feel with the hands

  How many childher did ye say ye had? God an that's a handlin an a half.

hanging together like a pair of trousers /haŋın təgɛər laik ə pɜr ə ᴛrauzərz/, adv. quite well.

  < OE 'hangian' = to hang

  How are you doin, the day?

  I'm ony rightly. I'm hangin together like a pair o' throusers.

hansel /hansəl/ noun and verb. (give a) present in the hope of giving good luck.

  < ON 'handsal' = giving the hand in bargain

  There was many ways o' hansellin a new house. If ye were goin for the first time, ye would a took three things: a lump o' coal that they might always have heat an light; a dhrop o' salt that their food would always be tasty; an a sixpence that there would always be money.

hap /hap/ verb. dress warmly, cover oneself well.

  < Sc 'hap' = cover, wrap

  Now hap you yourself well goin out. It's threacherous the night.

hard /hard/, adj. hard, mean.

  < OE 'heard' = hard

  It's as hard as the hammers o' hell!

  You're as hard as a hoor's heart.

hardy /hardi/, adj. cold but healthy.

  < OF 'hardi' = bold

  << OE 'heard' + '-y'

  That's a hardy one for you! (It's a cold day!)

(if/when) hardy comes to hardy /hardi kʌmz tə hardi/, adv. in an extremity.

  < ModE 'hardy' = blacksmith's tool

  If hardy comes to hardy, we can sell the place.

  When hardy comes to hardy them MacMahons is very clannish.

(By the Lord) Harry /(bai ðə lɔrd) hari/, exclam. polite swearing.

  < eModE 'Harry' = King Henry

  By the Lord Harry, I'll leave the thrack o' my belt across your legs the day!

*harl o' bones /harl ə bonz/, adj. very thin.

  < Sc 'harl' = roughcast + OE 'ban' = bone

That's dietin for ye! She was a wee ball o' butther before she went
till England an now look at her, a harl o' bones!

hasp /hasp/, noun. door fitting, part of latch.

< OE 'hæsp' = hinged fastening

That hasp'll not howl. Ye might as well fix it with a bit o' paper.
It reminds me o' saft John that barred the door with a sausage!

hate /hiət/, noun. tiny piece. In rural areas, Scottish-
influenced speakers tend to say 'Dale a hate' whereas
Irish-influenced speakers prefer 'Divil the bit'.

< ?OE 'hætu' = heat, single effort

We forced him up an down but dale a hate he'd give us.

have a notion of /hav ə noʃən ə/, verb. be romantically
interested in.

< OE 'habben' = to have + Lat 'notio' = idea

She has a brave notion o' thon boy. He has a nice face an a right
good way with him but you mark my words. If she marries a will
o' the wisp like thon, she'll not have her sorrows to seek!

haver /hiəvər/ verb. talk nonsense; behave indecisively.

< Sc 'haver' = talk nonsense

Och well now, the crayther's eighty odd (over eighty) *so ye*
don't be surprised if she havers a wee bit.

Thon boy can't make up his mind. Between haverin here an
switherin there, you mark my words, he'll end up an he won't
get a woman (wife) *at all.*

headbombadier /hedbʌmadir/, noun. person in charge.

< OE 'heafod' = head + Fr 'bombadier' = artilleryman

Did ye hear that Minnie's boy is headbombadier over in Bir-
mingham? He has done powerful well, so he has.

headbuckcat /hedbʌkkyet/, noun. person in charge.

< OE 'heafod' + 'buc' + 'cat' = head + buck + cat

If I'm livin an spared I'll see the headbuckcat about it in the
mornin.

headstaggers /hedstagərz/, noun. madness associated
with the moon.

< OE 'heafod' + ON 'stakra' = stagger

You'll give me the headstaggers, chile, with all this owl nonsense.
From the day an hour ye put your foot in that school, it's been
'gimme' an' 'get me'. For God's sake, give me head pace (peace).

head-the-ball /hed ðə bɔl/, noun. name for unpredictable
man.

< OE 'heafod' + ME 'bal' = ball
Sure who'd listen to head-the-ball?

hear tell of /hir tɛl ə/ verb. hear about.
< OE 'heran' + 'tellan' = to hear + to make known
Out she went one mornin for butthermilk an she was nether seen nor heerd tell of from that day ti' this. Sometimes I be puzzlin over it an I think owl Barney must a done her in.

hear the grass growing /hir ðə gras groɪn/, verb. have excellent hearing.
OE 'heran' + 'græs' + 'growan' = to hear + grass + to grow
It's very sad now. Our Mary could hear the grass growin an she can't sing a note.

(with a) heart and a hand /(wɪθ ə hart an ə han/, adv. with pleasure.
< OE 'heorte' + 'hand' = heart + hand
You can have it wi' a heart an a han an may you have all sorts o' good luck wearin it.

heart o' the hand /hart ə ðə han/, noun. centre of palm.
< OE 'heorte' + 'hand'
<< Gael 'croidhe na baise' = heart of palm
I could scratch the heart o' the han off myself. I'll be gettin a surprise.

heartscalded /hartskɔldəd/, adj. mortified, vexed.
< OE 'heorte' + Lat 'excaldare' = wash in warm water
<< Gael 'scallach croidhe' = upset, vexed ('scall' = scald, insult; 'croidhe' = heart)
I'm heartscalded with the whole o' yiz!

heartsome /hartsʌm/, adj. cheering
< OE 'heorte' + '-some'
There's nothing as heartsome as a good fire.

*heckle (USc) /hɛkəl/, noun. flax-dressing comb.
< Sc 'heckle' = flax comb
Thou grimmest far o gruesome tykes
Grubbin thy food by thorny dykes
Gude faith, thou disnae want for pikes
Both sharp and rauckle (strong);
Thou looks (Lord save's) arranged in spikes
A creepin heckle.
(Samuel Thompson (1766–1816))

heech /hix/, exclam. used to provoke an answer.

< ME 'heh' = exclamation

You've learned your lesson now, heech? Ye'll not be so uppity now, heech?

heel /hil/, noun. crusty end of the bread; part of palm nearest wrist.

< OE 'hela' = heel, buttom crust

You can't get the heel all the time. You may eat a slice like another body.

I knocked the end of it with the heel o' my hand.

hen-toe(d) /hen to(d)/, adj. and noun. pigeon-toed.

< OE 'henn' + 'ta' = hen + toe

Hen-toes an kaylegs (bandy-legs) *goes together.*

hesky /hɛski/, adj. overly hasty.

< OF 'hasti' = hasty (cf 'pest' and 'pesky')

Ye've no call (need) *to be hesky. Have a wee dhrop o' tay in your han and get yourself together. If ye rush at it like a mad bull ye'll do more harm than good.*

*****heth** /hɛθ/, exclamation.

< ?ME 'heh' = exclamation

Heth an I'll go with you if I'm livin an spared.

hide nor hair /(haid nər hɜr/, phrase. nothing at all.

< OE 'hyd' + 'hær' = skin + hair

They looked everywhere but they nivir foun' hide nor hair of her an that's the story of the woman that went for butthermilk.

*****hill-la-loy** /hɪl lə loi/, call. traditional call of a man selling salt herrings.

< unkn

Hill-la-loy with their mouths open

Pipes in their mouth an them smokin.

himself (HE) /hɪmsɛlf/, pronoun and noun. male head of house.

< OE 'him' + 'self' = himself

<< Gael 'é féin' = emphatic 'he'

I was wondherin is himself in.

hinch /hɪntʃ/, noun. hip, hip bone.

< OF 'hanche' = haunch

I've a touch o' rheumatics in my hinch.

hip-at-the-clinch /hɪp ət ðə klɪntʃ/, noun. someone with a limp.

< OE 'hype' + 'clencan' = hip + clinch
Thon fall did him no good. He's like hip-at-the-clinch ever since,
just nought an carry one.

hippity-tippity /hɪpɪti tɪpɪti/, adj. eager to have people and
things as tidy and organised as possible.
< Sc 'hippertie tippertie' = over punctilious
Your father was a hippity-tippity kind o' man. Good enough and
kind enough but a wee bit too finickity of himself if you take my
meanin.

hirple /hɜrpəl/, verb. hobble, walk with limp.
< Sc 'hirple' = hobble
Would ye quit your hirplin. You'd be nether lame nor lazy if a
body gave you the price of a black 'n tan (bottle of stout and a
glass of whiskey).

hives /haivz/, noun. skin eruptions.
< Sc 'hives' = skin rash
This good weather has brought the chile out in hives. Her back's
just alive with them.

hobbledyhoy /hɒbəldihoi/, noun. hunched-up goblin-
like person, usually male.
< eModE 'hobbard de hoy' = clumsy or awkward youth
I see ye've still your wee owl hobbledyhoy in the corner.

hobnob /hɒbnɒb/, noun and verb. one who is or who
behaves as if he is socially mobile upwards.
< ModE 'hob or nob' = to drink to one another in turns,
be familiar
People would make you laugh! Yankie Dolan puttin out that he's
a hobnob an him went till America without a shoe till his foot.

hochle /hʌxəl/, noun and verb. walk in a slovenly way.
< OE 'hoh(sinu)' = hamstring + '-le'
I'll break your mouth if ye don't lift your feet! Ye've got intil a
rotten, dorty habit o' hochlin instead o' walkin.

hod /hɒd/, noun and verb. hod for carrying bricks, carry
bricks in a hod.
< OF 'hotte' = pannier
Seven brick would be as many as ye could hod up two flight o'
stairs.

hogo /hogo/, noun. bad smell.
< Fr 'haut goût' = high flavour
There's a quare hogo o' thon boy's feet.

hoke /hok/, noun and verb. poke in the ground, uproot.
  < Sc 'howk' = dig, burrow
  << Gael 'tóch' = rooting, digging
  What is it you're lookin? If you'd only tell a body what you're
  lookin, I might know where it is an you could stop your hokin in
  the dhrawers.

hold foot to /haul fʌt tɪl/, verb. sustain such a level of
expenditure.
  < OE 'haldan' + 'fot' = hold + foot
  Nobody could howl foot ti' that. Ye'll have to be a bit more thrifty
  with your money.

hoodlum (HE) /hudləm/, noun. turncoat, person who plan-
ned to be a priest but changed his mind close to ordination.
  < ?Ger 'haderlump' = good-for-nothing
  He's a good enough wee fella but you don't like to see your
  daughther marryin a hoodlum.

hooley /huli/, noun. enjoyable get-together.
  < ?Gael 'hulach' = turmoil
  I hear yiz had a quare hooley out at your place las' night. I believe
  it was quare crack.

hoor /huər/, noun. whore.
  < OE 'hore' = adulterer
  An what do they call you, son? (What's your name?)
  Sometimes Mommy calls me a 'hoor's basket' (a whore's
  bastard).

hoor's get /huərz gɛt/, noun. whore's bastard.
  < OE 'hore' + ON 'geta' = to beget
  That'n is the two ends of a hoor's get. She wouldn't give ye
  daylight!

hot-press /hɒt pres/, noun. airing cupboard.
  < OE 'hat' = hot + ME 'presse' = cupboard
  Put them wet things in the hot-press. They'll be bone dhry by
  mornin.

hough /hɔx/ noun. back of leg.
  < OE 'hohsinu' = hamstring
  I get a cramp in me hough at night now an I've thried
  everything. There's corks undher the matthress an a magnet on
  the table but I'm still crucified with the cramp.

houthern /hʌðərn, hʌərn/, adj. untidy, slovenly (usually of
a woman)

< unkn
<< Gael 'ceatharnóg' = ungainly female
God an you're houthern! Will ye tidy yourself an the place up a bit?
howl your tongue/whisht /haul yər tʌŋ/ʍɪʃt/, exclam.
Don't talk.
< OE 'haldan' = to hold + eModE 'whist' = call for silence
<< Gael 'bí 'do thost' = be quiet
Would ye howl your whisht about Yankie Dan. He cleaned up afther the Yankies in the Hib Hall an to hear him ye'd think he was born an rared in America.
howlt /hault/, noun. fix, difficulty.
< OE 'haldan' = to hold
I got out o' the one prockus but I was still left in a howlt.
***huckaback** /hʌkabak/, noun. rough linen.
< ModE 'huckaback' = linen fabric
Their sheets are all made o' flourbags an they'd cut lumps out o' ye. It's like thryin to lie (sleep) on huckaback!
***huckleback** /hʌkəlbak/, noun and verb. lively dance.
< ?eModE 'huckle' = hip + OE 'bæc' = back
D'ye mine (remember) the Charleston an the huckleback? God, we had quare crack at the dances in them days!
huff /hʌf/ noun and verb. pique, 'strunt', avoid taking a man in draughts.
< eModE 'huff' = blow, bully
She has took the huff. God but people's aisy annoyed these days. You huffed so I can lift your man.
***huff** /hʌf/, noun. upper part of thigh.
< OE 'hohsinu' = hamstring
See her huffs? Ye could nearly see her navel! I just don't know what the young'ns is comin till!
hug-me-tight /hʌg mi tait/, noun. shawl, any garment for a woman that is close fitting.
< ON 'hugga' = comfort + OE 'me' + 'thiht' = me + tight
I could be doin with me hug-me-tight. There's no hate (heat) an the hall would foundther ye (make one very cold).
hum /hʌm/, noun. bad smell.
< eModE 'hum' = unpleasant smell
There's a quare hum o' thon boy's feet! A boy like that should be parboiled.

hum an' ha /hʌm ən ha/, verb. hesitate, put someone off.

   < Sc 'hum and hae' = prevaricate
Will ye quit your hummin an ha-in an give a body a sthraight answer.

humidity /hyumɪdɪti/, noun. very gentle rain.

   < Latin 'humidus' = moist + '-ity'
Sure that's not rain. It's what we would call the humidity fallin.

humour /hyumər/, noun. pus.

   < OF 'humor' = fluid, specimen of the body's four fluids
That knee's bieldin. I doubt we may open it an get the humour out.

humpy-dumpy /hʌmpi dʌmpi/, noun. Humpty Dumpty, short fat person.

   < ModE 'Humpty Dumpty' in rhyme
Mrs X hasn't her crosses to seek with thon owl humpy-dumpy clockin by the fire mornin, noon an night.

(like) hunger's mother /(laik) hʌŋərz mɔər/, adj. very thin.

   < OE 'hungor' = hunger + 'modor' = mother
All that dietin has torned a sancy wee blade intil a gation. She's like hunger's mother.

hungersome /hʌŋərsʌm/, adj. tending to be hungry.

   < OE 'hungor' + '-some'
Boys is hungersome. You need to give them something very fillin, like fresh soda bread.

hungry grass /hʌŋri gras/, noun. grass which makes those who walk on it hungry.

   < OE 'hungor' + 'græs' = hunger + grass
   << Gael 'féar gortach' = hungry grass (grass + hungry)
I never saw anybody pack away as much food as you, boy. You must a thramped on hungrygrass!

hunker(s) /hʌŋkər(z)/, noun and verb. haunches, squat down.

   < Sc 'hunkers' = haunches
When we were at school, we had to sit on our hunkers in the corner if we couldn't spell right.
Go on, chile. Hunker you down over there an don't let a peep out o' ye.

hunt /hʌnt/, verb. haunt and hunt.
    < OE 'huntian' = to hunt
    << OF 'hanter' = to haunt
    Can dead people really come back to hunt you?
    Ye give me a pup (a bad bargain). *Thon owl dog o' yours is out huntin crows from the crack o' dawn. I might as well not have a dog about the place.*
hurl /horl/, noun. ride.
    < Sc 'hurl' = bowl along, wheel
    If yous childher is good, we'll go for a we horl in the car the day.
hurley /horli/, noun. game for men, similar to hockey.
    < eModE 'hurling' = a game
    He clove him open wi' his horley bat. He got a quare bat (blow) *now.*
hushaby /hʌʃabai/, noun and verb. (sing a) lullaby.
    < ModE 'hushaby' = lullaby
    It's not everybody that can hushaby a baby to sleep. You have to have the gamut (knack) *of it.*
huxther /hʌkstər/, noun. house/property that is badly run down.
    < ?Du 'hoekster' = person who carries a backpack
    You're not thinkin o' buyin a place where the women hang their washin out on the sthreet? Sure a place like that would be no betther than a huxther or a dundherin-in.

I

ignorant /ignərənt/, adj. rude (a strong insult).
    < OF 'ignorant' = person lacking knowledge
    You're an ignorant plug! You don't know how to behave wi' daicent people.
illwill /ɪlwɪl/, noun. strong dislike.
    < ON 'illvili' = malevolence
    You may give up, chile. If a body has that much illwill agin you, you'll do no good. Let her have it an may all bad luck go with it.
*inchland /inʃlan/, noun. marshland, low land near water.
    < SG/G 'innis' = island + OE 'land' = land
    Lan's got out of all buyin, even inchlan. (Land has become too expensive to buy and this applies even to marshland.)

Indian male /ɪndiən miəl/, noun. maize (often associated with the hardship of the Great Famine in 1846ff).
  < OE 'Indea' + 'melu' = India + grain
  They forget the owl ass-hole that shit the Indian male. (Proverb. They forget that they once needed help, even if the help that was given was of little value to either the givers or the receivers.)
ingine /ɪndʒɪn/, noun. engine.
  < OF 'engin' = contrivance
  He must spend all his time talkin till his ingines because he nivir passes a word wi' another soul. By God an he learnt the owl sayin: 'A shut mouth makes a wise head!'
*inglenook /ɪŋəlnyuk/, noun. chimney corner seat.
  < SG/G 'aingeal' = light, fire + 'niuc' = corner
  Thon wee wasp nivir left the inglenyook! He was cowl-rifed. Winther or summer he was clockin half-way up the chimley.
insense /ɪnsɛns/, verb. convince, persuade.
  < Sc 'insense' = convince
  You might as well thry an make an impression on a rubber ball. You couldn't insense anything into the heads o' the youngsthers that's goin now.
insleeper /ɪnslipər/, noun. future visitor who will spend the night.
  < OE 'in' + 'slep' = in + sleep + '-er'
  If a torf falls out o' the fire, ye'll have ether an insleeper or an outsleeper, an if it's red, he'll come in scratchin himself.
intil /ɪntɪl/, prep. into.
  < OE 'in' = in + ON 'til' = to
  The light near left me eyes! Who did I bump intil in Leeds but thon owl peeodler from Moneymore. He was still bummin an blowin but I got away as quick as was daicent. It's as my mother always said: 'You can watch a rogue but you can't watch a liar!'
*ithergates (USc) /ɪðərgiəts/, adv. somewhere else.
  < Sc 'ithergates' = elsewhere
  I can't get me eyes together (get a little sleep) *with all the talkin. Could yiz not go ithergates?*
itinerant /aitɪnərɪnt/, noun. Gypsy, traveller.
  < Lat 'itinerans' = travelling
  Margaret McDonough is the smartest girl in the class. She's an itinerant an she has the longest hair.

its lone /its lon/, adv. on its own, alone.
  < eModE 'its' + 'lone' = solitary
  The bone stands its lone,
  The bone stands its lone,
  Hey ho me deary oh,
  The bone stands its lone.
  (Children's rhyme)

J

jack-easy /dʒak iəzi/, adj. very easy, no trouble.
  < ?'Jack' + OF 'aisié' = easy
  Now, it might give throuble till another body but it's jack-easy to
  me.
jag, jeg /dʒag, dʒeg/, noun and verb. prick, injection,
barb.
  < Sc 'jag' = prick, thorn
  That's a joke wi' a jeg in it!
*****jam** /dʒam/, noun. poor teacher, not fully qualified.
  < ModE 'Junior Assistant Mistress'
  Are you tellin me that she's puttin her nose up to be principal an
  her only a jam?
jap /dʒap/, noun and verb. splash with mud.
  < Sc 'jaup' = splash, drop of water
  My stockins were all japped.
jar /dʒar/, noun. sociable drink.
  < Fr 'jarre' = vessel
  We'll just have a wee jar to settle our nerves.
jarbox /dʒar bɒks/, noun. sink.
  < Sc 'jawbox' = kitchen sink
  Who left clothes steepin in the jarbox?
jaunt /dʒɒnt/, noun and verb. ride, trip for pleasure.
  < eModE 'jaunt' = make a trip
  Do you mine (mind = remember) *the time we used to go out of*
  a Sunday an we'd go to Omeath an we'd go for a jaunt to
  Calvary an Paddy Dhrumm would be singin: 'Enjoy yourself,
  it's later than you think'?
jessie /dʒesi/ noun. effeminate man.
  < Jessie = woman's name

Did you see your man (the one we've just been talking about) *out yesterday an him pushin a pram? A man, pushin a pram! He's turnin out to be a right wee jessie.*

jiffy /dʒɪfi/, noun. instant.

< ModE 'jiffy' = short time

Will ye howl (hold) *on a wee minute. Now, just a wee jiffy an I'll give ye all the assistance I can.*

jinty /dʒɪnti/, adj. and noun. small, small man.

< eModE 'Jenny' = woman's name, female of certain birds

The men from Belfast is all wee jinties. Ye'd see bigger things up a three (tree).

jinty wren /dʒɪnti ren/ noun. wren.

< eModE 'jenny' + OE 'wrenna' = wren

The jinty wren, she lays but ten

An rares (rears) *them up like gentlemen.*

(Children's rhyme)

joog /dʒug/, noun. hypercorrection of 'jug'.

< eModE 'jug' = vessel with handle

Don't shame a body! Get that big milkbottle off the table. Where's the wee delph joog?

joogle /dʒugəl/, verb. jiggle, shake.

< ME 'iugelere' = juggler

Will ye quit jooglin that chile. She's not a toy.

*jorum /dʒorəm/, noun. bowl for punch, punch.

< ModE 'jorum' = drinking bowl

In weather like this, the only thing that would warm you to the core is a wee jorum o' punch.

*jube /dʒub/, verb. suspect.

< ?Lat 'dubietas' = doubt

I wouldn't like to say who I jube now, because I'm not certain but I have my suspicions.

juke /dʒuk/, verb. peep, dodge, avoid.

< Sc 'jouk' = elude

He was jukin an keekin an lookin could he see what was goin on. You'll have to juke them or you'll have them clockin on you (visiting) *every night.*

jummle /ʒʌməl/, noun and verb. jumble.

< ME 'jombre' = move about in a disorderly way

There's a whole big jummle o' stuff in the attic. It'd take you the best part of a week to go through it.

junder /dʒʌnDər/, noun and verb. jolt, shove.
  < Sc 'jundie' = jolt, push
  My neck's desperate (in a bad state). *I was enjoyin myself
  dhrivin the two of us in a bumpin-car when some misbegotten
  eejit jundhered right intil us an sent us flyin.*
jundey /dʒʌndi/, verb. push or shove in an unmannerly
way.
  < Sc 'jundie' = jolt, push
  *Now a wee shove nivir hort nobody but thon timeservin get jus
  jundied himself to the front o' the queue.*

K

kackhanded(er) /kyakhandəd(ər)/, adj. and noun. left-
handed, clumsy.
  < eModE 'cack' = excrement + OE 'hand' = hand
  *It's not easy to work with a kackhander. You're workin one road
  an he's workin the other.*
kale /kyiəl/, noun. cabbage.
  < ME 'cole' = cabbage
  << Gael 'cál' = cabbage
  *There's nothin to touch a bit o' boiled ham with mashed potatoes
  an corly kale.*
keech /kyix/, noun and verb. excrement, defecate.
  < Sc 'keech' = defecate
  *Riddle me riddle me reech
  What do you do before you keech?
  Bend your knees
  Give a squeeze
  Out comes yella cheese.*
  (Children's rhyme)
*keek /kyik/, noun and verb. peep.
  < Sc 'keek' = peep
  << Gael 'caoch' = peep, wink
  Would ye take a wee keek in the windy (window) *to see is there
  anybody in.*
keeny (HE) /kyini/, verb. cry, wail.
  < Gael 'caoineadh' = mourn, lament
  That chile'll keeny somebody out o' the house.

keep /kyip/, noun and verb. board and lodgings, maintain.
   < OE 'cepan' = to keep
   Sure what's her keep? A board (bird) *would ate* (eat) *more!*
*keerog /kyirog/, noun. beetle.
   < Gael 'ciaróg' = cockroach, beetle
   Me heart's as low as a keerog's kidney (I'm very depressed
   but I can still joke about it).
kehee, kehoe /kyəhi, kyəho/, verb. laugh in a particular
way. To kehee is to whinny; to kehoe to laugh loudly.
   < unkn, perhaps onomatopoeic
   Yiz must be havin quare sport (good fun) *here the night. I could*
   hear the keheein an kehoin before I got half way up the hill.
*kelpie /kyɛlpi/, noun. spirit with black hair and green
eyes.
   < Sc 'kelpie' = water spirit
   << SG/G 'cailpeach' = heifer
   I'm afeard of her, if I'm to be honest. She's like a sheeoge or a
   kelpie. Thon green eyes can look through ye.
*ken (USc) /kyen/, noun and verb. knowledge, know.
   < Sc 'ken' = know, knowledge
   That's beyon' my ken now, chile an I'd say it'd be beyon' your
   thumb (it would be impossible for you to change it).
   A dinnae ken what's wrang wi' me;
   A'm vixed, A kennae why;
   A cannae talk, A cannae wark;
   My min's a' gang'd agley;
   A say sich foolish thin's at whiles
   My face is scorched wi' pain…
   O let them lave me tae mysel'!
   A jist wud be alane.
   (G.F. Savage-Armstrong, 1845–1906)
*kibben /kyɪbɪn/ noun and verb. dibbler stick for making
holes in the ground for planting seeds.
   < Gael 'cipín' = stick
   You don't see kibbens now.
   What's a kibben?
   A dibbler stick for kibbin.
*kile (USc) /kyail/, noun. small haystack, haycock.
   < Sc 'kile' = hayrick
   There's a tidy farmer for ye! All the grass cut an ricked in kiles.

kill /kyɪl/, noun. kiln.
  < OE 'cylene' = kiln
  I believe Joe got an awful jowlt (jolt). *The owl bogie come off the line an ran full butt intil the kill.*

kiltie /kyɪlti/, noun. man who wears a kilt.
  < ?ON 'kjalta' = skirt
  I like the kilties well enough but thon owl bagpipes would deeve (deafen) *you.*

*kinch /kyɪntʃ/, noun. knot.
  < ?Lat 'cingula' = girdle
  Now that's a kinch nut (knot). *They learn you to make the different nuts when you start wavin* (weaving).

kink /kyɪŋk/, noun and verb. fit of coughing or laughing; frizzy hair.
  < Sc 'kink' = twist, choke
  Well I got into that big of a kink I thought I'd a coughed me guts out. Them'ns has all a bit of a kink in their hair.

*kinnel /kyɪnəl/, noun. warm drink/food for a cow that has just calved.
  < Gael 'cineál' = foodstuff for cow during milking
  If ye hadn't a give the roney (red cow) *a kinnel, she'd a lifted her foot an clove ye open.*

kip /kyɪp/, noun. house of ill repute.
  They sent us till a place in Benidorm and, as God's my judge, the hotel was no betther than a kip. We were afraid to go out when it got dark an it gets dark brave an early out foreign.

*kish /kyɪʃ/, noun. rush basket.
  < Gael 'ceas' = coracle, basket
  Me mother could make kishes an they were the quare mark (very handy) *for carryin torf.*

kiss-me-quick /kyɪs mə kwɪk/, noun. kiss curl.
  < OE 'coss' + 'me' + 'cwic' = kiss + me + lively
  I can't stand these wee kiss-me-quicks that they're all growin on their foreheads. Your face doesn't be clean lookin if there's wee bits o' hair all over the place.

*kist /kyɪst/, noun. wooden chest.
  < ON 'kista' = chest
  Kists was always kep' in homes in the counthry until people started to bring in newfangled furniture like ottomans an poufees (pouffes).

*kitchen /kyɪtʃən/, noun and verb. stretch food out, sauce.

   < OE 'cycene' = kitchen

   She can kitchen it well or, as she would put it, she can make a meal out o' nothin.

   Hunger makes the best kitchen. (Proverb)

kitter /kyɪTər/, noun. left-handed person, fool.

   < Gael 'citeóg' = left-hander, clumsy

   It's not often ye sit between two kitthers!

kitterdy /kyɪTərdi/, noun. foolish person.

   < Gael 'citeóg' = left-hander, clumsy

   Och it's sad! Ony (only) the one daughther an her a kittherdy!

kittle /kyɪtəl/, verb. have kittens.

   < Sc 'kittle' = have kittens

   Ye may watch the cat. She's about ready to kittle.

kittlen /kyɪtlən/, noun. kitten.

   < Sc 'kittlin' = kitten

   Wee kittlens is nice but ye can't have too many about the place.

   The bucks (tomcats) *'d be afther them in no time.*

kneecap /nikyap/, verb. punish by shooting in the knee.

   < OE 'cneow' + 'cæppe' = knee + cap

   Tom O. has a terrible limp!

   They kneecapped him. Did you not know?

*kyoch /kyox/, adj. still raw, not fully cooked.

   < unkn

   << Gael 'ceoch' = disease

   I don't like loaf bread (shop-bought bread). *It's ap* (liable) *to be kyoch in the middle.*

L

*labscouse /labskaus/, noun. stew, mess.

   < unkn

   << Gael 'lábaireacht' = plastering

          'leadhbachtas' = untidiness

   She knows more about a bad breakfast than she knows about cookin. I went in last Sunday an sure it wasn't a dinner at all they were atin. 'Goulash', she called it! Labscouse more like!

lachter /lɒxtər/, noun. only child in phrase 'a cuckoo's lachter'

   < ON 'latr' = nest

How could he be other nor (than) a wintherstale (weakling) an him a cuckoo's lachther.

lacing /liəsɪn/, noun. quite severe beating.

   < ME 'las' = snare, to lace

You're askin for a quare lacin, boy, an you'll get it too the minute we get home.

lambaste /lambiəst/, verb. beat severely.

   < eModE 'lambaste' = thrash

   << ON 'lemja' = beat

The father'll lambaste him when he gets home. I wouldn't rare (rear) an uncivil (rude) chile. He had no business to torn his tongue on ye (answer you back) or give back cheek.

lambeg drum /lambeg drʌm/, noun. large drum played only by Protestants.

   < Lambeg (place name)

Ye need to be quare an strong to lift a lambeg not to mention playin it.

*langle /laŋəl/, noun. tether tying the front and hind legs together.

   < eModE 'langelyn' = bind together

   << Gaelic 'langal' = spancel from front to hind leg

The buckgoat wants away (to go after the nannygoats). The spancel (rope for goats) now isn't enough. You may langle him.

lap /lap/, verb. wrap, wrap up.

   < ME 'wrappe/wlappe' = wrap

Lap that parcel a bit tidier now. Where's a body goin to write the addhress on a rough article like that?

Now lap up warm. That night would foundher ye!

larn, learn /larn, lɜrn/, verb. learn, teach.

   < OE 'leornian' = learn, teach

It's a boy (a strange phenomenon) when the childher's learnin their mother.

lash /laʃ/, verb. spend lavishly.

   < eModE 'lash' = be lavish

They've lashed out on the weddin because apart from the one wee girl, they have neither chick nor chile.

lashings /laʃɪnz/, noun. plenty (usually of liquid).
  < eModE 'lash' = be lavish + '-ings'
  Och now, they put up a powerful spread (great reception).
  There was full an plenty, lashins an lavins. I'm tellin you, no
  cotther (poor person) *lives there.*
lather, lether /laðər, laər, lɛðər, lɛər/, noun. ladder.
  < OE 'hlæder' = ladder
  You have the handiest wee lather I've ever seen. The nixt time
  I'm decoratin I'll send for the len' (loan) *of it an take a wee thrick*
  out of it (use it).
laugh /laf/, noun in phrase 'badly a laugh for'. greatly in
need of.
  < OE 'hlæhhan' = laugh
  You were badly a laugh for a woman when you took thon owl
  targe (woman who scolds a lot).
leather /lɛðər/, verb. beat severely.
  < OE 'lether' = skin, thong
  O Lammity Father! He leathered the lad somethin shockin.
*lee (USc) /li/, verb. lie.
  < Sc 'lee' = to tell an untruth
  He'll no listen ti' her. She was aye a leear (liar). *She would lee as*
  lief as look at ye!
*leelang (USc) /lilaŋ/, adj. live-long.
  < Sc 'leelang' = livelong
  The bairns would play
  All the leelang day!
  (Traditional ballad)
*leesome /lisʌm/, adj. pleasant.
  < Sc 'lousome' = lovable, affectionate
  O, a leesome enough wee body an canny wi' a shillin.
*(Peggy's) leg /pegiz leg/, noun. striped stick of rock.
  < female name + ON 'leggr' = limb
  I don't want the barley sugar sticks. I want a Peggy's leg.
length /lɛnθ/, noun. as far as.
  < OE 'lengthu' = length
  We'll go the lenth o' the mainroad with you.
length of one's tongue /lɛnθ ə wʌnz tʌŋ/, noun. reprimand,
scolding.
  < OE 'lengthu' + 'tunge' = length + tongue

I knocked his door an told him he had a big nail in the front wheel an instead o' thankin me, I got the length of his tongue about not mindin me own business.

lep /lɛp/, adj. and verb. lap; leap, jump up.

< OE 'hleapan' = to leap

I have no time for lep dogs. Some o' them weemen thinks more o' them wee dogs than they would of a chile.

There was a time I could a lep that river an nivir a looked back an now I'm lookin for stones so that I can sthriddle across.

let in /lɛt ɪn/, verb. leak.

< OE 'lætan' + 'in' = let in

The owl shoes is not seaworthy at all now. They're lettin in badly.

let on /lɛt ɔn/, verb. 1. pretend 2. reveal.

< OE 'lætan' + 'on' = let on

1. I'll let on that I'm Charlene an you can let on you're Lucy.
2. Now don't let on ye got anything for he won't let you spend it. You know what he's like about wilful waste makin woeful want!

(cat's) lick /(kyɛts) lɪk/, noun. superficial wash.

< OE 'liccian' = to lick

I haven't time to wash the floor properly so a cat's lick will have to do it for the time being.

lift /lɪft/, verb. 1. steal 2. arrest, intern 3. understand 4. cheer up.

< ON 'lypta' = raise

1. Don't you lave (leave) that bag there. Ye could get it lifted.
2. She had two boys lifted on the 9th an the father lifted on the 10th.
3. What did he say? I didn't quite lift it.
4. Put on a wee bit o' music there. It might lift my mind (cheer me up).

lig, liggety /lɪg, lɪgɪti/, noun. fool. ('Lig' is often male and 'liggety' female.)

< unkn

<< Sc 'lig wi' = consort with

<< Gael 'liog' = maimed limb

Would ye listen to thon lig! There's wiser in Omagh (Lunatic Asylum in Tyrone).

light /lait/, noun. sight.
   < OE 'leoht' = light
   The light near left me eyes when I opened the door an seen your man (the one we've been talking about).
light /lait/, adj. thin, translucent (of material).
   < OE 'leoht' = of little weight
   His hair's gettin very light on it. (He's going bald.)
   It's that light, ye could spit peas through it!
light boys /lait boiz/, noun. irresponsible young men.
   < OE 'leoht' + ME 'boie' = boy
   He has got in wi' a bad click (group) *o' light boys, goin to card schools* (places where cards are played for money) *an out till all hours.*
lightsome /laitsʌm/, adj. light on one's foot.
   < OE 'leoht' = light + '-some'
   It must be quare good news! Tommy's away down the road as lightsome as a lamplighter.
line /lain/, noun. doctor's certificate, certificate.
   < OE 'line' = thread-like mark
   If ye're not goin to work, ye may get a line from the docthor. Did anybody see my lines? I had them all in this handbag, marriage lines, birth certificates, an now I can find nothin.
link /lɪŋk/, verb. go arm in arm.
   < ON 'hlenkr' = loop in chain
   It wasn't ony (only) *linkin, they were. They were oxthercoggin other!*
links /lɪŋks/, noun. sausages.
   < ON 'hlenkr' = loop
   << OE 'hlincas' = undulating ground
   Is them links the day's (Were those sausages freshly made today)?
lint /lɪnt/, noun. the inside of flax.
   < ME 'lynnet' = lint flax, dressing
   In them days, the inside o' the flax was called lint. That's the bit that they torn into linen.
lintwhite /lɪntʍait/, noun. linnet.
   < OE 'linetwige' = linnet
   And to the lintwhite's piping
   The many's a tune I played.
   (Traditional ballad)

lip /lɪp/, noun. cheek.
< OE 'lippa' = lip
We'll have less o' your lip, my girl. When you start bringin in a wage you can start dictatin but not before.

loaf /lof/, noun. shop-bought bread with a crust on two sides only.
< OE 'hlaf' = loaf, bread
Do you want a loaf or a pan loaf (one with a crust on each side)?

loanin /lonən/, noun. narrow country lane, path.
< OE 'lane' = lane + SG/G '-ín' = diminutive marker
Did ye manage to dhrive up that wee loanin?

lock /lɒk/, noun. few.
< eModE 'lock' = few, not many
He gave me a lock o' sweets in my hand an told me to go home.

lone /lon/, noun. alone.
< ME 'al ane' = alone
Was he left his lone? No wondher he took aff (complained). I wouldn't like to be left me lone in a big ramblin house like this!

(think) long /(θɪŋk lɔŋ/, verb. meditate, contemplate.
< OE 'lang' = long
She does be thinkin long about when she was young an she can mind everythin she done when she was a child but sure, betimes, she doesn't know that she has her dinner ate.

long-headed /lɔŋ hedəd/, adj. deep-thinking, highly intelligent.
< OE 'lang' + 'heafod' = long + head
<< Gael 'ceann fada' = intelligent (head long)
Our'ns were all brave an smart, thank God. They all passed the 11+ an that but I'd say the chile was the best. He was long-headed from the day an hour he was born.

longnebbed /lɔŋnebd/, adj. nosy.
< OE 'lang' + 'nebb' = long + nib, tip
Golong you longnebbed crayther. Don't you stick your long, quiverin nose in my business again.

longsome /lɔŋsʌm/, adj. slow to act.
< OE 'lang' = long + '-some'
She's a right good dhressmaker. I'll give her that, but she's longsome about doing things.

look /lʌk, luk/, verb. want.

  < OE 'locian' = see, look

  What are you lookin? If you're lookin spuds, we're sowl (sold) *out.*

loss /lɔs/, verb. lose.

  < OE 'losian' = to lose

  I thought ye said he was young! He was an owl man, for God's sake. Ye could loss a penny in every wrinkle!

lough /lɔx/, noun. lake.

  < SG/G 'loch' = lake

  They say there was a town dhrownded in the lough an when the wine's (wind's) *rough, ye can hear the chapel bells ringin.*

*loughryman /lɒxriman/, noun. short man with magical powers (not a dwarf or elf).

  < Gael 'luchorpán' = pigmy

  Thon'n is a loughryman if ever I seen one. Even the boards (birds) *is afeard of him!*

*lowp /laup/, verb. leap.

  < ON 'hlaupa' = leap

  Wouldn't ye wondher where the childher gets the energy from? They're out there, lowpin an kehoin from mornin till night.

low-set /losɛt/, adj. short in stature.

  < ME 'lah' = not tall + OE 'settan' = to set

  Och, ye must know Billie B. He's the wee, lowset man that's saved. Och ye see him every weekend in the square prayin an singin an preachin. The childher says he sings:

  The bells of hell go tingalingaling

  For you but not for me.

  O death, where is thy stingalingaling?

  I know the Lord loves me.

loy /loi/, noun. narrow-bladed spade.

  < Gael 'láighe' = spade

  Loys is handy when ye're on a stony place.

luckpenny /lʌkpɛni/, noun. small return when a bargain has been struck.

  < Du 'luc' = fortune + OE 'penig' = penny

  He paid eighteen hundhred in cash for the car an had to fight for a luckpenny of five pounds!

luckybag /lʌkibag/, noun. potluck.

  < Du 'luc' + ON 'baggi' = container

It's a bit like a luckybag. You might do all right or you might come away with nothin.

luder /luDǝr/, verb. beat severely, hit heavily.
< Gael 'lúdradh' = beating, buffetting
It wasn't what ye would call a fight! It was a ludherin match. His face was pure pulp.

lug /lʌg/, noun. ear.
< Sc 'lug' = ear
Be careful what you say in front of the chile. Wee jugs has big lugs, ye know.

*lum /lʌm/, noun. chimney.
< Sc 'lum' = chimney
Ye never see a chimley sweeper now. I have to set fire to clear my chimley out when it won't dhraw. But there was an owl fellow years ago that came round an he always said the same thing: 'One an a tanner to redd out your lum (7.5 pence to sweep your chimney).'

lump /lʌmp/, noun. good size, when applied to a child.
< ME 'lump' = lump
Your youngest must be a right lump of a lad now.

Lurgan shovel/spade /lorgǝn ʃʌvǝl, spiǝd/, noun. very long face.
< Lurgan = placename + OE 'scofl/spadu' = shovel/spade
Thon boy would have a long face to wash in the mornin (i.e. he is bald). He's as long in the face as a Lurgan shovel.

*luvesome (USc) /lüvsʌm/, adj. loveable, affectionate.
< OE 'lufu' = love + '-some'
Lassies are luvesome whenever they're wee (girls are affectionate when they're young).

M

mad /mad/, adj. angry.
< ME 'amad' = excited, furious
I was spittin mad! Imagine invitin a body roun' special an then not askin had I a mouth on me (if I'd like something to eat or drink).

*maggymore (HE) /ˈmagimor/, noun. big fair.
  < Gael 'margadh mór' = big fair
  There's no crack at the maggymores like there used to be.
magobbler /məgɒblər/, noun. term of address and reference for a child, often a naughty one.
  < Gael 'mo ghaobaire' = my witty person
  An what about magobbler? Has she not got a mouth on her (are you not going to offer her something to eat and drink)?
make /miək/, noun. halfpenny.
  < ?OE 'macian' = to make
  It's a make, not a moke. A moke's a donkey. That's a make; that's a wing (penny); *that's a tanner* (sixpenny piece) *an that's a bob* (shilling).
male /miəl/, noun. meal.
  < OE 'melu' = meal
  Did ye hear who's dead?
  Biddy behin' the bed.
  Did ye hear who's in jail?
  A wee bag o' mail.
  (Children's rhyme)
*malecyartin /miəlkyartən/, noun. chilblain.
  < unkn
  << Gael 'maol-troigh' = bare foot
      'maoil-dearg' = red like a boil
  God himself ony knows why we called chilblains malecyartins. Maybe we just didn't know any betther.
man /man/, noun. husband; and in phrases: 'man above', God, and 'your man', the one just referred to.
  < OE 'man' = man
  << Gael 'an fear suas' = God (the man above)
  My man's out workin the day.
  Ye can mock me but ye can't mock the man above.
  Says your man to me, says he: 'Any chance of a sale, Mrs Woman?'
man dear /man dir/, exclam. Good Lord.
  < OE 'man' + 'deore' = man + dear
  Man dear, but you're behin' the times. Miniskirts is back in again!
mane /miən/, adj. mean.
  < ME 'mene' = inferior, ignoble
  That'n is too mane to live. He's as mane as get out so he is.

*march /martʃ/, noun and verb. boundary, be adjacent to (of land only).
　< OF 'marche' = boundary
　This is what was called 'march land'.
　Their land marched on our own.
market /markyət/, noun. market, age to be married.
　< ME 'market' = market
　<< Gaelic 'margadh' = market, contract.
　Ye'll pull that scarf as long as a market stockin.
　She'd take a cripple on a cross for she's near past her market.
*markins /markyənz/, noun. toeless socks, over-socks.
　< unkn
　<< Gael 'máirtín' = type of stocking
　The warmest day nivir seen the markins off.
*marl(ey) /marl(i)/, adj. mottled like marble.
　< OF 'marle' = type of clay
　<< Sc 'marl' = mottle
　An for the working tops, I'd like a light grey with a marl finish, if you know what I mean.
*marl(ey) /marl(i)/, adj. confused.
　< ?Sc 'marl' = mottle
　My head's a marley with all this noise. I can't think with that television on so loud!
mart /mart/, noun. market.
　< eModE 'mart' = fair, market
　Now the cattle mart is of a Thursday an to the best o' my knowledge, they sell flowers on a Thursday too but I couldn't tell you for sure now whether there's anything else at the mart for it's the beasts that I'm interested in.
mass (HE) /mas/, noun. esteem, high regard.
　< Gael 'meas' = valuing, estimating
　I have no mass in clothes or them things.
mate /miət/, noun. food, meat.
　< OE 'mete' = food, meat
　Och now, he's not the whack. He's off his mate an that's nivir a good sign.
*maun (USc) /mɔn/, verb. must.
　< Sc 'maun' = must
　A maun thole! (I have no option but to put up with it.)

may /me/, verb. must.

< OE 'mæg' = may, be able

Ye may stop the car this very minute for I'm goin to boke.

meeting house /mitɪn haus/, noun. place for non-conformist church services.

< OE 'gemeting' + 'hus' = meeting + house

Och, it was the loveliest wee meetin house ye ever clapped eyes on an it was goin for nothin (very cheap) *but it was in a bad area* (area where there the troubles are bad).

meet up with /mit ʌp wə/, verb. encounter.

< OE 'metan' + 'up' + 'with' = to meet + up + with

It's not who they gout (go out) *wi' that you worry about. It's the company they meet up wi' when they are out.*

melt /mɛlt/, noun. often used as an insulting word for 'offspring, spawn'; stuffing.

< OE 'milt' = spleen in mammals

<< Sc 'milt' = sperm

<< Gael 'málaid' = bag, foolish person.

It'd be a poor day that I'd let a hoor's melt (whore's offspring) *check* (reprimand) *me.*

I thought he was goin to knock the melt out o' me!

*meskin /mɛskɪn/, noun. crock of butter, crock.

< Gael 'meascán' = pat of butter, small dish

They don't make meskins now but they were the quare mark (very useful) *after chornin.*

message /mesədʒ/, noun. errand.

< OF 'message' = communication

Hear, wee boy, will ye run a message for me?

midden /mɪdɪn/, noun. dunghill.

< ME 'mydding' = manure heap

The place was like a midden! God knows now but it has went to loss (has deteriorated badly) *since the mother died, God rest her.*

midge /mɪdʒ/, noun. gnat, small fly.

< OE 'mycge' = gnat-like insect

I'm not too good at readin the paper now, but I could see a midge at Maghery.

*mig /mɪg/, noun. scream, squeal.

< Gael 'míog' = cry of bird, bleat

She let a mig out of her that ye'd a thought she was a-stranglin.

mind /main/, verb. remember; look after.

< OE 'gemynd' = memory

I can mine things a done fifty years ago but I can hardly mine what I had for me dinner the day.

I don't want to be mindin the chile all the time. Is there nobody else can mind her?

minging /mɪŋɪn/, adj. child's word for 'very dirty'.

< unkn

<< Sc 'mingmang' = confusion, disorder

It was really mingin. There was no place to sit even.

mingy /mɪndʒi/, adj. mean.

< ? 'm(ean) + (st)ingy' = mean

They're a terrible mingy click (group). *They talk as if they hadn't even the nails for ti' scratch wi' but sure everybody knows they're loaded* (very well off).

miscall /mɪskɔl/, verb. denounce, slander.

< eModE 'miscall' = revile

He miscalled me for all the owl torfmen (he cast doubt on my reputation).

mischievious /mɪschiviəs/, adj. mischievous.

< OF 'mischief' = playful malice + '-ious'

Boys is mischievious of themselves. As Masther Willie used to say: 'Whenever you see a wee boy, give him a kick on the ass, because if he's not comin from doin somethin wrong, he's on his way to do it.'

misdoubt /mɪsdaut/, verb. disbelieve.

< eModE 'misdoubt' = suspect

I don't misdoubt it. I always said there'd be a day at the catchin o' thon boy (that boy would get his just deserts).

miserable /mɪzərəbəl/, adj. mean.

< OF 'misérable' = wretched, avaricious

He's too miserable to live, always pleadin a poor mouth an him wi' more money than he knows what to do with.

misfortunate /mɪsfɔrtʃənət/, adj. unfortunate.

< eModE 'misfortune' = ill luck + '-ate'

There's some people an' if they fell intil the wather, they'd come up dhry but our ones is misfortunate. They couldn't get wather if they went to the well!

mismake /mɪsmɪk/, verb. give oneself away by showing surprise.

< Sc 'mismake' = disturb, trouble

I never mismade myself. I just looked at her. 'Is that right?' says I. 'Well now, that's news to me!' Her face fell a mile. I could see she was gunked.

mitch /mɪtʃ/, verb. play truant.
   < OE 'mycan' = to steal
   The girls hardly ever mitch or skive.

mither /maiðər/, verb. scold, nag in a whining tone.
   < unkn
   << ModE 'moither' = confuse, perplex
   Would ye for God's sake quit mitherin! Gimme pace (peace) to get me head shired, will ye?

mizzle /mɪzəl/, noun and verb. light rain.
   < Du 'miezelen' = drizzle
   Sure that's not rain. It's not even mizzle. It's just the humidity fallin, as my mother used to say.

*moilly /moili/, adj. hornless.
   < Gael 'maol' = bald + '-y'
   It's that cowl it'd blow the horns aff a moilly goat.

mommy /mɒmi/, term of address and reference. mother.
   < ModE 'Mom' = mother + '-y'
   Mommy doesn't be out much these days. She hasn't really been at herself since that fall she took (had).

mooch /mutʃ/, verb. idle around.
   < ME 'mouche' = skulk
   Och I know there's nothin for them, like no work or nothin, but ye'd still think they could do somethin betther than moochin around the corners.

moonlight flit /munlait flɪt/, phrase. move without paying debts.
   < OE 'mona' + 'leoht' = moon + light + ON 'flytja' = move
   You mark my words, all these big dos (parties) is goin before somethin. They wouldn't be the first nobs (rich people) that done a moonlight flit an them owin the counthry (owing money to everyone).

*morrow /mɒra/, verb. borrow until the following day.
   < ME 'morwe' = day after + OE 'borgian' = take on pledge
   They were only morrowin it, they said, an that was six months ago an we haven't seen the shoe last since.

mortal /mɔrtʃəl, mɔrtəl/ adj. very.
  < ME 'mortel' = fatal, deadly
  I'm very sorry indeed. I forgot all about it but if I'm livin an spared, I'll get it for ye this mortal night.
moss /mɔs/ noun. turf bog.
  < OE 'meos' = bog, swamp
  I won't shake hands with ye, daughther, if ye don't mind. We've been workin all day in the moss an me hands is the colour o' torf.
mouth /mauθ/, noun. in various phrases, 'in the mouth o' Christmas' (very close to Christmas), 'poor mouth' (pleading poverty), 'shoe mouth' (opening of the shoe).
  < OE 'muth' = mouth
  << Gael 'i mbéal' = close to (in the mouth)
            'béal bocht' = pleading poverty (mouth poor)
  A death's bad at any time but it's desperate in the mouth o' Christmas.
  I never seen ye but ye had a poor mouth on ye (you were pleading poverty).
  The snow's thick now. It was over the shoe mouth when I come in.
mowl /maul/, noun. mould.
  < ON 'mygla' = mould
  If ye take that wee clippin (cutting) *an put it in torf mowl an a wee toty dhrop o' wather on it, ye'll have a lovely plant this time next year.*
  Away an cla (claw) *mowl on yourself* (get lost).
*muckle (USc) /mʌkəl/, noun. large amount.
  < Sc 'muckle' = a great deal
  Manny's a mickle macks a muckle (Proverb, Every little bit counts).
muck out /mʌk aut/, verb. clean.
  < ON 'myki' = dung + OE 'ut' = out
  An what'll ye give me if I muck out the byres?
mucky /mʌki/, adj. dirty, muddy.
  < ON 'myki' = dung
  << Gael 'muc' = pig
  It's mucky enough now workin in the claypit but the money's clean.
(like a) Mullingar heifer /(laik ə) mʌlɪngyar hɛfər/, adj. fat and beefy.

< Mullingar = placename + OE 'heahfre' = heifer
She's beef to the ankle, like a Mullingar heifer.

munchees /mʌntʃiz/, noun. marshy area, turf bogs.
< Gael 'móinte' = moors, peat bogs
You can always tell a muncheeman : clobber (mud) to the knee.

***musheroon** /mʌʃərun/, noun. mushroom.
< OF 'mousseron' = mushroom
God but he was as white in the face as a well-washed musheroon!

N

***nae** (USc) /ne/, adv. no, not.
< Sc 'nae' = no, not
Is there nae room at your feet?
I'll nae be seein him the day.

***nane** (USc) /nen, niən/, negative pronoun. none.
< Sc 'nane' = none
Ye'll nae gee'm (give him) nane.

nap /nap/, noun and verb. knock softly.
< Sc 'nap' = blow with hammer
*Were ye nappin long? I thought a heard a wee nap at the door but
I wasn't sure.*

***nary** /neri, nɜri/, adv. emphatic not.
< OE 'næfre' = not ever
How many did ye get?
Nary a wan (not a single one).

nate /niət/, adj. neat.
< OF 'net' = clean, trim
That chile's as nate as ninepence.

***natural draft** /nɛkərl ᴅraft/, noun. living image.
< OF 'naturel' = innate + ME 'draht' = sketch
*God but thon chile's the neckerl dhraft o' the grandmother. She's
owl Mary on the sod.*

naw /nɔ/, negative answer. no.
< OE 'na' = no
*Naw, I will not. I may have neither chick nor chile (I am totally
alone in the world) but I'm nobody's cotther (I'm not in
anyone's pocket).*

nayger /niəgər/, noun. mean person.
  < ON 'hnoggr' = mean person
  Now there's some people would give you the clothes off their back an there's others wouldn't give ye the skin of their skitther, but now I've been alive since I was born an a while before it an I have yet to meet a bigger nayger than that tight-fisted crayther you brought into the house last night!

near /nir/, adj. mean.
  < ON 'nær' = closer
  I doubt your friend is a bit near of himself. Imagine comin to spend a couple o' days with us an him with his two hands the one length (without a present).

nearbegone /nirbəgɔn/, adj. very mean.
  < ON 'nær' + ME 'begone' = go away
  That nearbegone owl misert! Sure ye know what they say about him? They say that if he had nine gold watches, he wouldn't tell the time till his blind sisther!

nearhand /nirhan/, adv. almost.
  < Sc 'nearhaun' = almost
  You nearhan sned (cut) *the leg o' that boy!*

*neave (USc) /niv/, noun. fist.
  < ON 'hnefi' = fist
  That crakin (whining), *crabbit* (cross) *crayther! Who does he think he is, shakin his neave at the childher if they as much as go near his front gate.*

neb /neb/, noun. nose (impolite).
  < OE 'nebb' = nib, tip
  Get your neb out o' this. It's of no concern to you.

neddy /nɛdi/, noun. donkey.
  < Ned + '-y'
  There's a whole lot o' different words for 'donkey'. There's 'ass': 'He knows his road like a beggin ass'; an there's 'cuddy', though that's usually a grey boy; an there's 'moke' an there's 'neddy'. Neddies is almost like pets, I suppose.

neggin /nɛgɪn/, noun. measure of alcohol.
  < eModE 'noggin' = quantity of liquor
  << Gaelic 'noigín' = vessel holding about a litre
  They had a couple o' five-neggin bottles o' whiskey an a dhrop or two o' brandy but that was about all. It was a very dhry wake!

neighbour's childer /niəbərz tʃɪlDər/, noun. children who are specially attached to each other because they were brought up almost as siblings.
> < OE 'neahgebur' + 'cildru' = neighbour + children
> *Sure he could do nothin else but to throw a wee bit o' business Harry's way. Weren't they neighbour's childher?*

*newance /nyuəns/, noun. novelty, something unexpected.
> < OE 'niwe' = new + '-ance'
> *Begod an that's newance for ye. That's new light through tired windies* (windows)*!*

New aZealand /nyu azilən/, noun. New Zealand.
> < placename
> *They were all runagates, them'ns. There's a boy or two in Australia an a couple in America an now the daughter's away till New aZealand.*

newfangled /nyufaŋəld/, adj. modern.
> < eModE 'newfangled' = new fashioned
> *I have no time at all for these newfangled songs. Sure they're not songs at all. They've neither top, bottom nor sides to them. It's just people keenyin like a bunch o' banshees!*

*nicht (USc) /nɪxt/, noun. night.
> < Sc 'nicht' = night
> *The bogle's due this aye nicht* (poltergeist's due this very night)*.*

nick /nɪk/, verb. steal.
> < ModE 'nick' = cheat
> *The fancy ways people has o' talkin! They don't say he was lifted for stalin* (stealing)*. Aw naw, it's he was accused o' nickin somethin!*

*nim /nɪm/, verb. steal.
> < OE 'niman' = to steal
> *Them's the very boys would nim the eye out o' your head!*

nip /nɪp/, noun and verb. pinch.
> < Sc 'nip' = pinch
> *That was no nip. Ye took the lump clean out o' me with them big scoops* (long nails) *o' yours.*

nippy /nɪpi/, adj. chilly (of wind).
> < Sc 'nip' + '-y'
> *It's not too bad. It's still a bit nippy but it's nothin to what it was last night.*

nivir /nɪvɪr/, adv. never.
  < OE 'næfre' = not ever
  That'n'll nivir comb a grey hair (that one will die young).
no harm in /no harm ɪn/, adj. without sin or guile.
  < OE 'na' + 'hearm' + 'in' = no + harm + in
  He was the best crayther that ever faced the clay. There was no harm in him.
*****no that well** (USc) /no ðat wil/, phrase. not very well.
  < OE 'na' + 'thæt' + 'wel' = no + that + well
  He's no that well at the minute.
nob /nɔb/, noun. important person.
  < ?Du 'knob' = knob, knot
  << ModE 'hobnob' = be on good terms with
  The nobs is all left since the throuble started up an there's anybody livin in their houses.
(Jack) Nod /dʒak nɔd/, noun. sleep.
  < name + ME 'nodde' = nod
  He can't keep his wee eyes open. I'd say Jack Nod's comin on.
nor /nər/, conj. than.
  < ME 'nor' = nor
  << Gaelic 'ná' = than
  He was a wee bit fatter nor me.
notion /noʃən/, noun. fancy, admiration, affection.
  < Lat 'notio' = idea
  Thon boy has the quare notion of himself.
not wise /nɒt waiz/, adj. insane.
  < ME 'noht' = not + OE 'wis' = learned
  Have a titther o' wit. It's not just a wee want. Sure the man's not wise.
nought and carry one /nɔt ən kari wɔn/, adj. and nickname for someone who is lame.
  < OE 'nowiht' = nothing + OF 'carier' = to carry + OE 'an' = one
  Did ye see nought an carry one? He's neither lame nor lazy since the daughther moved back in with him.
numbskull /nʌmskʌl/, noun. fool, dunderhead.
  < ModE 'num(b)skull' = dolt
  Is the childher learnin nothin in school these days? They're a bunch o' numbskulls an dundherheads. I asked a wee boy where Cork was an he said 'At home in a bottle!' They're not only stupid, they're uncivil with it.

*(deaf) nut /def nʌt/, noun. nut with no kernel.
< OE 'deaf' + 'hnutu' = deaf + nut
Them Brazil nuts is a bad buy! Half o' them's deaf nuts. There's nothin at all in them.

nyam /nyam/, noun and verb. noise made by a cat.
< onomatopoeic
Did you hear the nyammin last night? There's too many buck cats about the place.

(buck)nyay /(bʌk)nyeɪ/, noun. insult, term of contempt.
< unkn
<< Gael 'bochtán' = poor person
Who does he think he is an him dhressed up like a bucknyay.

nyiffnyaff /nyɪfnyaf/, noun. trifle, small ornament.
< ModE 'knick-knack' = trifle
Och, I'm awful fond o' them wee nyiffnyaffs.

nyeeher /nyihər/, noun and verb. noise made by a horse.
< onomatopoeic
Horses can be as bad tempered as people, ye know. Me da had one horse. Och he was spunky but he had to be learnt his place. He would suddenly rust (refuse to draw the cart), *let a nyeeher out of him an stan on his back legs, throwin me da and the full contents of the cart on to the road.*

nyimf,nyimp /nyɪmf, nyɪmp/, noun. tiny bit.
< unkn
<< Gael 'neamh-thuis' = thing of no importance
Not as much as a nyimf o' beef did I get!

nyook /nyuk/, noun. nook, alcove.
< Sc 'neuk' = corner
You've got nyooks in every room an they're quare an handy. Robert's new house now hasn't got any nyooks. They don't build wi' chimneys any more.

O

obligement /obledʒmənt/, noun. favour.
< OF 'obliger' = pledge + '-ment'
I was ony lookin for a wee obligement but she hadn't the goodness in her for to do it.

och-hanee-o /ɒxanio/, exclam. alas!
  < unkn
  << Gael 'ochaoideacht' = moaning
Och-hanee-o! I'm sick, sore an tired o' bein stuck in the same place day in an day out!

(what) odds /ʍat ɔdz/, exclam. it doesn't matter.
  < eModE 'odds' = difference
I lost my wee purse. Och but sure what odds! It had very little in it.

*odious /odʒəs/, adv. very, extremely.
  < OF 'odious' = hateful
He's an odious big man, now. He must be close on seven feet.

often as fingers and toes /ɔfən əz fɪŋərz ən toz/, adv. up to ten times.
  < ME 'ofte' = often + OE 'finger' + 'ta' = finger + toe
  << Gael 'comh minic is atá méireanna coise agus láimhe orm' = as often as I have toes and fingers on me (fingers of feet and fingers of hand)
He's out an about like a good'n. He's in town every day an out visitin as often as fingers an toes.

old /aul/, adj. disparaging epithet.
  < OE 'ald' = old
He's a right owl skinflint!

old-fashioned /aul faʃənd, old faʃənd/, adj. advanced for one's years.
  < ModE 'old-fashioned' = cunning
That's not a child! It's a wee, owl-fashioned man!
The DHSS money isn't goin to the right people. There's owl-fashioned boys on the double (on the dole but also working) *an they're gettin everything an there's people without tuppence gettin nothin.*

old lip /aul lɪp/ noun. cheek.
  < OE 'ald + lippa' = old + lip
I'll take none of his owl lip. I'll cut the mouth of him (slap him on the mouth) *the next time I see him.*

*Old Year's Night /aul yirz nait/, noun. New Year's Eve.
  < OE 'ald' + 'gear' + 'niht' = old + year + night
There'll be a bit of a do on Owl Year's Night.

*oot (USc) /üt/, adv. and prep. out.
  < OE 'ut' = out
He let it oot o' the bag!

orange /ɔrndʒ/, adj. and noun. Protestant.

< William of Orange

He's as orange as a lily (symbol of some Protestant groups).
D'ye not mine (remember) *Orange Lily? Och, she used to go
out on the Twelfth wearin a union jack? Well the crayther was
found dead at the foot of her stairs this mornin. She must a took a
terrible toss.*

other /ɒðər, ɒər/, pronoun. one another.

< OE 'other' = one of two

*They're powerful fond of other. Ye never see one o' them out their
lone.*

*outby /autbai/, adv. out of doors.

< Sc 'ootby' = outside

She's not far now. She's outby an if ye go the length (as far as) *o'
the hedge, ye may* (must) *see her.*

out-mouthed /aut mauθt/, adj. with protruding teeth.

< OE 'ut' + 'muth' = out + mouth

*The polite word for it is 'out-mouthed' but we usually say
'bucktoothed'. It's like having the sort of teeth where you could
eat an apple through a letterbox.*

*ower (USc) /oər/, adv. and prep. over.

< Sc 'o'er' = over

It's a' ower the head (because of) *o' oor Johnnie.*

*owercome (USc) /oərkʌm/, noun. message, import.

< Sc 'o'ercome' = issue, outcome

An aye the owercome of his sang (and the entire message of
his song)

Was 'Wae's me for Prince Chairlie'.

(Traditional ballad)

*oxther /ɒkstər/, noun. under one's arm, armpit.

< OE 'ohsta' = armpit

*So, hear dear, didn't she stick the parcel undher her oxther an
away back to Woolies with it.*

*oxthercog /ɒkstərkɔg/, verb. go arm in arm.

< OE 'ohsta' + ME 'cogge' = armpit + cog in wheel

*Ye'll not enthermeddle if you're wise. They may be fightin the
day but they'll be oxthercoggin the morrow.*

P

pace /piəs/, noun. peace.
< ME 'pais' = peace
Would ye give my head pace wi' your owl shenannigans. Ye'll have to learn that a body's not made o' money. Wi' you, it's not 'Can I have'. It's 'Gimme' an' 'Get me'.

pad /pad/, noun. narrow path, footway
< OE 'pæth' = footway
<< eModE 'pad' = road
The owl dog for the hard road an' the pup for the pad. (Proverb)

pachal /paxəl/, noun. uncomplimentary term.
< unkn
<< Gael 'pachaille' = a bunion
'padhail' = an old cow
Get up an get yourself cleaned. You great big pachal sittin an you not dhressed at half eleven!

pag /pag/, noun. unflattering term.
< unkn
<< Gaelic 'peacach' = sinner
He's nothin betther than a pag. He'll neither work nor want.

paling /piəlɪn/, noun. fence, fence post.
< eModE 'paling' = pointed stake
It's the loveliest wee place now with a palin all the way round.
He's not expected to do (live). *He got a palin stuck in his eye an it must have penetrated the brain.*

panbread /panbred/, noun. shop-bought long loaf with crust on all sides, usually sliced.
< OE 'panne' + 'bread' = pan + bread
There was no panbread in my day. It was all baps an barnbracks an soda farls.

pannady /pəniədi/, noun. boiled bread with milk and perhaps raisins.
< eModE 'panade' = pulped bread with flavouring
She's not well at all. She's hardly fit to swallow. I've thried her on Complan and Build-Up but it's as much as she can do to take a wee bit o' pannady.

parlatic /parlatɪk/, adj. very drunk indeed.

< eModE 'paralytic' = one whose mobility is impaired
He was more than half cut, if you ask me. He was bloody parlatic!

pass-remarkable /pas rəmarkəbəl/, adj. prone to offer an unsolicited comment.

< OF 'passer' = to pass + eModE 'remarkable' = remarkable
She's not a bad crayther, a bit pass-remarkable maybe but she means well.

pass oneself /pas wʌnsɛlf/, verb. behave according to protocol.

< OF 'se passer' = pass one another
Sure my voice is away with it with the smokin (smoking has ruined my singing) but I had to pass myself so I sung 'Danny Boy'.

peeodler /piodlər/, noun. naughty or mischievous person (not always critical).

< unkn
<< Gaelic 'piadóir' = meddler
What did he do? Cowp (turn over) the hay float (hay waggon)? He's a peeodler all right. He doesn't know what to be up to, to be bad enough.

peezle /pizəl/, noun. penis in the phrase 'bull's peezle'.

< eModE 'peezel' = bull's penis
Them shoes is as hard as a bull's peezle!

pick /pɪk/, noun. bit of fat in phrase 'not a pick'.

< Me 'pek' = measure
There's not a pick on him! I doubt he's not well.

*pick /pɪk/, noun. lid of churn.

< Gael 'peic' = measure, tub.
Take the pick off the chorn there chile an see is it ready for skimmin.

pickle /pɪkəl/, noun. small amount.

< Sc 'pickle' = grain
I wondher if you'd have as much as a wee pickle o' sugar, just to taste the chile's tea?

picker /pɪkər/, noun. person with a small appetite.

< ME 'pic' = pointed object + '-er'
She has always been a picker. The longest day I knew Anne, a board (bird) would a ate more!

piddle /pɪdəl/, noun and verb. urine, urinate.
  < eModE 'piddle' = urinate
  O, Mary's/Tommy's blue/white etc drawers
  O, Mary's/Tommy's blue/white etc drawers
  A wee hole in the middle
  For Mary/Tommy to piddle
  O, Mary's/Tommy's blue drawers.
  (Children's teasing song)
piece /pis/, noun. sandwich lunch.
  < ME 'pece' = portion
  I never know what to give Robert in his piece. He's very finickity. One day, ye give him ham an he eats it all; another day, ye give it to him an he brings his whole piece home.
pigging /pɪgɪn/, adj/ very dirty.
  < Me 'pigge' = pig + '-ing'
  The place was piggin. You could see that it had went to loss since the wife died.
*****piggy** /pɪgi/, noun. a variant of 'cat and bat', a game played with a bat and a piece of wood sharpened at both ends. The person who is 'in' hits the sharpened end of the wood causing it to rise in the air. It is then hit again as far as possible while the batsman runs.
  < ModE 'piggy' = wood sharpened at both ends
  Piggy was safer than bat'n ball because the stick didn't break as many windows.
pig's back /pɪgz bak/, noun. condition of comfort and ease.
  < ME 'pigge' + OE 'bæc' = back
  << Gael 'ar dhrom na muice' = lucky (on back of + the pig)
  Thanks be to God, things couldn't be betther! I'm on the pig's back since my man got a good job an if he keeps it for a year or more we'll be able to put somethin by (save something) *an then we'll be as high on the hog* (as well off) *as another body.*
pills /pɪlz/, noun. goat and sheep droppings.
  < eModE 'pill' = pill, pellet
  Thon eejit couldn't even throw a goat's pill. (Comment on the inaccurate throw of a sportsman.)
pinchers /pɪntʃərz/, noun. pincers, pliers.
  < ME 'pinsours' = pincers
  Get the pinchers out o' the dhrawer. I can't get a purchase (firm hold) *on this screw at all.*

pish /pɪʃ/, noun and verb. urine, urinate.
   < OF 'pisser' = urinate
   Arra, health to your sowl (soul)
   Will ye buy me a bowl
   For to howl (hold) *King Willie's wather?*
   For the rattle of his pish
   Would scare all the fish
   That live in the River Boyne's wather.
   (Traditional Catholic children's chant)
pishmire /pɪʃmaiər/, noun. ant, very cross person.
   < ME 'pissemyre' = ant
   Is there something eatin you? You're like a pishmire all day!
pish-the-bed /pɪʃ ðə bed/, noun. dandelion, bed-wetter.
   < ME 'pissabed' = dandelion
   The childher won't play with dandelions any more not since
   Micky R. towl them they were pish-the-beds.
pishogues /pɪʃogz/, noun. superstitions.
   < Gael 'piseog' = witchcraft, spell
   It's only pishogues she does be tellin from one day's end to the
   next. Sure she'd have you believe she could milk ducks.
pitter, pretty /pɪtər, prəti/, noun. potato.
   < ModE 'potato'
   < Gael 'préataí' = potatoes
   She's a boy for pitters (she eats a lot of potatoes) *or 'pretties'*
   as she calls them.
planter /plantər/, noun. outsider.
   < eModE 'planter' = owner of plantation
   The place is full o' planters now with everybody marryin outside
   (outside the village).
planting /plantɪn/, noun. plantation, wood.
   < ModE 'planting' = coppice
   All the courtin couples diz be walkin up to the hagginblock or the
   plantin, as you might call it.
plaster /plasTər/, noun. unpleasant person, also sometimes
unreliable.
   < OE 'plaster' = remedy applied to skin
   John's the right owl plasther! He hasn't a friend till his name.
play yourself /ple yərsɛlf/, verb. play, try to get away
with something.
   < OE 'plegian' = exercise oneself

Go youse on outside an play yourselves.
Ye can play yourself, John, but I howl you (I'm sure) *you'll not get away with it twice.*

playboy /pleboi/, noun. person (not necessarily male) who behaves in an extravagant or unexpected manner.

   < OE 'plegian' + ME 'boie' = boy
Begod an you're a playboy! What time do you think this is to be comin to a daicent (decent) *body's house?*

please /pliz/, verb. satisfy, gratify.

   < ME 'plaise' = gratify
I wouldn't please them to see that I was all cut. I just let on that it didn't take a fidge out o' me.

plot /plɒt/, noun. grave.

   < OE 'plot' = small piece of ground
When you're pickin a plot, pick a right big one for there's six of us to get intil it.

*ploodacha (HE) /pludəxə/, adj. full to the brim.

   < Gael 'ploduighthe' = thronged
I'm more than full to the gills! I'm ploodacha!

plump /plʌmp/, noun and verb. sudden shower; boil vigorously.

   < ME 'plompe' = fall down
   << Sc 'plump' = shower, fall into water
That was a terrible plump, now. I'm dhrownded.
Lave (leave) *the kettle till it's plumpin, chile, or it's not tay* (tea) *at all ye'll be makin.*

*plunk /plʌŋk/, verb. fail exams.

   < unkn ?'plug' + 'flunk'
Pass, me ass! (He certainly did not pass.) *He plunked one hundred percent an that takes some doin!*

po /po/, noun. chamberpot.

   < Fr 'pot' = pot
I was watchin the Antiques Road Show an you'll never believe the price they put on a wee delph po.

*pock /pɒk/, noun. smallpox.

   < OE 'poc' = pustule
God bless us an save us but her face was all lumps like one o' them rubber mats ye put in the bath. They say she took the pock disaise (disease) *when she was a chile but thank God that's all done away wi' now.*

podion ball /podʒən bɔl/, noun. big, round, hard ball.
　< unkn
*How would I know what hit him? Sure I wasn't there. But by the
look o' thon lump on the back of his head, it could a been a podion ball.*
poke /pok/, noun. icecream cone, cone-shaped container,
bag or headgear.
　< OF 'poche' = pouch
Mammy, will you buy us (me) a poke?
Put the nails in a wee paper poke there.
What happened my pixie (headgear), the one wi' the poke?
pollute /pəlut/, verb. irritate by pestering.
　< ME 'pollute' = render impure
*That chile has my head polluted this day with talk about clothes.
I'll be glad to get out to get me head shired.*
poogh /püx/, noun and verb. puff.
　< ?Fr 'pouf' = puff of breath
He just gave a wee poogh an he was dead.
*poortith (USc) /pürtɪθ/, noun. poverty.
　< Sc 'puirtith' = poverty
*My mother had a lot of Scotch in her speech even though she was
born and reared in Antrim. I remember one word of hers was
'poortith'. She would talk about how some people had to live in
poortith, but I don't think ye'd hear that word now except from
an old, old person.*
poteen /pɒtʃən, pɒtʃin/, noun. locally brewed alcohol.
　< Gael 'poitín' = small pot, whiskey
*Them'ns an their bummin (bombing)! They've desthroyed the
counthry. Ye couldn't get a dhrop o' the crayther (illicit
whiskey) now for love or money. When them helicopters see
smoke, they're flyin over an a body's poteen's desthroyed.*
*poureen /porin/, noun. little potato.
　< Gael 'póirín' = little seed
*The spuds is all bad now, all poureens or spachans (small
potato for planting).*
pour /por/, verb. rain heavily.
　< ME 'poure' = emit in a stream
*It's not takin time to pour! It's just bucketin out o' the heavens!
Since last week, it has been rainin stair-rods. I'm alive since I
was born an a while before it an I never seen anything like it!*

pouse /paus/, noun. dust.
 < Fr 'poussière' = dust
There was three kinds o' dust in the facthory. There was stoor.
That stayed low down. An there was pouse that settled round
the looms. An then there was flock that could get up a body's
nose.

*pow /pau/, noun. head, often a bald head.
 < ?ME 'pol' = head
He had a big bald pow on him och an you know what childher's
like. We tortured him askin him if he took a long time to wash his
face in the mornin.

power /pauər/, noun. large number.
 < ME 'pouer' = body of armed men
I go through (use) a power of eggs in the week. There's a big
housefull of us an everybody wants a fry or a gugg (boiled egg)
in the morning.

powerful /pauərfʌl/, adj. and adv. great, very.
 < eModE 'powerful' = mighty
Isn't the weather powerful?
Them'ns is all powerful smart (intelligent).

press /pres/, noun. cupboard.
 < OF 'presse' = large cupboard
I'm gettin all new presses in. The boss made a few pounds on the
horses an we're goin to brightify the kitchen.

prickles /prɪkəlz/, noun. gooseflesh.
 < OE 'pricel' = sharp bump on skin
Prickles is like freckles. Some people is prone to them.

prime /praim/, adj. and adv. very well, excellent.
 < eModE 'prim' = of first rank
I'm sure ye can do it prime. It's like ridin a bisylik (bicycle). You
never loss the gamut of it.
She was a prime lookin lassy, I'm tellin you.

prockus /prɒkəs/, noun. trouble, palaver.
 < Gael 'prácás' = hotch-potch
That's a right prockus ye've give Liam. I'm tellin ye that'll make
him scratch his head for a day or two!

prog /prɒg/, noun and verb. large quantity of good
things; steal apples from an orchard.
 < ModE 'prog' = prowl for food

Davy would go to Belfast every Sathurday an he'd come home with a quare prog. They filled his bags wi' fruit cake an apples an oranges for the childher.

I haven't progged an orchard since I was a chile.

puke /pyuk/, noun and verb. disagreeable person; cough.

    < eModE 'pewkishnesse' = prone to vomit

    << Gael 'píochán' = hoarseness

    Thon owl puke would annoy a saint, always whingin.

    The chile's pukin. A howl ye (I'm certain) he has the whoopin cough.

pull /pʌl/, noun and verb. smoke, puff.

    < OE 'pullian' = drag, tug at

    Give us (me) a shode (puff) o' your pipe, just one or two pulls there. I've give up smoking, ye see.

pumpture /pʌmptʃər/, noun and verb. puncture.

    < eModE 'puncture' = perforation

    I think the bike must have a slow pumpture. No matther how many times I pump the wheel, it never gets hard.

*puss (HE) /pʌs/, noun. long face.

    < unkn

    << Gael 'pus' = lip, mouth

    If ye don't take that puss aff ye this minute, I'll give ye somethin to girn about.

put on you /pʌt ɔn yə/, verb. put one's clothes on.

    < OE 'putian' = put

    Would ye put on ye, chile or you'll be late for school.

put past/by /pʌt pas, pʌt bai/, verb. save.

    < Sc 'pit by' = save

    I'd say they'd have a brave bit (good amount) put past.

puzzler /pʌzlər/, noun. riddle.

    < eModE 'pusle' = perplex + '-er'

    It would make ye think now. It's a puzzler. Like, if Adam an Eve was the only people, did brothers have to marry their sisters? Maybe ye're as well not thinkin o' them things.

Q

quake /kwiək/, verb. tremble.
  < OE 'cwacian' = tremble, shake
  Well, hear boy, when I die of old age, you may quake with fear!
quare /kwɜr/, adj. and adverb. good, nice, very.
  < eModE 'queer' = odd, strange
  He's a quare worker. He doesn't know what it means to be tired!
  He's got a quare nice manner with him. I love to listen to him.
  Och but sure, ye can't beat education!
quare and /kwɜr ən/, adv. very.
  < eModE 'queer' + OE 'and' = and
  He might have a rough way with him but he's quare 'n good to
  the (his) mother now.
quare man your da /kwɜr man yər da/, exclam. Your
father did a good job! (Also occurs as 'Brave man your
da!')
  < eModE 'queer' + OE 'man' = man
  You done well, chile! Quare man your da!
*queels /kwilz/, noun. combs.
  < ?Fr 'quille' = skittle
  She has her hair all dolled up an it kept in place wi' silver queels.
quick of himself /kwɪk əv hɪmsɛlf/, adj. fast and accurate.
  < OE 'cwic' = alive, swift
  He's the best workman goin, reliable an very quick of himself.
quilt /kwɪlt/, noun. rascal.
  < ?OF 'cuilte' = coverlet
  Thon owl quilt! I wouldn't give him bad money (I wouldn't
  give him my custom again even if I could pay him with
  counterfeit money.)

R

rack and ruin /rak ən ruən/, noun. dilapidated state.
  < eModE 'rack and ruin' = destruction
  The father worked himself till an early grave ti' build up the
  business an thon boy has dhrunk the bit out an let everything go
  ti' rack an ruin.

rage /riədʒ/, noun and verb. anger, be furious.
  < OF 'rage' = madness
  She's just ragin. Anne come in to see her new carpets and she
  walks in wi' her owl spags (sensible walking shoes) *all glaur*
  (heavy mud) *and thramps* (walks all over) *the house. The*
  carpet's desthroyed.
rag /rag/, noun. temper.
  < Sc 'rag' = temper
  << Gael 'ráig' = fit of anger
  Don't loss your rag with me. I don't know what happened your
  car but I didn't ate it.
ragnail /ragniəl/, noun. torn skin near nail.
  < ME 'ragge' = scrap + OE 'næglan' = nail
  Now, thanks be to God, I've never had a ragnail since I got the
  charm (traditional cure) *but there's others biz prone to them.*
*rail /riəl/, noun. load of turf or blocks (i.e. logs).
  < Gael 'ráil' = load (of turf)
  C'mere boy. What are ye chargin for a rail o' torf these days?
ramstam /ramstam/, adv. headlong, without due care.
  < Sc 'ramstam' = rush headlong
  He was a wild boy that. He rushed ramstam into things an never
  seemed to heed what another body said.
*rann /ran/, noun. stanza.
  < Gael 'rann' = stanza
  Give us a song there, Bridie. Go on, ye girl ye, give us a rann or
  two to pass yourself.
rare /rɜr/, verb. rear, bring up.
  < OE 'ræran' = to rear
  Thon woman couldn't rare a cat! She has an ignorant plug of a
  son and the kindest thing a body could say about him is 'Them
  that rared him would dhrown nothin.'
rath /raθ/ noun. ghost, spirit, wraith.
  < unkn
  << Gael 'rathughadh' = forewarning
  As God is my judge, I seen her rath comin through the
  door.
*ratten /ratən/, noun. coarse material, poor clothes.
  < ?Fr 'ratine' = thick material
  << Gael 'raitín' = coarse cloth

God be with the days when the Muncheemen would come till a dance, thinkin they were dhressed ti' kill an them thricked out in the best o' ratten.

rattling /ratlɪn/, intensifying adv. extremely.

   < ?eModE 'ratlin' = nautical rope

We had a rattlin good evenin. There was lashins an lavins (drink and food in abundance).

rave /riəv/, verb. ramble, dote, 'have a dwam'.

   < OF 'raver' = be senseless

Sure isn't he as well ravin there as in bed?

ravel /ravəl/, verb. tangle, fray at edges.

   < eModE 'ravel' = entangle

Don't be playin wi' that wool. Ye'll have it all ravelled and fankled (tangled) *an it won't be worth a knittin.*

reach /ritʃ/, verb. stretch for and pass to.

   < OE 'ræcan' = stretch out, extend

Reach me that book, will ye, the one on the top shelf.

read up /rid ʌp/, verb. recite all the things which one has done and would rather forget.

   < OE 'rædan' + 'up' = to read + up

She read /red/ me up from ass-hole ti' breakfast time. A body'd need ti' have a clean slate ti' get the betther of Alice.

red /red/, noun. rid.

   < ME 'ruden' = set free

I can't get red o' this owl chest at all. I got the wheezles a couple o' months back an' I just can't shift it.

red /red/, adj. red-haired.

   < OE 'read' = red

   << SG/G 'ruadh' = red, red-haired

Is it Black Paddy or Red Paddy ye mean?

redd up /red ʌp/, verb. tidy up.

   < ?ON 'rythja' = clear a space

Give us a wee hand ti' redd up, chile, an then we can sit down an have a wee shannach (comfortable gossip).

reed /rid/, noun. life, vital parts (invariably female).

   < ?OE 'hreod' = reed

   << Gael 'rudaí muc' = entrails

You could put out your reed for some people an they'd never say thanks.

*reek /rik/, noun and verb. smoke.

OE 'rec' = smoke

You're chimney's reekin, so it is. Ye should born it (set it on fire) *the first good day we get.*

*reevogue /rivog/, adj. 'borrowing', only in the phrase 'reevogue days'.

< unkn

<< Gael 'riabhóg' = anything streaked

The 'reevogue days' was the days borrowed from March ti' kill the straked cow. (Traditional saying)

render /rɛnɒər/, verb. melt down.

< OF 'rendre' = hand over

You could rendher that suet down a wee bit an use the fat for fryin.

renegade /rɛnəgiəd/, noun. term of abuse for a Catholic who has given up his religion or for a priest who has left his ministry.

< Lat 'renegatus' = apostate, deserter

Take no notion (pay no attention) *of what he says. The father was a renegade and thon boy is the two ends of one* (also a complete renegade).

renegue /rəniəg/, verb. go back on one's word, betray; shirk.

< Lat 'renegare' = refuse, renounce

Nobody wants that kind of a man in any organisation. Ye couldn't thrust him. He'd renegue on ye as soon as look at ye. He's workshy. He'd renegue at a daicent day's work. Sure, look at him. The coat's still on him an it dinner time. (He hasn't taken his coat off or rolled up his sleeves and it's close to midday.)

rensh /rentʃ/, noun and verb. wash quickly, rinse.

< OF 'rincer' = to wash out

Would you rensh them few dishes an I'll redd up the table.

rhyme /raim/, noun and verb. repetition, repeat over and over.

< ModE 'rhyme' = sound chime

Make a wee rhyme of your exercise (lesson) *an ye'll be able to mind* (remember) *it betther.*

rib /rɪb/, noun. strand of hair

< Gael 'ribe' = single hair, bristle

<< OE 'rib' = curved bone

She rugged the hair out o' me as if she didn't want to leave a rib on me head.

rick /rɪk/, noun and verb. small stack of hay, between a 'stook' and a 'stack'.

< OE 'hreacc' = hay rick

First, ye stool the hay an then ye put it in ricks.

riddle /rɪdəl/, noun and verb. riddle, puzzle.

< OE 'rædels' = enigma

That's a riddle for ye, eh? That's a puzzler and a half. Here, riddle me this one:

High it hangs on leather strings.

It's all men's mate (food) an no-one ates it.

(Traditional riddle for 'breast')

rift /rɪft/, noun and verb. belch.

< ME 'rift' = split

If I could only rift, I'm sure I could get red (rid) of this indigestion.

rigging /rɪgɪn/, noun. roof ridge.

< ?ON 'rigga' = to wrap + '-ing'

The lightnin hit the riggin an we thought the whole house would be down on top of us.

right /rait/, adj. and adv. very acceptable, pleasing; very.

< OE 'riht' = right, equitable

That's a right wee blade I seen ye with last night. You could do a lot worse!

Your father's a right fat man, isn't he?

right and /rait ən/, adv. very.

< OE 'riht' + 'and' = right + and

He's right an canny with his money. Doesn't put the hand in the pocket too often, if you get my meanin.

rightify /raitəfai/, verb. rectify.

< OE 'riht' + '-ify'

You may take that car to the garage an have the brakes rightified because the hills around here is no joke.

right hand /rait han/, noun phrase. attempt.

< OE 'riht' + 'hand' = right + hand

You made a right hand o' the decoratin. Lord knows but you have the place lovely.

rightly /raitli/, adj. quite well.

< OE 'rihtlice' = correctly

I'm feelin rightly the day, thank God. I couldn't do a day's work in the moss like, but I could pass myself if the work wasn't too heavy.

rigout /rɪgaut/, noun and verb. outfit.

    < ?ON 'rigga' = wrap up + OE 'ut' = out

    Man but ye had the quare rigout on ye last night. It must have cost a bob (shilling) *or two.*

    It's not cheap to rigout a child for school these days. Even gutties (cheap tennis shoes) *is out of all buyin.*

rings round /rɪŋz raun/, adv. profusely, better than.

    < OE 'hring' = ring + ME 'rond' = round

    I was that sick I was vomitin rings round me.

    She was ony a chile but she was talkin rings round the politicians an hobnobs.

road /rod/, noun. direction.

    < OE 'rad' = way

    Could ye tell me am I on the right road ti' Lisburn?

    I didn't know my road o' hokin (what to do in order to get maximum benefit).

*roan /ron/, noun. roof gutter.

    < ?ModE 'roan' = leather used in bookbinding

    << Gael 'ronn' = bond, drip

    The roan's blocked with them dead leaves.

roast /rost/, verb. burn in hell.

    < OF 'rostir' = cook by exposure to open fire

    Hell roast him! Them that rared a son like that was fond o' childher!

roney (HE) /roni/, noun. red calf or cow.

    < OF 'roan' = animal of variegated colours

    << Gael 'ruadhan' = reddish-brown animal

    Everybody likes a roney about the place. They're lucky now.

rong /rɔŋ/, noun. rung, chair support.

    < OE 'hrung' = rung

    Don't you be standin on the rong o' that chair, chile. Ye'll cowp it (cause it to fall over).

rosner /rɒznər/, noun. drink (usually of whiskey).

    < unkn

    << Gael 'roisín' = ration

    Och, ye'll have a wee rosner now before ye go, just a wee dhrop for luck!

rounds of the kitchen /raunz ə ðə kɪtʃən/, noun. beating.

< ME 'rond' = round + OE 'cycene' = kitchen

If you ever put your foot in her house again, I'll give you the rounds o' the kitchen.

ructions /rʌkʃənz/, noun. loud commotion.

< ModE 'ruction' = disturbance

There'll be ructions when my Ma sees that you have the windy (window) broke.

rug /rʌg/, noun and verb. pull, tug, yank.

< Gael 'rug' = carry off, seize

I've lost me wee comb! I'll never get another like it! It was a well-behaved wee comb. Not one o' them boys that would rug every hair in your head!

run /rʌn/, noun and verb. distil poteen; chase.

< ME 'ronne' = run

Was that poteen well run? I know people took a dhrop that wasn't well run an begod they paid for it. A dhrop o' bad stuff could kill ye!

Thon blade would run you if you put as much as a foot on her property.

runagate /rʌnəgiət/, noun. wanderer, person who is always on the go.

< eModE 'runagate' = runaway, deserter

She'll be a runagate, that wee blade, if ye don't put a corb on (restrain) her.

runt /rʌnt/, noun. small person or thing.

< ModE 'runt' = small breed of cattle

The youngest child or the smallest of a litther was called a runt.

rust /rʌst/, verb. refuse to move.

< ?OE 'rust' = coated with layer of rust, deteriorate

On we went till we come to the oak threes near the Sanatorium an lo an behold, the owl horse rusted. He would not budge...

S

saft /saft/, adj. soft, foolish, innocent.
  < OE 'softe' = soft, compliant
  Hm! That's for ye! Saft John barred the dure (door) wi' a sausage.
  How soft the wool grows on you! (i.e. Nobody can be as innocent or foolish as you seem.)

*saibies /saibiz/, noun. spring onions, scallions.
  < ?Gael 'saidhbheog' = butterwort
  They were always 'saibies'. Then a body took ti' callin them 'scallions'. We'll be callin them 'spring onions' next.

sally /sali/, noun. willow.
  < Gael 'saileog' = willow tree
  They used to make canes from sally wattles and a quare crack they could give you.

sancy /sansi/, adj. healthy, good-looking.
  < SG/G 'sonas' = healthy
  She was as sancy a wee blade (girl) as ever I clapped eyes on.

sang /saŋ/, exclamation.
  < Fr 'sang' = blood
  'By my sang,' says wee Mick, 'you're a tarra (terrible).'

sate /siət/, noun. chair, seat.
  < ON 'sæti' = seat
  Ye got in me sate brave an nifty. I wondher would you be in me grave as quick?

*sausenger /sɒsɪndʒər/, noun. sausage.
  < ME 'sausige' = sausage
  Put us on two or three o' them big sausengers when ye have a minute.

scad /skad/, noun. shadow, faint colour.
  < Sc 'scad' = faint colouring
  << Gaelic 'scaid' = husk of grain
  You have a red scad to your hair since you started dying it.

scald /skɔld/, noun. tea.
  < ME 'scalde' = burn with hot liquid
  Put us on a wee dhrop o' scald there when ye're on your foot.

scalded /skɔldəd/, adj. very upset.
  < ME 'scalde' = burn, hurt
  << Gael 'scallach croidhe' = upset (scald + heart)
  You have the heart scalded on me, chile.

scaldy /skɔldi/, noun. very young bird with few or no feathers.
  < ON 'skalli' = bald
  Sure how could a boy like that expect luck? Didn't he rob nests an kill the wee scaldies?
scantlins /skantlınz/, noun. scraps.
  < OF 'escantillon' = sample, small amount
  She's that canny of herself, she could make a feast out o' scantlins.
scobe /skob/, verb. scrape, eat fruit with the front teeth.
  < unkn
  << Gael 'scíob' = scoop
     'scuab' = brush
  I don't like pears ye have ti' scobe.
scollop /skɒləp/, noun and verb. thick, badly cut piece of meat or bread, cut something roughly.
  < OF 'escalope' = scallop
  << Gaelic 'scolb' = loop to secure the thatch
  Would you look at the scollop he lifted out of it!
  Don't scollop it! A body'd like it as sthraight as you can get it.
scoosh /skuʃ/, noun. gush, swish.
  < Sc 'scoosh' = rush of water
  My spoutin (spout) broke and it give one big scoosh and my house (room) was dhrownded (very wet).
scrab /skrab/, noun and verb. scratch.
  < ON 'skrapa' = remove layer
  Mind that cat doesn't scrab you.
*scran /skran/, noun. bad luck.
  < unkn
  Bad scran ti' ye! That ye may never see Sunday!
scrake /skriək/, noun. screech, scream.
  < ON 'skrækja' = screech
  << Gaelic 'scréach' = screech, scream
  Well, she let a scrake out of her. We all ran in for to see what had happened. Man dear, she had a face on her that would a torned milk. 'It was a banshee,' says she. 'I seen it out through the windy (window)...'
scrape /skriəp/, noun and verb. scratch, write.
  < ON 'skrapa' = scratch
  You were away a month and not one wee scrape of the pen out o' ye.

screed /skrid/, noun and verb. long document, reel out.
  < OE 'screade' = shred
  She doesn't talk much but when she writes she can screed it out
  like a good'n.
scringe /skrɪndʒ/, verb. noise like fingernail on wood or
glass.
  < unkn ? scratch + cringe
  I can't stand that scringin. It goes sthraight to my teeth.
scroof /skruf/, noun. dandruff.
  < OE 'scurf' = scales of epidermis
  Tidy yourself up a bit now and take that scroof off your jacket.
scrunt(y) /skrʌnt(i)/, adj. and noun. small, mean person.
  < Sc 'scrunt' = miser, puny person
  He's a wee owl scrunt of a man. Och, he's no man at all. Just an
  excuse of a man.
scuffed /skʌft/, adj. well worn.
  < Sc 'scuff' = rub, wipe
  << Gaelic 'scaifeach' = refuse, waste
  They have a carpet but it's well scuffed and the three piece
  (suite) is well scuffed too.
scundher /skʌnDər/, noun and verb. strong dislike.
  < Sc 'scunner' = feeling of aversion
  << Gael 'scondaire' = dunce
  In the War, I ate that much brown sugar I took the scundher
  agin it.
*scutch(in) /skʌtʃ(ɪn)/, adj. and verb. process used in
preparing flax.
  < OF 'escousser' = dress fibre by beating it
  There was two or three scutchin mills about here once but sure
  the linen thrade's away with it (finished).
see (me) down /si mi daun/, verb. outlive.
  < OE 'seon' + 'dune' = see + down
  Look at her. She's eighty if she's a day and as fit as a flea. A howl
  ye (I assure you) she'll see me down.
sell your hen on a wet day /sɛl yər hen ɒn ə wɛt de/, verb.
fail to make the most of yourself or your possessions.
  < OE 'sellan' + 'henn' + 'wet' + 'dæg' = sell + hen +
  wet + day
  That planter (i.e. outsider) does nothin but bum an blow. She
  wouldn't sell her hen on a wet day!

*sevendable /səvɛndəbəl/, adj. excellent.
  < ?OE 'seofon' + OF 'doble' = seven + double
  << Sc 'sevendle' = steadfast, secure
  That's a sevendable day now! A body could be doin with more of the same.

shade /ʃiəd/, noun and verb. hair parting.
  < OE 'sceadan' = part or divide
  Don't put a shade in my hair now. Ye'll give me a sore head (headache).

shade /ʃiəd/ = noun. shed
  < ME 'shadde' = shed
  You're not gettin that bike into the house! Put it out in the shade like a sensible body.

shaking ague /ʃiəkın iəgi/, noun. severe flu.
  < OE 'sceacan' = shake + OF 'ague' = fever
  A body doesn't get the shakin agues now. There's pills ye can take to get ye on your feet.

shank /ʃaŋk/, noun and verb. leg of meat, walk.
  < OE 'sceanca' = tibia, shin
  Ye'll get no bus the night. Ye may shank it.

shannach /ʃanax/, noun. a good chat, comfortable gossip.
  < Gael 'seanchaidheacht' = storytelling, gossip
  It was always the quare ceili-in house. Many's the right shannach I heard thundher (yonder).

shannachie /ʃanaxi/, noun. storyteller.
  < Gael 'seanchaidhe' = storyteller,
  I'm the last o' the breed. When I die, there'll be no more shannachies an the owl stories an words o' wisdom'll be forgot.

shanty /ʃanti/, noun. small house.
  < Gael 'sean tí' = old house
  They've come up in the world for they were all born an' rared in a shanty!
  I am the little Irish boy
  That lives in the shanty.
  (H.D. Thoreau, *Journal*, Nov. 26, 1850)

*sheebone /ʃibon/, noun. snowdrift, heavy fall of snow.
  < Gael 'síobán' = shower of rain, hail or snow
  Should the snow be lyin sheebone, when the morrow comes, I'll go.

sheeogue /ʃiog/, noun. fairy, changeling
< Gael 'sí + óg' = fairy (fairy + young)
That's not me da ye'r makin' all this fuss about, a said,
that's a sheeoge.
A what? me ma said, laughin'. A sheeoge, a said, a wee
changeling - can't ye see what's happened, ma, the fairies have
took me real da away an' left that wee wizen sheeoge in hes place?
(Frances Molloy, 1985)

Shelta /ʃɛlta/, noun. secret language, mixture of English,
Irish and back slang.
< unkn
Like in Shelta now, you change the words. Like, if you want to
say 'doras' (Gaelic 'doras' = door), you call it 'rodas'...

shilpit (USc) /ʃɪlpɪt/, adj. thin and puny.
< Sc 'shilpit' = emaciated
God stiffen ye, ye wee shilpit, sleekit skitther! (said to a dog)

shin,skin /ʃɪn, skɪn/, verb. climb up.
< ?OE 'scina' = shin
He could skin up a three like a monkey.

shire /ʃaiər/, adj. and verb. rest, relieved (only of
heads).
< ?Sc 'skyre' = bright, limpid
Go out for the day an shire your head.
I can't get me head shired wi' them bagles (noisy children).

shite /ʃait/, exclam. noun and verb. excrement, excrete.
(The past tense and past participle are 'shit'.)
< OE 'scitan' = to excrete
That's thanks for ye! They've forgot the owl ass-hole that shit the
Indian male (meal).

*shooler (HE) /ʃulər/, noun. walker, wanderer, 'tinker'
< Gael 'siubhlóir' = walker
Breed, seed and generation of them was all shoolers.

shoot the boots off /ʃut ðə buts ə/, verb. annihilate.
< OE 'sceotan' + 'bot' = shoot + boot
Somebody should shoot the boots o' that fella.

shower /ʃauər/, noun. unpleasant person or group of people.
< ?Sc 'shouer' = paroxysm
?Sc 'scour' = scamper, rush
I wouldn't want a child o' mine to get in with a shower like that.
The mother was dacent enough but she rared bad childher.

shuch /ʃʌx/, noun. ditch, trench with water in it.
   < SG/G 'sruth' = brook, stream
   << Sc 'sheuch' = trench, ditch
   He's as full as a shuch (very drunk)*!*
sickener /sɪknər/, noun. terrible disappointment.
   < OE 'seoc' = sick + '-ener'
   He's not the whack now. He had a right sickener last Sathurday
   an he hasn't overed it yit. He gave the youngsther a pound to put
   on a horse an the horse come in at twenty to one but the child had
   give the money to the mother.
simmet /sɪmət/, noun. man's vest or undershirt.
   < ?Fr 'chemise' = vest
   Winther or summer he always wears a simmet.
*sinther /sɪnTər/, verb. separate.
   < OE 'syndrian' = to put apart
   Them chickens would need to be sinthered if ye want to make
   anything of them. Put the weest of them in a place by themselves
   an they'll do betther.
sitting-down /sɪtɪn daun/, noun. house and land.
   < OE 'sittan' + 'dune' = to sit + down
   Thon blade would be worth a-marryin. She has a quare wee
   sittindown.
skelly /skɛli/, adj., noun and verb. squint.
   < Sc 'skellie' = squint-eyed
   'Wall-eyes', 'skelly-eyes', 'tully-eyes' and 'four o'clock eyes',
   they're all near enough the one (same) *thing. It's for somebody*
   with a cast or a torn in their eyes.
skelp, skelf /skɛlp, skɛlf/, noun. splinter of wood; beat
severely.
   < Sc 'skelf' = splinter
   < Sc 'skelp' = beat
   << Gaelic 'sceilp' = splinter; slap
   Would ye look is there a scelf in me foot?
   He needs a quare good scelpin, thon boy.
skiboo /skɪbu/, noun. nobody in particular.
   < ?Sc 'skybal' = contemptible person
   Who did that?
   It must've been skiboo.
skidaddle /skɪdadəl/, verb. go away quickly.
   < ModE 'skidaddle' = retreat hastily
   Ye may skidaddle till England. There's no place to hide here.

skiff /skɪf/, noun and verb. light shower.

   < Sc 'skiff' = shower

   *You're a quare mollycoddled boy you, afeard to go out an it ony
   (only) a wee skiff. Sure ye're not made o' sugar. Ye'll not melt.*

skimf /skɪmf/, noun. tiny amount.

   < ? Sc 'scrimpit' = frugal

   *Could you put a wee skimf o' butther on that, just a toty wee bit
   to taste it* (to make it tasty).

skinnymalink /skɪnɪməlɪŋk/, noun. very thin person.

   < unkn

   << eModE 'skinny' = emaciated

   Skinnymalink melodeon legs big banana feet
   Went to the pictures an couldn't get a seat.
   When he got a seat, he fell fast asleep.
   Skinnymalink melodeon legs big banana feet.

   (Children's chant)

skin of your skitter /skɪn ə yər skɪtər/, the least of things.

   < OE 'scin' = skin + ON 'skita' = excrement

   *Give you the lend of his hook? Sure thon man wouldn't give ye
   the skin of his skitther.*

skite /skait/, noun and verb. splash, usually with muddy
water; quick dash cf 'bletherskite'.

   < ON 'skjota' = shoot with water

   I got skit when the car went through the puddle.

   Maybe you'll get a wee skite home at the holidays?

skitter /skɪtər/, noun and verb. 1. diarrhoea 2. term of
abuse.

   < ON 'skita' = excrement

   1. *I've had the skitther on an off for a week now.*

   2. *Ye wee skitther ye! Ye have no manners!*

slabber /slabər/, noun and verb. untidy person, talkative
person, term of abuse.

   < eModE 'slabber' = behave in a slovenly way

   << Gael 'slob' = mud, soft-fleshed person

            'liobar' = untidy person

   Thon slabber! Doesn't know when to keep his thrap (mouth)
   shut.

slack /slak/, noun. cheap type of coal, often powd-
ery.

   < ME 'sleck' = poor quality coal

*Put on a good back o' slack before you go out an the fire'll
still be on when I get home.*
slane /sliən/, noun. long-bladed spade for cutting turf.
< Gael 'sleaghán' = turf spade
*Some slanes has only one wing an others have two, but
there's nothin like a slane for cuttin torf.*
*slap /slap/, noun. gap in a hedge.
< Sc 'slap' = gap
He'd be (He ought) to fill in thon slap before it gets any bigger.
sleekit /slikɪt/, adj. sly, untrustworthy.
< Sc 'sleekit' = unctuous
*You were badly a laugh for (desperately in need of) a man
when ye started goin out wi' thon sleekit wee upstart. Could ye
not do any betther for yourself?*
slob /slɔb/, noun. a soft person, man who cries when
he's drunk.
< Gael 'slob' = soft-fleshed person
<< ModE 'slab' = wet, slushy
*He means well but he's a bit soft. It's not that he has a wee want.
He's a bit of a slob.*
*slog (HE) /slɔg/, noun and verb. mouthful, eat in big
bites
< Gael 'slog' = swallow, devour
He'd torn you (turn your stomach) the way he slogs his dinner.
sloot(d)er /sluт(D)ər/, noun and verb. clumsy oaf; to behave
oafishly.
< Gael 'sladaire/slutaire' = plunderer
*They'll have throuble wi' thon boy. You mark my words. There'll
be a day at the catchin of him (he'll be caught out one day) for
he's a lazy, big sloother.*
slootery /sluтəri/, adj. clumsy, untidy.
< Gael 'slutaire' = plunderer
She has a sloothery way o' walkin for a girl.
slope off /slop ɔf, af/, verb. steal away.
< ModE 'slope off' = decamp
They slope off early so that they don't get the cleanin up to do.
*slouster /slausтər/, noun and verb. flatterer who lacks
the art of flattering successfully; butter someone up.
< Gael 'slus' = dissimulation
        'slusaire' = dissembler, wheedler

I can't stand that blade. She's too sweet to be wholesome. Always sloustherin a body up an then she acts that nice! As my ma always said, the saftest part o' that blade is her teeth.

smidgeon /smɪdʒən/, noun. tiny amount

< Gael 'smioda + ín' = piece + diminutive marker

Could ye just put a wee smidgeon o' butther on the bread, like a good girl. I could never eat dhry bread, not even in Lent.

*smig (HE) /smɪg/, noun. chin.

< Gael 'smeig' = chin

I just can't stand that man. He's just full of himself an the owl smig stuck out, tellin everybody what to do an when to do it!

smit /smɪt/, verb. infect.

< OE 'smitan' = to hit

I'll not sit near ye for ye're full o' the cowl (cold) *an ye could smit me. D'ye mind* (remember) *what Paddy Reagan used to say: 'Always sit on the windy side of a bad breath.'*

smithereens /smɪðərinz/, noun. tiny fragments.

< Gael 'smiodar + ín' = fragment + diminutive marker

It was broke in a thousand smithereens.

*smoor /smur/, noun. fine, wet mist.

< Gael 'smúr' = embers, dross, mist, vapours

<< OE 'smorian' = to suffocate

That smoor'd wet ye more nor rain.

*sned /sned/, noun. wooden shaft of scythe.

< OE 'snæd' = handle of scythe

Ye hardly ever see sneds now. It was aisy enough to rightify the blade if it got blunted but sneds was a different matther. There was quare work in a sned, for a good man would shape it till your arm.

sned (USc) /sned/, verb. cut.

< Sc 'sned' = chop off, prune

You should send for Joe if ye want to get the door off your car. He sned the doors o' two breadvans an you nivir seen a neater job!

snib /snɪb/, noun and verb. door latch.

< Sc 'snib' = catch, bolt

Put the snib on the door. We'll have no visitors now.

snipe /snaɪp/, noun. person with long nose.

< ME 'snipe' = bird

He wasn't 'Snipe' till his own name. That's the name ye give a body that has a long thin nose. They say that an inch is a dale (large amount) *in a man's nose but the breed o' that boy had nebs that would buck a pig.*

snood /snud/, noun. scarf used to cover the hair completely and tied in a knot at the front of the head.

   < OE 'snod' = hair band

   Ye'd think a body could dhress herself an not go everywhere in thon owl snood.

snug /snʌg/, noun. private room in pub.

   < ?eModE 'snug' = secure against bad weather

   Well, ye see, women didn't get into public houses, well, at least not on their own. But an odd (occasional) *woman might go into the snug with her man, more to see that he didn't spend the few ha'pence they had than to get a dhrink, like.*

(Old) Sod /aul sɔd/, noun. earth, Ireland.

   < eModE 'sod' = piece of earth

   << Gael 'fód' = sod

   A kinder woman never walked the sod!

   I hear ye're lavin the Owl Sod? Is it England ye're goin to?

soople /supəl/, adj. active, supple.

   < ME 'souple' = supple

   He's a great man for eighty, an a dale (good deal) *soopler than many's a man half his age. He fought in the Boer War, ye know, an rides into town every month to get his pension.*

sore /sor/, adj. aching.

   < OE 'sar' = painful, sore

   My head's very sore. Would ye have such a thing as an aspro?

***spachan** /spaxan/, noun. small potato for planting.

   < Gael 'spochadh' = gelding, cutting part off

   Them's spachans or cutlins, as you'd call them. Them'ns isn't ate. They're spachans, ye know, for plantin.

spags /spagz/, noun. very sensible shoes.

   < unkn

   << Gael 'spág' = foot, claw, hoof

   She wasn't at a dance in spags? Pull the other one. Sure nobody would be that daft!

spay /spe/, verb. foretell, see the future.

   < ON 'spa' = foretell

   I knowed they shouldn't a went. I spayed thon accident as sure as there's a haft in a beetle.

***spalpeen** (HE) /spɔlpin/, noun. labourer, spade.

   < Gael 'spailpín' = labourer, term of abuse

I'd a clove (split) *him open wi' a spalpeen if I had a got within a hound's gowl* (short distance) *of him.*

speel /spil, ʃpil/, verb. climb nimbly.

   < Sc 'speil' = game, match

We called them 'Monkey' because they could shpeel up a dhrainpipe as nifty as a monkey.

*spencel, spancel /spɛnsəl, spansəl/, noun. rope used to tie up goats.

   < ?OE 'spannan' = to yoke

There should be an owl spancel in the shade. They had it for the goat.

spit /spɪt/, noun and verb. close likeness; rain lightly.

   < OE 'spittan' = eject saliva

Ye're the dead spit o' your father, Robert.

Och, ye'll hardly need a coat. It's only spittin.

splah /spla/, noun. flat feet, pointing out.

   < eModE 'splay' = spread out

   << Gael 'spléacht' = squint

The whole breed of the O'Neills walks with a splah and some o' them has torned-in toes into the bargain.

sprachal /spraxal/, adj and verb. sprawl, stretch out lazily.

   < OE 'spreawlian' = to spread out

   < Gael 'spreachall' = spatter

Where is he? He's lyin sprachalled across the road.

spree /spri/, noun. a drinking bout.

   < ModE 'spree' = boisterous frolic

   << Gael 'spreidh' = scatter, squander

He was a good man till he went on the spree an when he was on a spree he'd a dhrunk the Jordan dhry.

spricklybags /sprɪklibagz/, noun. stickleback spawn.

   < Sc 'spreckled' = spotted + ON 'baggi' = bag

   << ModE 'sticklebacks'

Many's an hour I whiled away hokin in the wather for spricklybags.

spud /spʌd/, noun. potato.

   < ModE 'spud' = potato

   << Gael 'spad' = clod

I'm fond of a spud now. I wouldn't feel full if I didn't have me spuds every day.

spunk /spʌŋk/, noun. courage.
  < Sc 'spunk' = bravery
  Now, no matther what ye say, they showed quare spunk to face odds like that!

squint /skwɪnt/, verb. provide for.
  < ME 'squynt' = squint
  I'd be hard pushed to squint for a wife an childher as well as myself.

starve /starv/, verb. die of cold, feel very cold.
  < OE 'steorfan' = die of hunger or cold
  I'm starvin. I left home without a coat for I thought it was warm but the day would foundher ye.

stays /stiəz/, noun. corsets.
  < OF 'estaie' = stay, support
  You may slacken these stays o' mine because I'm a-chokin. Sure what good will it do yiz if I have a good figure an me dead?

steady /stɛdi/, adj. well-balanced.
  < eModE 'steady' = firm, fixed
  That child's as steady on his foot as a three-legged pot.

sticking out /stɪkɪn aut/, adj. very impressive.
  < OE 'stician' + 'ut' = to stick + out
  You're lookin great! Stickin out a mile!

stime /staim/, noun. something very small.
  < ?Sc 'styme' = glimpse, glimmer
  Ye can see the stime in my eye an ye can't see the plank in your own!

stocious /stoʃəs/, adj. very drunk.
  < ?Sc 'stot' = stagger
  He's like many a man. He's either stone cold sober or he's stocious. He doesn't know the meanin o' moderation.

*stook (HE) /stuk/, noun. twelve sheaves of corn, turf stack.
  < ME 'stouk' = stack of corn
  << Gael 'stuaic' = pinnacle, wall
  Ye stool the torf into stooks.

stool /stul/, noun and verb. stool, arrange in order.
  < OE 'stol' = stool, seat
  Ye have to stool the torf first for to let it dhry. God chile, are ye stupid altogether? What are they teachin you at your fancy school?

stoor /stur/, noun. dust.
  < Sc 'stour' = dust
  When ye were weavin there was always stoor. It come off the web
  (woven cloth).
*stoon (USc) /stün/, noun and verb. pain, suffer.
  < Sc 'stoun' = ache, pain
  When a think aboot the bonny lass
  I'll never see again
  My eyes grow wet wi' oft-shed tears
  An me hert, it stoons wi' pain.
  (Traditional song)
stoppage /stopədʒ/, noun. stammer, speech
impediment.
  < OE 'stoppian' = to plug
  He had a wee bit of a stoppage like but sure if ye towl him ti' sing
  sure ye wouldn't a knowed there was a thing wrong wi' him.
stravague /strraviəg/, verb. wander around without much
purpose.
  < Sc 'stravaig' = gad about
  Och ye'd have to feel sorry for owl Granyawail (itinerant
  singer). *It's all very well to be stravaguin in good weather but it*
  must be cat (very unpleasant) *when it's lashin down* (raining
  heavily).
*stredlegs /strɛdlegz/, adj. astraddle.
  < eModE 'striddlings' = astride
  Ye'd be as well to wear throusers now if ye're goin to be ridin
  sthredlegs.
streeler (HE) /strrilər/, noun. prostitute, immoral woman.
  < Gael 'straoille' = loose garment, untidy person
  Didn't they keep a kip (house of ill repute) *an her nothin*
  betther nor (than) *a sthreeler.*
striddle /strrɪdəl/, verb. walk uncomfortably, with an
unusual gait.
  < Sc 'striddle' = straddle
  Quit you your striddlin an walk right.
stroup /strrup/, noun. spout.
  < Sc 'stroup' = spout
  Be a wee bit canny when you pour out the tea, chile. That owl
  stroup lets it all out of a whoosh.

strunt /strʌnt/, noun and verb. sulk, be obstinate.
 < Sc 'strunt' = sulk
 Ye wouldn't think a chile could be so thick-witted (stubborn)!
 This one was huffin an sthruntin since she was in the creddle
 (cradle).

stummle /stʌməl/, noun and verb. attempt.
 < ON 'stumla' = stumble, trip
 *You're to be congratulated now. You made a quare stummle at
 the French with them foreigners!*

stump /stʌmp/, noun. (apple) core.
 < eModE 'stump' = stub, end bit
 I say, hi! Will ye lave us (give me) *your stump an I'll give
 you a ride on the bike?*

stutter /stʌtər/, noun and verb. speech impediment.
 < ME 'stutten' = stutter
 *Naw, a stoppage an a stutther is not the same thing at all. A
 stoppage now is when ye can't get anything out an a stutther is
 when ye keep sayin the same thing over an over. Ye can sing the
 words if ye have a stoppage. It's not so easy to sing them if ye
 stutther.*

subumptious /səbʌmʃəs/, adj. joke word 'comme il faut'.
 < unkn ? sublime + scrumptious
 Quite subumptious, mademoiselle!

*suggin /sʌgɪn/, noun. hayrope used by farm workers
for tightening their trousers at the ankles to prevent
fieldmice running up their legs during harvesting.
 < Gael 'súgán' = hayrope, strawrope.
 You'd need somethin stronger nor (than) *a suggin to tie him up wi'.*

suit /sut/, verb. look good in something.
 < eModE 'suit' = be agreeable
 You suit (look very good in) *that dress lovely.*

summer seat /sʌmər sit (siət)/, noun. garden bench.
 < OE 'sumor' = summer + ON 'sæti' = seat
 *My mother used to enjoy sittin at the front on the summer seat
 an havin a wee crack with everybody that went past.*

supturate /sʌptʃəriət/, verb. suppurate.
 < ModE 'suppurate' = cause to form pus
 *Ye'd be as well to get the charm for that leg now. It's supturatin
 badly.*

swither /swɪðər, swɪər/, verb. dither, go backwards and forwards, be uncertain.

  < Sc 'swither' = hesitate

  I swithered one way an another for years.

swotty /swɒti/, adj. well-dressed.

  < ?ModE 'swot' = study hard

  You're lookin quare an swotty the night, boy! I doubt (i.e. strongly suspect) *you have a lady to see.*

T

tail /tiəl/, noun. prostitute, loose woman.

  < OE 'tægel' = posterior of animal

  What in the name o' God are you goin around with an owl tail like that for? You'll have the counthry talkin about you.

tail /tiəl/, noun. hem, edge of garment.

  < OE 'tægel' = extremity of animal

  Will ye sew the tail o' my skirt for me? I caught it with the heel o' my shoe.

taildraft /tiəlɒraft/, noun. following.

  < OE 'tægel' + ME 'draht' = that which is drawn behind

  You never see Mary but she has a taildhraft with her.

tail o' the day /tiəl ə ðə de/, noun. end of the day, late evening.

  < OE 'tægel' + 'dæg' = day

  < Gael 'earball an lae' = tail of the day

  It used to be that a body would go for a ceili at the tail o' the day but that owl wireless (television) *has the counthry desthroyed.*

tail of the eye /tiəl ə ði ai/, noun. corner of the eye.

  < OE 'tægel' + 'eage' = tail + eye

  I just seen him wi' the tail of my eye.

take a hand out of /tɪk ə han aut ə/, verb. make fun of.

  < OE tacan' + 'hand' = to take + hand

  Don't you be so friendly with that playboy. He'd take a hand out of his own mother!

take a toss /tɪk ə tɔs/, verb. fall heavily.

  < OE 'tacan' + eModE 'toss' = throw

  She took a terrible toss now. She hit her head an broke her glasses. A toss like that could come agin her in later years.

take a trick out of /tɪk ə ᴛʀɪk aut ə/, phrase. use.
   < OE 'tacan' + OF 'trique' = trick
   << Gaelic 'feidhm a bhaint as' = use (= trick to take out)
   Can I take a thrick out o' your new dhress? I'll be very careful.
take bad /tɪk bad/, verb. become unwell.
   < OE 'tacan' + ME 'badde' = take + bad
   He took bad on Friday at twelve an he was dead by Sunday.
take off you /tɪk af yə/, verb. remove your clothes.
   < OE 'tacan' + 'of' = take + of/off
   Take all off you, chile, an have a good warm bath.
take someone's toe /tɪk sᴧmwᴧnz to/, verb. get into one.
   < OE 'tacan' + 'ta' = take + toe
   *I don't know what has took Muriel's toe the way she hasn't been
   in to see me this three days.*
take soup (HE) /tɪk sup/, phrase. give up one's religion for
material well-being.
   < OE 'tacan' + OF 'soupe' = soup
   *How is it that some Murphys are Catholics and others Protestants?
   Some o' them took soup at the time of the famine. They were dyin
   of hunger so I suppose you shouldn't blame them but that's why
   from that day to this you say that a body took soup if they turn
   (change their religion).*
take up with /tɪk ᴧp wə/, phrase. go to live with.
   < OE 'tacan' + 'up' + 'with' = take + up + with
   I hear she has took up wi' a widaman (widower).
talk from the teeth out /tɔk frɒm ðə tiθ aut/, verb. be
hyprocritical, speak hypocritically.
   < ME 'talken' + OE 'teth' = talk + teeth
   *That'n only talks from the teeth out. I howl ye (I suggest) he
   says more nor his prayers an he whistles them.*
*tapping hen /tapɪn hen/, noun. hen with high feathers
on its head.
   < OE 'topp' + 'hen' = crest/tuft of feathers + hen
   *A tappin hen's not lucky about the place. Ye'd be as well to make
   soup of a boy like that.*
targe /tardʒ/, noun. bad-tempered woman.
   < OE 'tergan' = to irritate, annoy
   *She may be a targe but she's game (brave). I'm tellin you she
   wouldn't let her bone go wi' a dog (she would defend herself
   and her belongings fiercely).*

tarra /tara/, noun. terrible thing.

  < OF 'terrour' = fear, terror

It's a tarra! He didn't last long! I'm very sorry for your throuble.

taste /tiəst/, noun. small amount.

  < OF 'taster' = to try, touch, taste

Me ma says will you lend her a taste o' polish for me da's shoes.

taties /tiətiz/, noun. potatoes.

  < Sc 'tatty' = potato

Taties is nice this time o' the year. They're like balls o' flour.

tatie-hoking /tiəti hokɪn/, phrase. potato picking.

  < Sc 'tattie howker' = potato picker

They used to give the childher a week off school for tatie-hokin but it's like many things. It's all done away wi' now.

tats /tats/, noun. knots in hair.

  < Sc 'tatty' = matted

I told the nurse just to cut the tats out of her hair. I didn't want her hurtin my mother in any way, shape or form.

taw /tɔ/, noun. marble, usually a metal one.

  < ModE 'taw' = large fancy marble

*The childher's out playin taws. Many's the game o' taws I played myself. I used to be a dab-han*d (expert) *at pinkin* (getting the marble to stop near a specified spot).

(on the) tear /ɒn ðə tɜr/, phrase. on a drinking spree.

  < OE 'teran' = to pull apart, tear

That poor crathure hasn't her sorrows to seek. That man's on the tear constant now.

tears /tɜrz/, noun. haste.

  < OE 'teran' = to pull apart, tear

You shoulda seen the tears o' him down the road. Ye would a thought that the divil in hell was afther him.

teehee /tihi/, verb. mock, make fun of.

  < ME 'tehee' = derisive laughter

How do you know they were teeheein you? Could they not just a been laughin at somethin funny?

teem /tim/, verb. rain very heavily.

  < OE 'teman' = to bring forth

  << Gael 'taom' = leak, overflow, torrent

Rainin! It's not takin time to rain! It's teemin!

them /ðem/, adj. those.

  < ME 'theim' = them

I was taught them things a long time ago an I'm not likely to stop believin them now.

they (USc) /ðe/, adj. those.

< ME 'thei = they

You'd be ti' (ought to) cut they rosie bushes.

*thereaway /ðɜrawe/, adv. thereabouts.

< Sc 'thereawa" = thereabouts

'Tis twenty year or thereaway I first met Kitty Bawn.
(Traditional song)

thick /θɪk/, adj. stupid, stubborn; intimate.

< OE 'thicce' = dense

Ye couldn't insense knowledge intil a boy like that! He's as thick as champ.

They're dacint enough people now, hardworkin an kind but they're as thick as mud (stubborn) to the last dhrop of them (and that includes every relative).

They're very great, very thick, if you take my meanin.

thickwitted /θɪkwɪtəd/, adj. stubborn.

< 'thicce' + 'wit' = understanding, sense

That child is very thickwitted now. When she gets a notion intil her head, nothin in hell'll shift it.

thin as a rake, rail /θɪn əz ə riək, riəl/, adj. very thin.

< OE 'thynne' + 'raca' ME 'reyle' = thin + rake/rail

<< Gaelic 'réal' = silver sixpence

When he was a child he was as thin as a rail and now he's as fat as a ball o' butther.

think long /θɪŋk lɔŋ/, verb. meditate, cogitate.

< OE 'thencan' + 'lang' = to think + long

He'd never do anything on the spur of the moment. He sits an thinks long about everything, even about buyin a pair o' socks!

*thoat /θot/, noun. throat.

< OE 'throte' = throat

Thon boy would cut your thoat as soon as look at ye!

thole /θol/, verb. endure patiently.

< OE 'tholian' = to suffer

Well, like all I can say is if you don't like it you may thole.

thon /ðɔn/, adj. yon.

< OE 'geon' = yon

Do you not see thon chimley stack? Ye've no eyes at all. When I was your age, I could a seen a midge (small fly) at Maghery.

thonder /ðʌnDər/, adv. yonder.

    < ME 'yonder' = yonder

    I seen him over thondher not above ten minutes ago.

*thow /θo/, noun and verb. throw.

    < OE 'thrawan' = to throw

    Go on, thow us the ball. One, two, thee, thow it.

thrapple /ʈrapəl/, noun and verb. throat, choke.

    < OE 'throt-bolla' = windpipe

    She catched your man (the one we've been talking about) *by the thrapple an whammled him right into the pig's through. Thon boy had a wee want. He'd a come up to you all smiles an then got a howlt* (hold) *o' your tie to thrapple you wi'.*

thraw /ʈra/, verb. pull against, draw back, usually in the fixed phrase 'pullin an thrain'.

    < ?Lat 'trahere' = to draw

    They may be pullin an thrain among themselves but they'd ate you without salt if you enthermeddled (interfered).

*thrawin /ʈraən/, adj. headstrong, stubborn.

    < Sc 'thrawn' = twisted, distorted

    He's a thickwitted wee upstart! A thra-in, good-for-nothin get!

throughother /ʈruɒðər/, adj. and adv. confused, untidy; within the same family or group.

    < OE 'thurh' + 'other' = through + other

    << Gael 'tré na céile' = upside down; among/through friends

    I'm sorry the house (room) *is a wee bit throughother.*

    Mind what ye say. They're all married throughother.

*thruppence /ʈrʌpɪns/, noun. three pence.

    < OE 'thri' + 'penegas' = three + pennies

    Sixpence take away thruppence an you're left with thruppence.

tickieman /tɪkiman/, noun. pedlar, salesman who sold things 'on tick', collecting their money every week.

    < eModE 'ticket' + OE 'man' = ticket + man (one who gives credit)

    Sure there wasn't a child in the town that would a had a shoe to their foot if it hadn't a been for the tickiemen.

tiddleyhoy /tɪdəlihoi/, noun. friendly joking word for private parts.

    < unkn

    Dhraw up to the fire now an warm your tiddleyhoy.

tig /tɪg/, noun and verb. game which involves the catcher touching or 'tigging' one of the other players.
   < ME 'tik' = touch lightly
   It's like 'Hide-and-go-seek' only we call it 'Tig'.
tight /tait/, adj. mean, ungenerous.
   < OE 'thiht' = firm, solid
   Thon blade's as tight as a willock (whelk). *She wouldn't give you the skin of her skitther!*
till /tɪl/, prep. to, till.
   < OE 'til' = to, till
   << ON 'til' = to, till
   You're late, you're late, it's a quarther till eight.
   You're in time, you're in time. It's a quarther past nine.
   (Children's chant)
timorsome /tɪmərsʌm/, adj. timid, nervous.
   < OF 'temoros' = fearful
   She's got till an age when she's timorsome, afraid ti' go to bed without the light on.
tinker's time /tɪŋkərz taim/, phrase. late, slow.
   < ME 'tinkler' = worker in tin + OE 'tima' = time
   I wouldn't arrange to go anywhere with my first daughther. She runs at tinker's time, if ye get my meanin.
tip /tɪp/, noun and verb. dump.
   < ME 'tip' = overturn, empty out
   You can always tell how a woman keeps her house by lookin at the step. If it's not well kept, ye may look out. An if it's very dirty, she'll have the house like a tip.
tishie /tɪʃi/, adj. and noun. tissue.
   < OF 'tissu' = fabric
   The sheets were as thin as tishie paper. Ye had ti' lie brave an canny not ti' put your foot through them.
tit /tɪt/, noun. growth, wart, untidy lock of hair.
   < ?OE 'tit' = teat
   It's not every tit ye can get removed, ye know. As we always say: 'If the tit grows above the breath (above the mouth and nose) *don't enthermeddle with it.'*
   You're all dhressed up an you've a tit stickin out at the back of your head.
toerag /torag/, noun. inferior person, second-class citizen.

< ModE 'toe-rag' = rag put into shoe that is too big for wearer
I'm damned if anybody's goin to make a toerag out o' me!

tongue /tʌŋ/, noun and verb. tongue, scold.
< OE 'tunge' = tongue
She has a tongue on her that would shave a mouse.
She's not bad but she's got intil the habit of tonguin a body. A body biz cankersome if they're left on their own too much.

(have a) tongue on you /tʌŋ ɒn yə /, verb. ask.
< OE 'tunge' = tongue
How could you have got lost? Had you no tongue on you (Could you not ask)?

topcoat /tɒpkot/, noun. overcoat.
< OE 'topp' = crest + ME 'cote' = coat
It's a topcoat ye'd need on a day like that, not a wee flimsy bit of a thing.

tord /tord/, noun. turd, term of abuse.
< OE 'tord' = turd
He's as mane as get-out. He wouldn't give his tord till a dog!

torf /torf/, noun. sod of peat, peat.
< OE 'turf' = turf
If you have the last torf on the fire, make people believe you have a stack in the yard (garden).

*to themselves may be told /tə ðəmselvz me bə taul/, adv. 'I'm telling you the absolute truth and not even the people concerned could deny it.'
< OE 'tellan' = to narrate
There was a family down by the Lowside, a family of girls an they were all educated. First they called their mother an father 'Ma an Da', but that wasn't good enough so they changed it to 'Mama an Papa'. Then they took to callin them 'Kate an James' an then, to themselves may be towl, they all ended in the asylum.

toty /toti/, adj. tiny, very small.
< Sc 'tottie' = tiny
Och, it's a toty wee house but it's just beautiful. You'd be as warm as a cruddled (coddled) *apple in there.*

townland /taunlan/, noun. region around a town.
< OE 'tun' + 'land' = town + land
How many would ye say would there be in the townland o' Dungannon? Would you say there'd be fifteen thousand?

trail /trɪəl/, verb. drag or follow behind.
  < OF 'traillier' = drag along
  Don't you be thrailin afther me.
trail the wing /trɪəl ðə wɪŋ/, verb. sulk so as to evoke
sympathy.
  < OF 'traillier' + ON 'vængi' = wing
  What's wrong with me da?
  Divil a thing. He's thrailin the wing an the rest of us is supposed
  to be sorry for him.
trake /trɪək/, noun and verb. long, slow walk.
  < OF 'trac' = path
  We must a thraked for hours. It was one o' them sthraight roads
  that never winds an never ends.
trap /trap/, noun. mouth.
  < OE 'træppe' = contrivance for catching animals
  Keep you your thrap shut.
trasby /trasbi/, noun. row, misunderstanding, usually
between members of the same family.
  < Gael 'trasnuigh' = contradict, forbid, oppose
  << Sc 'thrawn' = twisted, distorted
  There's a wee bit of a thrasby goin' on between Kitty and the
  (her) *mother.*
*trawnyeen /trɔnyin/, noun. small bit of a stone.
  < Gael 'traithnín' = dart, arrow, blade of grass
  He took the eye out o' me with an owl thrawnyeen of a stone. (He
  hit me on the eye with a small stone.)
trevally /trəvali/, noun. crowd of children; uproar.
  < Sc 'trevallie' = disturbance
  You could enjoy Sarah-Ann's crack if she didn't always have a
  whole threvally o' childher with her.
  King Billy was a Dutchman like Kruger I suppose.
  He was married till a Papish an he had a Roman nose.
  But in yearly jubilation all Ulsther people join
  For a Dutchman bate a Scotchman at the Battle o' the Boyne.
  An we're towl to keep the mem'ry green or orange, sthrong an
  hot
  Of that long ago threvally when a Dutchman bate a Scot.
  (Children's rhyme)
trick /trɪk/, noun. breed, family; go.
  < OF 'trique' = cheat, attire

There's breeds is good at makin money an there's others good at singin but the whole thrick o' the Ms. was good at pleadin poverty.

I was wondherin could a take a thrick out o' (wear) your blue dhress.

*trig /trɪg/, adj. tidy (of a woman).

< Sc 'trig' = neat, smart

She may be forty but she's a thrig wee body an has a tidy bit (large piece) o' land.

trouble /trʌbəl/, noun. death in the family.

< OF 'truble' = mental distress

I'm very sorry for your throuble, now.

troubles /trʌbəlz/, noun. violent times.

< OF 'truble' = distress, disturbance

I doubt (strongly believe) these throubles'll never stop.

trough /trɔx/, noun. receptacle for food or water for animals.

< OE 'trog' = vessel for liquid

He has a mouth on him like a bucket.

Bucket, how are ye! It's more like a through.

trough /trɔx/, exclamation.

< OE 'truwian' = believe, trust

Through an for two pins I'd throw the lot down his own jarbox (sink).

*truff /trʌf/, verb. steal.

< Sc 'truff' = steal, pilfer

They were known to have the long finger (to steal) or to thruff, if I would put it right.

trumf /trʌmf/, noun and verb. trump.

< eModE 'triumph' = trump card

If you play that one, you can thrumf her.

trummicky /trʌmɪki/, adj. upside down, back to front, topsy turvy.

< Gael 'tromach' = topsy turvy

You've a thrummicky (awkward) way o' doin things.

tully eye /tʌli ai/, noun. squint.

< ?Gael 'taoladh' = shedding tears

He has a terrible tully eye, God bless the mark! That's why we call him 'One-Lamp-Louie'.

*turl /torl/, verb. ring an old-fashioned bell.
  < ?OE 'tollian' = to toll a bell
  << Sc 'tirl' = rap, knock
  St Magdalen at Peter's Gate torled at the rope.
  She had led a wicked life below and wasn't filled wi' hope.
  (Children's verse)

turn /torn/ verb. change one's religion.
  < OE 'turnian' = to turn
  Nether of them torned. She said she would go her road an he
  would go his but ye could spey (foretell) what would happen.
  When the childher come along, nobody went nowhere.

*turrey /tʌri/, noun. young pig.
  < Sc 'torr' = call to pigs
  My father always said that if it took longer than thirteen weeks
  to fatten a turrey, then ye lost money on it.

*twangs /twaŋz/, noun. leather pieces at the back of a boot,
used for picking the boots up.
  < OE 'thwangs' = thongs
  God but he had little to do when he cut the twangs o' the chile's
  boots.

twig /twɪg/ verb. catch on, understand.
  < ModE 'twig' = understand
  << Gael 'tuig' = understand, comprehend
  Och, ye're as thick as champ! Ye don't twig aisy. Ye don't folly
  (follow).

typewriter /taipraitər/, noun. person who types.
  < Lat 'typus' = impression + OE 'writan' = to write +
  '-er'
  You have to be a good typewriter to manage computers.

U

uilleann pipes /ɪlən paips/, noun. elbow pipes.
  < Gael 'píob uileann' = elbow pipes
  Is it hard to play uilleann pipes?
  Well, it's hard to listen to them if ye don't play them right.

*umberstick /ʌmbərstɪk/, noun. umbrella.
  < Lat 'umbra' = shade + OE 'sticca' = stick

She bought me the most beautifullest umberstick you ever clapped eyes on.

unbeknownst /ʌnbənonst/, verb. without anyone knowing.

< eModE 'unbeknownst' = unknown to

An then, unbeknownst till a crayther, they flitted and from that day to this nobody has seen hide nor hair of them.

uncivil /ʌnsɪvəl/, adj. unmannerly.

< OE 'un-' + OF 'civil' = courteous

He's what I would describe as an uncivil gadherman (impolite term for a man lacking in principles). *He's too mane* (mean) *to live. You see him regular in a big motor an it empty and he would dhrive over you quicker than give you a lift.*

unction(HE) /ʌŋtʃən/, noun. reduced form of 'Extreme Unction', (usually pronounced 'Extra Munction'), the last rites of the Catholic Church.

< Lat 'unctio' = rite of anointing

They say that some sick people come round after the unction but, by the looks of her, I'd say she'll not do (survive).

untholable /ʌnθoləbəl/, adj. incapable of being endured.

< OE 'un-' + 'tholian' = to endure + '-able'

Ye can thole many's a thing but that man's cross was untholable. It would a broke anybody's back.

uppity /ʌpəti/, adj. snobbish.

< OE 'up' = up + 'ity'

You'll find that the uppitiest ones are the ones with no breedin. A man with a bit of breedin is as much at home with a tinker as a toff.

usen't to /yusəntə/, verb. negative of 'used to'.

< ME 'be used to' = be accustomed to

He usen't to touch a dhrop before his accident but his nerves is bad now an he dhrinks very heavy.

V

vause /vɔz/, noun. vase.

< Lat 'vas' = vessel

I've always fancied a couple o' them nice delph vauses.

venter /vɛntər/, verb. venture.
  < eModE 'venture' = chance, adventure
  Little boats stay near the shore.
  Larger vessels may venther more.
venturesome /vɛntərsʌm/, adj. adventurous.
  < eModE 'venturesome' = adventurous
  Boys is venturesome now. Ye need to watch them or they'd get up
  to somethin dangerous.
visions /vɪʒənz/, noun. premonition.
  < OF 'vision' = sight, thing seen
  Move that wee ornament further back for I have visions of it
  fallin an brekkin into smithereens.
***vocable** /vokəbəl/, noun. spoken vocabulary.
  < OF 'vocable' = word
  She has the very son at the elocution. When I asked her if she
  wasn't afraid o' turnin him intil a nancy she said that a boy had
  every bit as much need of his vocables as a girl.

W

wadden /wɒdən/, noun. cotton wool.
  < eModE 'wadding' = padding, cotton wool
  If you put a wee bit o' wadden over that cut heel, your shoes
  wouldn't festher it (cause it to get worse).
wadge /wɒdʒ/, noun. big piece.
  < ModE 'wodge' = lumpy object
  Don't give me such a wadge o' cake. I'm watchin me figure. Just
  a wee nyimf now to taste me mouth.
wag /wag/, verb. shake, wave.
  < OE 'waggian' = to totter, sway
  Don't you wag your finger at me!
  Wag that boy down. There's an accident a mile or two down the
  road an you wouldn't want anybody to dhrive intil it unbek-
  nownst like.
wag-o'-the-wall /wag ə ðə wɔl/, noun. clock with pendulum.
  < Sc 'wag-at-the-waa' = wallclock
  You could be doin with something on that wall, a nice picture or a
  wag-o'the-wall.

wain, we'un /wiən, wen/, noun. child.
   < Sc 'wean' = child
   Six wains at the last count an she's little more than a wain herself!

wake /wiək/, noun and verb. time after a death when the body is kept in the house for a period of time and when friends and relatives come to pay their respect.
   < OE 'wacu' = vigil
   Now mind you (remember) *what I'm sayin. I want to be waked the full two nights in me own house. Don't be puttin me in the chapel the last night. An I don't want a dhry wake either* (i.e. there should be alcohol at the wake).

walk /wɔk/, noun and verb. procession, process.
   < OE 'wealcan' = to go by foot
   Don't tell me he's away walkin? Sure he's not fit for that kind o' nonsense.

want /wʌnt/, noun. mental deficiency.
   < ON 'vant' = deficiency
   Them childher with wee wants is very lovin, very affectionate.

want /wʌnt/, verb. lack.
   < ON 'vanta' = be without
   How, in the name o' God, can you say I'm fat an me wantin a pound o' being ten stone (when I am only 9 stone 13 pounds)?

weather /wɛðər, wɛər/, noun. time, now, at the moment.
   < OE 'weder' = direction of wind
   How are yiz all doin this weather?

web-toed /web tod/, adj. web-footed, a good swimmer.
   < OE 'web' + 'ta' = web, membrane + toe
   You're brave an web-toed. Well, you'll never dhrown anyway.

wee /wi/, adj. small, young, usually with affectionate overtones.
   < ME 'wei' = small
   I hear your wee blade got a call (won a scholarship) *to University.*
   He's a wee wart of a man, no come-along (friendliness) *with him at all at all.*

wee problem /wi prɒbləm/, noun. alcoholism.
   < ME 'wei' + OF 'problème' = difficulty

Och, ye shouldn't be so hard on him. He has a wee problem, ye know, an he's doin his bit to bate (beat) *it.*

wee wasp /wi wɔsp/, noun. bad-tempered person with a sharp tongue.

< ME 'wei' + OE 'wæsp' = wasp

She seemed a civil enough wee blade when she married, but she's torned out to be a wee wasp, wi' a tongue that would clip a hedge!

weemen /wimɪn/, noun. women.

< OE 'wifman' = woman

When weemen gets wicked, they're a tarra (terrible).

well-heeled /wel hild/, adj. well-to-do.

< OE 'wel' + 'hela' = well + heel + '-ed'

Don't you know rightly why she married an owl baldy man like thon? Sure he's terrible well-heeled an she'll want for nothin.

well-mended /wel mendəd/, adj. fatter and healthier.

< OE 'wel' + ME 'mend' = restore to wholeness + '-ed'

I'm tellin you (emphatic phrase), *thon holiday done you the world o' good. You're terrible well-mended an you've a quare colour in your chicks* (cheeks).

well-put-on /wel pʌt ɔn/, adj. well dressed.

< OE 'wel' + 'potian' + 'on' = well + to put + on

Now she's a credit to the counthry! Left a widawoman wi' a big family an she fed them all an everyone o' them was well put on. Sure the crayther killed herself workin for them.

welt /wɛlt/, verb. beat severely.

< ME 'walt' = strip of leather

He got a quare weltin. The father took lumps out of him but ye nivir seen such an improvement in anybody. The father learnt him his place an although I don't howl (hold) *wi' batins* (beatings), *thon boy was askin for it.*

whack /ʍak/, noun. share, slice, large piece; in good form.

< ?OE 'thaccian' = to beat, thwack

Look at the whack he took out o' that loaf.

I'm not the whack since I had the flu. I'm as wake (weak) *as wather and nothin seems to have any taste.*

wheasel /ʍizəl/, noun. weasel.

< OE 'wesule' = weasel

He's as contrary as a bag o' wheasels.

wheen /ʍin/, noun. few, several.
  < Sc 'wheen' = several
  We haven't had sunshine like this in a wheen o' Sundays.

wheezle /ʍizəl/, noun and verb. wheeze, whistle.
  < ON 'hvæsa' = hiss, wheeze + '-le'
  I'd be as right as rain if it wasn't for this owl wheezle in me chest.

whenever /ʍənivər/, conj. when.
  < OE 'hwenne' + 'æfre' = when + ever
  Whenever he was in Belfast last week, he called to see us.

whid /ʍid/, noun. scent, usually metaphorical.
  < ?Sc 'whidder' = blow in gusts
  << Gaelic 'faoidh' = voice, cry (cf O'Faoilean = Whelan)
  *I might be wrong, but I got a whid o' what they were plannin an
  I'd say they're up to no good.*

while /ʍail/, verb. spend time pleasurably; lure.
  < OE 'hwilum' = at some time
  It's wonderful (strange) *how childher can while away the time
  with a wee doll or wee odds an ends.*
  He has the beautifullest voice ye've ever heerd (heard)*! I'm
  tellin you, thon boy could while the boards* (birds) *down o' the
  bushes!*

whillaballoo /ʍilabalu/, exclam.
  < unkn
  << ModE 'hullaballoo' = noise
  *The Magees was fond o' wandherin. Whillaballoo an they're
  here an whillaballoo an they're away again.*

*whillocky (HE) /ʍiləki/, noun. white bird.
  < Gael 'faoileog' = seagull
  *I knowed it, sure I knowed it. When I seen thon whillocky, I
  knowed there'd be throuble.*

whin /ʍin/, noun. gorse.
  < Sc 'whin' = gorse
  She came in like a blaze of whins (fast and very angry).

whinge /ʍindʒ/, noun and verb. cry, whine.
  < ?OE 'hwinan' = whine
  *Would you quit your whinging. Just give me peace for a wee
  while an let me get my head shired.*

whisper /ʍispər/, noun. rumour.
  < OE 'hwisprian' = whisper
  << Gael 'cogar' = whisper, hint

You must a got a whid (scent) *of it.*
Aye, well I got a whisper of it yesterday.
whisht /ʍɪʃt/, noun and verb. quiet, be quiet
   < eModE 'whisht' = call for silence
   << Gael 'bí i do thost' = be quiet
   Howl (hold) *your whisht, woman dear, there's not a word o'*
   thruth in that story.
white /ʍait/, adj. fair-haired.
   < OE 'hwit' = white
   << Gael 'bán' = white, fair-haired
   Noreen Bawn was White Noreen an that means she had lovely
   fair hair.
*****whitehead** /ʍaithed/, noun. loved one, pet.
   < OE 'hwit' + 'heofod' = white + head
   << Gael 'buachaill bán' = beloved boy (boy white)
   He liked all the childher but Joe was the whitehead.
white in the face /ʍait ɪn ðə fiəs/, adj. unnaturally pale.
   < OE 'hwit' + OF 'face' = countenance
   She's as white in the face as a cat in labour.
whittle /ʍitəl/, noun. inflammation near the nail.
   < ME 'whitflaw' = whitlow
   I've a whittle on the inside of my thumb and it's givin me jip.
*****whutherit** /ʍʌðərət/, noun. white-throated weasel.
   < OE 'hwit' + 'throte' = white throat
   What in the name o' God are ye killin things for? Sure them
   whutherits only do good about a place.
widowman /wɪdaman/, noun. widower.
   < OE 'widewe' + 'man' = widow + man
   << Gaelic 'baintreabhach fir' = widower (widow +
   man)
   The place was full o' widamen an widaweemin.
wild /wail/, adv. very, exceptionally.
   < OE 'wilde' = wild
   That bull's wild tame.
willy-wagtail /wɪli wagtiəl/, noun. wagtail.
   < eModE 'wagtail' = bird
   They used to call a wren a jinty-wren but the only name I know
   for a wagtail is a willy-wagtail.
windy-stool /wɪndi stul/, noun. window sill.
   < ON 'vindauga' = window + OE 'syll' = sill

Many's the time I sat on the windystool wi' your mother.
Them was the days!

*wine /wain/, noun. wind.
  < OE 'wind' = wind
When the wine's from the north
It's good for coolin broth.
When it dhrives from the south
Ye'll get dust in your mouth.
When the wine's from the east
It's woe for man an beast.
When it comes from the west
That the wine we love the best.
(Traditional rhyme)

winter /wɪntər/, verb. spend the winter in service.
  < OE 'winter' = winter
I winthered in Scotland so I could summer anywhere.

wirsch (USc) /wɪrʃ/, adj. bitter,
  < Sc 'wairsh' = insipid, bitter
Them berries I ate was that wirsch they nearhand withered the
tongue aff me.

wit /wɪt/, noun. good sense.
  < OE 'wit' = understanding, sense
Have a titther o' wit, will ye. Catch yourself on!

wobbling brush /wɒblɪn brʌʃ/, noun. shaving brush.
  < ModE 'wobble' = move from side to side + OF
  'broisse' = brush
God, it's comin till a quare pass when a man's wobblin brush is
lifted an put past (tidied up).

(be) woe /woˈ/, adj. low, depressed.
  < OE 'wa' = misery, misfortune
Och me heart was woe but I had to swally the lump an go.

wrought /rɔt/, verb. worked (usually manual work).
  < ME 'wrogt' = worked
You wrought hard an sore for them childher so if they can give
you a wee lift (help) *now, that's all to the good.*

Y

yahoo /yahu/, noun. ignorant, rough person.
< ModE 'yahoo' = brute in human form
He's an ignorant gobberlooney, an owl yahoo!
yammer /yamər/, verb. cry, complain.
< Sc 'yammer' = complain, fret
Wouldn't ye wondher that childher don't get tired yammerin?
yap /yap/, noun and verb. scold, nag.
< Sc 'yap' = nag, whine
<< OE 'gielpan' = to yelp, whine
Will ye quit your yappin! My ears is bizzin wi' your constant mitherin!
yard /yard/, noun. garden, yard.
< OE 'geard' = fence, enclosure
We thried to brighten up the back by plantin flowers in the yard but the childhren played with them that much they never came to anything.
yardbrush /yardbrʌʃ/, noun. strong brush for outside use.
< OE 'geard' + OF 'broisse' = brush
It must be nice to have hair that sits nice and doesn't be tatty.
My hair's strong, Lord knows, but it sits like a yardbrush.
*yarkan /yarkən/, noun. stiffening in a slipper.
< Sc 'yerking' = side seam of shoe
I'm walkin on the yarkin o' my slipper since I let Kathleen wear them. She must have powerful feet to walk the back down!
ye /yə, yɪ/, pronoun. unstressed form of 'you' singular.
< OE 'ge' = you
Ye've a quare pair o' hands on ye. (You're very handy.)
yella /yɛla/, adj. uncomplimentary term in the phrases 'yella laugh' and 'yella liver'.
< OE 'geolu' = yellow
<< Gael 'gáire buidhe' = yellow laughter
Thon owl yella laugh! It would turn (upset) you for ye know that he's false.
That's the second man she has seen down. I doubt she has a yella liver (i.e. is in some way responsible for the death of her two husbands).

yellaman /yɛlaman/, noun. rock (hard type of sweet).
    < OE 'geolu' + 'man' = yellow + man
    Did ye thrait (treat) *your Mary Anne*
    To some dullice an yellaman...
    (Traditional ballad)
yoke /yok/, noun. disparaging term for person.
    < OE 'geocian' = to yoke
    In the name o' God, who does thon yoke think he is!
your man, woman /yər man, wʌmən/, noun. 1. husband,
wife; 2. man or woman we've just been discussing.
    < OE 'eower' + 'man, wifman' = your man, woman
    1. *I hear your man's got a job. That's great news now.*
    2. *So your woman come up to me an she said...*
youse, yiz, yousuns /yuz, yɪz, yuzənz/, pronoun. 'you'
plural.
    < OE 'eow' = you + '-s/ones'
    Yiz is quare an crafty. The rest of us is out toilin an yousuns is
    sittin warmin your tiddleyhoys.
yowl /yaul/, noun and verb. howl with pain.
    < Sc 'yowl' = howl
    << yell + howl
    Ye'll have to put that owl dog down. Sure the yowls of him is
    pitiful.

SECTION THREE

ENGLISH – NORTHERN IRELAND ENGLISH

A

abduct, verb. lift.
abnormal, adj. freety, pishogues.
abundant, adj. galore, lashings and lavings.
abroad, adv. foreign.
absurd, adj. daft.
accent, noun. brogue.
accident, noun. mischance.
accost, verb. check.
ache, noun. brash, sore, stoon.
aching, adj. sore.
acknowledge, verb. let on.
acquainted, adj. acquent.
acquire, verb. come by, huff.
acrimony, noun. trasby.
across, adv. and prep. through.
active. adj. soople.
acumen, noun. gumption.
adamant, adj. positive.
(in) addition, adv. forby.
addle-brained, adj. away in the head, astray.
admiration, noun. mass, notion.
adolescent, noun. youngster, lump of a boy/girl.
adroit, adj. canny, handy.
adult, noun. body, man, woman.
(in) advance, adv. and prep. afore.
advanced for one's years, adj. old-fashioned.
adventurous, adj. venturesome, (act the) playboy.
affable, adj. feasant.
affection, noun. graw, mass, notion.
affectionate, adj. luvesome.
affluent, adj. well-heeled, well set up.

afraid, adj. afeard.
afternoon, noun. evening.
against, prep. agin, firnenst.
age (to be married), noun. market.
aghast, adj. dumbfoundered.
agile, adj. soople.
ago, adv. back, since.
ague, noun. boy, shaking ague.
aid, verb. lend a hand.
airing-cupboard, noun. hot-press.
alas, exclamation. och-hanee-o.
(illegal) alcohol, noun. the crayther, poteen.
alcoholism, noun. wee problem.
alcove, noun. nyook.
alert, adj. no dozer.
alive, adj. to the fore.
alley, noun. close, entry.
allow, verb. get one's way, let.
(be) allowed, verb. get.
almost, adverb. nearhand.
aloft, adv. and prep. aboon.
alone, adj. alane, one's lone.
alternately, adv. time about.
always, adv. aye.
amaze, verb. bumboozle, dumbfounder, flabbergast.
amenable, adj. biddable, feasant.
am I not, verb. amina.
am not, verb. amn't.
amount, noun. dribble, dribs and drabs, lock, lot, lick, muckle, pick, pickle, prog, skimf, smidgeon, stime, taste, wadge, whack.
anger, noun. rage.
(be) angry, adj. and verb. mad, rage.
animal, noun. beast.
annoy, verb. fash, faze, be heartscalded.
ant, noun. pishmire.
anus, noun. eye of the ass.
apiece, adv. the piece.
apparition, noun. banshee, boggyman, bogle, rath.
(unripe) apple, noun. crab.

apprehend, verb. lift, nab.
apprehensive, adj. timorsome.
April, noun. Aprile.
argument, noun. trasby.
armpit, noun. oxther.
armsful, noun. gwall.
aroma, noun. hogo, hum.
arrange in order, verb. stool.
arrest, verb. lift.
arrogant, adj. consaty.
ascend, verb. shin, skin, speel.
as far as, prep. the length of.
ashes, noun. greeshy.
ask, verb. axe.
(be) asleep, verb. Jack Nod's come on.
asparagus, noun. sparrow grass.
(cast) aspersions, verb. miscall.
ass, noun. cuddy, neddy.
assist, verb. further, give a hand.
association, noun. click.
asthma, noun. wheezle.
astray, adj. agley.
astride, adv. and prep. stredlegs.
astute, adj. canny.
astuteness, noun. gumption.
asylum, noun. big house.
arse, noun. ass, bum, case o' pistles, tiddleyhoy.
at all, adv. ava.
atom, noun. atomy, hate, stime.
attempt, noun. right hand, stummle.
attraction, noun. graw, mass.
attractive, adj. bonny, sancy.
austere, adj. dour.
authority, noun. headbuckcat.
aversion, noun. scundher.
avoid, verb. jook.
await, verb. wait on.
awkward, adj. ass about face, clootie, fyuggy.

B

babble, verb. blether.
baby, noun. bairn, child, wain.
back garden, noun. back.
back to front, adv. ass about face, trummicky.
backside, noun. ass, bum, case o' pistles, tiddleyhoy.
bad, adj. desperate.
bad luck, noun. scran.
bad-tempered, adj. crabbit, crabby, cyarnaptious.
bad-tempered person, noun. attercap, pishmire.
bag, noun. poke.
bake (an apple), verb. cuddle.
bald, adj. baldy, moilly.
bale, noun. bottle.
(cannon) ball, noun. podion ball.
ballad, noun. come-all-ye.
bandy, adj. boolie, kayleg.
bar, noun and verb. snib.
barbed wire, noun. bucky wire.
basket, noun. creel, kish.
bastard, noun. by-blow, get, hoor's get.
bauble, noun. folderdol.
beak, noun. bake, neb.
bear, verb. thole.
beard, noun. baird.
beast, noun. baste.
beat, verb. belt, dunt, give what Paddy gave the drum,
give the rounds of the kitchen, hammer, lace, lambaste,
leather, lick, luder, morder, skelp.
beating, noun. hiding, lacing, leathering, ludering,
skelping, what Paddy gave the drum, welt.
beautiful, adj. bonny, sancy.
become ill, verb. take bad.
beck and call, noun. bidding.
bee, noun. bumbee.
beef, noun. flesh, fleshmeat.
beetle, noun. clock, daleclock, keerog.
before, adv. and prep. afore, firnenst.
beg, verb. cadge, plead a poor mouth.

beggar, noun. beggarman, gaberlunzie.
beginning, noun. crack.
beguile, verb. while.
behave according to protocol, verb. pass oneself.
behave indecisively, verb. haver, swither.
behave sensibly, verb. catch oneself on.
behind, adv. and prep. ahind, aback, back.
belch, noun and verb. rift.
believe, verb. doubt.
bellicose, adj. crabbit, crookit.
bellow, verb. gulder.
bellows, noun. bellowses.
belongings, noun. bardicks.
beloved, noun. blue-eye, whitehead.
berry, noun. fraun.
beseech, verb. plead like a cripple on a cross.
beside, adv. and prep. nearhand.
besides, adv. forby.
bespatter, verb. jap.
betray, verb. renegue.
between, prep. atween.
bewail, verb. keeny.
bewilder, verb. dumbfounder.
bicycle, noun. bicylic.
big, adj. clever, muckle.
bin, noun. ark.
bird, noun. board, lachter, scaldy.
bitter, adj. wirsch.
(heavy) blow, noun. clout, dig.
board, noun. boord.
board (and lodgings), noun. keep.
boast, verb. bum.
bog, noun. moss, munchees.
boil, noun. bile.
bomb, noun and verb. bum.
booth, noun. snug.
border, noun. march.
borrow, verb. morrow.
boss, noun. headbuckcat, headman.
bother, verb. fash.

bottom, noun. ass, bum, case o' pistles, tiddleyhoy.
boundary, noun. march.
box, noun. kist.
boy, noun. boy, cub, lump, lad.
braces, noun. gallisses.
bramble, noun. brammle.
brat, noun. beggar's get, by-blow, get.
brave, adj. game.
brawl, noun. ructions.
bread, noun. bannock, bap, barmbrack, fadge, farl,
loafbread, panbread, panloaf, pannady.
breast, noun. diddy.
breed, noun. trick.
brew, verb. draw.
brighten, verb. brightify.
bring, verb. fetch.
bronchitis, noun. brownkittlies, brownchitis, wheezle.
broom, noun. bizzum.
brothel, noun. kip.
bull's penis, noun. peezle.
bumblebee, noun. bumbee.
bump, noun and verb. dunch, dunt.
(unemployment) bureau, noun. beroo.
burn, verb. roast.
buzz, verb. bizz.
buzzing noise, noun. bizz.

C

cabbage, noun. corly cale, cale.
cabinet, noun. armory, press.
cancer, noun. quare fake.
candy, noun. yellaman.
cane, noun. sally wattle.
cannot, verb. cannae.
cantankerous, adj. crabbit, cranky, crookit, wee wasp.
cap, noun. bonnet, duncher, pixie.
capable, adj. crafty.
capacious, adj. clever.

caprice, noun. crack, gag.
capsize, verb. cowp.
carcase, noun. cyarkidge.
careful, adj. canny.
carouse, noun. spree, tear.
cat, noun. beelie, cat.
catch, noun and verb. glam, nab, lift.
catch on, verb. twig.
caterpillar, noun. grannygreybaird.
Catholic, noun. fenian, left-footer.
Catholic church, noun. chapel.
cattle, noun. bastes.
censure, verb. check.
certificate, noun. line(s).
chair, noun. sate.
chamberpot, noun. chanty, po.
changeling, noun. sheeoge.
change religions, verb phrase. turn.
chase, verb. run.
chat, noun and verb. collogue, crack, shannach.
cheap, adj. chape.
cheat, verb. bumboozle, chate.
cheek, noun. brass neck, chick, guff, impidence, lip, owl lip.
cheeky, adj. bold, impident.
cheerful, adj. heartsome.
cheer up, verb. brightify, lift.
chest, noun. ark, kist.
chew, verb. chaw.
(brood of) chickens, noun. gailin.
chilblain, noun. malecyartin.
child, noun. bairn, brat, chile, cub, cuckoo's lachter, faggot, magobbler, wain.
children, noun. childer.
chilly, adj. cold-rifed, nippy.
chimney, noun. chim(b)ley, lum.
chimney seat, noun. inglenook.
chin(s), noun. chullers, smig.
choke, verb. kink.
chores, noun. messages.

chubby, adj. sancy, well-mended.
church, noun. chapel, church, meeting-house.
churning movement , noun. brash.
churnlid, noun. pick.
cinder, noun. clinker.
clamour, noun. trevally.
clean up, verb. muck out, redd up.
clear throat, verb phrase. clocher.
clever, adj. smart.
climb, verb. shin, skin, speel.
cliquish, adj. clannish.
clock, noun. wag o' the wall.
close (eyes), verb. bat.
close (of the day), noun. tail o' the day.
clumsy, adj. clootie, corry-fisted, footery, fyuggy, kack-handed, kittery, slootery.
coal, noun. slack.
coax, verb. while.
cockroach, noun. clock, dale-clock, keerog.
cold, adj. cowl, hardy, foundered, starving.
cold, noun. cowl, founder, the boy.
colic, noun. skitter.
comb, noun. queel.
comely, adj. sancy, trig.
(extremely) comfortable, adj. on the pig's back.
commonsense, noun. wit.
commotion, noun. bizz, glow, ructions.
company of people, noun. ceili.
compel, verb. gar.
compendious, adj. clever.
complain, verb. girn, yammer.
conceited, adj. consaty.
confer, verb. collogue.
confound, verb. bumboozle, dumbfounder.
confused, adj. a marley, throughother.
congeal, verb. cruddle.
container for grain or flour, noun. ark.
contemplate, verb. think long.
contrary, adj. crooked, thrawin.
controversy, noun. trasby.

convince, verb. insense.
cooing dove, noun. croodling doo.
copy, verb. cog.
core (of fruit), noun. stump.
corn bin, noun. ark.
corner, noun. nyook.
corpse, noun. corp.
correct someone, verb. check.
corsets, noun. stays.
cost, noun. damage.
costume, noun. rigout.
cottonwool, noun. wadden.
cough, noun and verb. kink, puke.
courage, noun. spunk.
court, noun and verb. coort.
cover, verb. hap.
coward, noun. cyavvie, hag.
cowardly, adj. cowl.
cowpat, noun. clap.
cowshed, noun. byre.
cradle, noun. creddle.
cradle in one's arms, verb. croodle.
creak, noun and verb. crake.
creature, noun. crayther.
crew, noun. trevally.
cripple, noun. bedther, hip-at-the-clinch, nought-and-carry-one.
criticise, verb. cyast up.
crock, noun. meskin.
crockery, noun. delph.
cross, adj. contrary, cranky, mad.
cross person, noun. attercap, pishmire.
cross woman, noun. barge, targe.
crowd, noun. trevally.
crumb, noun. crummle.
crumble, verb. crummle.
crust of bread, noun. heel.
cry, verb. blert, greet, keeny, whinge, yammer.
cry-baby, noun. blert.
cunning, adj. fly.

cupboard, noun. armory, glory-hole, press.
cur, noun. bagle.
curdle, verb. cruddle.
curds, noun. bonnyclobber, cruds.
cure, noun. charm.
curl, noun. kink, kiss-me-quick.
currant, noun. corn, curn.
curse, verb. blink.
cut, verb. cleave, collop, hack, scollop.
cutting remark, noun. dig.
cut turf, verb. clamp.

D

damage, verb. destroy.
damp, adj. kyoch, humid.
dance, noun. borl, hucklebuck.
dandelion, noun. clock, pish-the-bed.
dandruff, noun. scroof.
dapper, adj. trig.
dare, verb. dar.
dark-haired, adj. black.
dark-skinned, adj. darkavised.
darling, noun. child, croodlin-doo, daughter, dote, hen, son.
date steadily, verb. go strong.
dawn, noun. crack o' day.
daze, noun. dwam.
daze, verb. dumbfounder.
deafen, verb. deeve.
deal, noun. dale, lock.
(close to) death, adj. a-waitin-on.
death, noun. end, trouble.
death rattle, noun. clocher.
debate, noun. barney.
decamp, verb. flit.
decaying, adj. fusted.
decent, adj. daicent, feasant.
decline in health, verb. fail.

defecate, verb. keech, shite.
defect, noun. want.
defiant, adj. bold.
deformed, adj. backy, gammy.
dejected, adj. low as a keerog's kidney.
delicate, adj. downy.
deluge, noun and verb. bucket, pour, teem.
delve, verb. hoke.
demented, adj. astray in the head/mind.
demur, verb. haver, swither.
denounce, verb. miscall.
dent, noun and verb. dinge.
derelict (building), noun. dunderin-in, shanty.
desire, verb. think long.
desolate, adj. drachy.
destitute person, noun. cotter, gaberlunzie.
devil, noun. dale, divil.
devilment, noun. divilment.
dexterous, adj. canny.
diarrhoea, noun. skitter.
dibbler stick, noun. kibben.
dice, noun. die.
die, verb. dee.
dig, verb. hoke.
diploma, noun. line.
direction, noun. road.
dirt, noun. clabber, clart, glaur.
dirty, adj. bogging, clatty, glaury, mucky, pigging.
disappointment, noun. sickener.
disaster, noun. mischance.
disbelieve, verb. misdoubt.
disentangle, verb. unfankle.
disgorge, verb. boke, vomit rings round.
dish, noun. ashet, ramekin.
dishevel, noun. ravel.
dislike, noun. ill-will, scundher.
distant, adj. far-out, foreign.
distaste, noun. scundher.
distil whiskey, verb phrase. run.
distrust, verb. misdoubt.

disturb, verb. annoy.
ditch, noun. bruch, shuch.
dither, verb. haver, swither.
divulge, verb. let on.
dizziness, noun. dwam, light head.
do, verb. dae.
dock, noun. docken.
document, noun. line, screed.
dodge, verb. jook.
dog, noun. bagle, coolie, grew.
dolt, noun. lig, liggety.
donkey, noun. ass, cuddy, neddy.
doorcatch, noun. latch, sneck, snib.
dote, verb. rave.
doubt, verb. misdoubt.
doughnut, noun. gravyring.
dove, noun. doo.
downpour, noun. teem.
drag, verb. rug, trail.
dragonfly, noun. divil's needle.
dregs, noun. groundshels.
drenched, adj. drookit, drowned, wringing.
dress warmly, verb. hap, put on one.
dribble, verb. slabber.
drinker, noun. druth.
drinking bout, noun phrase. spree, tear.
drip, noun and verb. dreep.
drizzle, noun. mizzle, skiff.
(animal) droppings, noun. pills.
dross, noun. glit.
drum, noun. boron, lambeg.
drunk, adj. blootered, half-cut/tore, footless, full, parlatic, stocious, (have) a drop on him, a drop taken.
dry, adj. fair.
dry sticks, noun. brosny.
dryness, noun. druth.
duck, verb. jook.
dull, adj. dreech.
dump, noun. tip.
dunce, noun. dunderhead, eejit.

dunghill, noun. duchill, midden.
dust, noun. flock, pouse, stoor.
dyke, noun. ditch.

E

ear, noun. lug.
earwig, noun. coolygullen, eariwig.
easy, adj. jackeasy.
easily, adv. aisy.
(piece of) earth, noun. clod.
earthenware, noun. crock, delph.
economical, adj. tight.
elastic, noun. elasket.
elbow, noun. elbuck.
electricity, noun. electric.
elopement, noun. runaway.
elsewhere, adv. ithergates.
elude, verb. jook.
emaciated, adj. away to scrapings, failed, like a sleigh-hook, shilpit.
embarrass, verb. break, cut.
ember, noun. greeshy.
encounter, verb. meet up with.
encourage, verb. egg on.
encouraging, adj. heartsome.
endure, verb. abide, thole.
enmity, noun. ill-will.
entangle, verb. fankle.
entice, verb. while.
escort, noun. taildraft.
esteem, noun. mass.
errand, noun. message.
evade, verb. jook.
evil-eye, noun. heavy-eye.
excellent, adj. sevendable.
except, adv. and conj. barring.
excrement, noun. keech, shite, skitter.
excrete, verb. come speed, keech, shite, skitter.

exist, verb. be to the fore.
expert, noun. dab-hand.
extraordinarily, adv. powerful.
eye(s), noun. ee(n).
eye matter, noun. blear.

F

(long, miserable) face, noun. grouse, puss.
fail examination, verb. plunk.
faint, noun. dwam.
fair, noun. maggymore, mart.
fair, adj. fair-avised, white.
fairly well, adv. bravely, middling, rightly.
fairy, noun. banshee, bogle, sheeoge.
fall heavily, verb. take a toss.
family, noun. care.
famish, verb. starve.
fancy, noun. graw, notion.
fart, noun and verb. blitter.
fastidious, adj. finnickity.
fat person, noun. buddley.
fatter (and healthier), adj. well-mended.
favour, noun. obligement.
favourite, noun. blue-eye, whitehead.
feeble-minded, adj. feckless.
feed, noun and verb. fother.
feel very cold, verb. starve.
feet, noun. cloots.
feign, verb. let on.
fence, noun. paling.
fester, verb. bield.
festering, adj. cankersome.
few, noun. lock, wheen.
film, noun. glit.
filthy, adj. bogging, clatty, glaury, mucky, pigging.
fine, adj. bra, brave, sevendable.
fire, noun. ingle.
first cousin, noun. full cousin.

fist, noun. neave.
fit, noun. dwam.
flabbergast, verb. dumbfounder.
flannel, adj. and noun. flannen.
flat feet, noun. splah.
flatterer, noun. slouster.
flavour, noun and verb. kitchen.
(inside of) flax, noun. lint.
flea, noun. flay.
fledgling, noun. scaldy.
flog, verb. bate, lambaste, leather, looder.
floor, noun. flure.
flu, noun. the boy, the cowl, the founder.
fluctuate, verb. haver, swither.
fly, noun. clag, midge.
fodder, noun and verb. fother.
follow behind, verb. trail.
following, noun. taildraft.
food, noun. comestibles, cuddy, kinnel, mate.
fool, noun. clift, cod, dunderhead, dilsy, eejit, gam, goat's toe, gobberlooney, gomeril, kitter, kitterdy, lig, liggety, numbskull.
fool, verb. bumboozle, cod.
foolish, adj. daft, saft.
foolishly in love, adj. daft (in the head).
footpath, noun. footpad.
footstool, noun. pouffie.
forbode, verb. spay.
foretell, verb. spay.
forewarning, noun. rath, vision.
forge, noun. smiddy.
fork (agricultural), noun. grape.
forward, adj. brazen, old-fashioned.
fowl's crop, noun. croppin.
foxglove, noun. deadman's fingers, fairy fingers.
fractious, adj. crabbit.
fragments, noun. smithereens.
frail, adj. like death-upon-wires, failed, a gation, away to scrapings.
frantic, adj. astray in the head/mind.

fray, verb. ravel.
freckles, noun. farntickles.
freeze to death, verb. starve.
frenzy, noun. whillaballoo.
frequently, adv. as often as fingers and toes.
fret, verb. fash.
fried potatoes and leftovers, noun. boxty.
friendly, adj. big, great.
(in) front (of), prep. firnenst.
frosty, adj. hardy, nippy.
frugal, adj. canny, tight.
fuel, noun. firing, kibben.
full to the brim, adj. full as a shuch/trout, ploodacha.
fumble, verb. fummle.
funeral celebration, noun. wake.
furrow, noun. bruch.
furze, noun. whin.

G

gable, noun. gavle.
gadfly, noun. clag.
gallows, noun. gallowses.
game, noun. beddies, camogie, hurley, piggy, taws, tig.
gap, noun. slap.
gape, verb. gawp.
garbage, noun. gorbitch.
garden, noun. yard.
(close-fitting) garment, noun. hug-me-tight.
garrulous, adj. blethery, gabby.
gaunt, adj. failed, like a gation.
generous, adj. daicent, flahool.
genius, noun. long-headed person.
get something for nothing, verb. cadge.
get into someone's head, verb. take someone's toe.
get-together, noun. ceili(dhe), hooley.
ghost, noun. banshee, boggyman, bogle, rath.
giddy, adj. kittery, liggety.
Gipsy, noun. itinerant, tinker.

girl, noun. blade, child, cutty, lass.
give up Catholicism, verb. take soup.
glance, noun and verb. gleek, keek.
(small) glass of whiskey, noun. half'n.
globules of fat on soup, noun. glit.
glutton, noun. gorb.
gnat, noun. midge.
go, noun. trick.
go, verb. gang, skidaddle.
go arm-in-arm, verb. link, oxthercog.
go on, verb. be afoot.
go to live with, verb. take up with.
gobble, verb. gollop.
God, noun. dear, God, Man Above.
good, adj. brave, quare.
(be in) good form, noun. (be) at oneself.
good-looking, adj. chancy, sancy.
good-tempered, adj. civil.
gooseberry, noun. goosegob, goosegog, grossart.
gooseflesh, noun. prickles.
gorse, noun. whin.
gossip, noun. ceili, collogue, shannach.
grab, noun. glam.
grace note, noun. twiddle.
grain of corn, noun. ear.
grate (i.e. drain cover), noun. grating.
gratify, verb. please.
grave, noun. plot.
gravy, noun. dip.
grazing-land, noun. grass.
great, adj. powerful.
grey, noun. gugglin-grey.
greyhound, noun. grew.
grieved, adj. heart-scalded.
grievous, adj. grievious.
grimace, noun and verb. girn.
grip, noun. glam.
grope, verb. fummle.
growl, noun and verb. gowl.
grumpy, adj. crabbit, crooked.

gulp, noun and verb. gollop.
gurgle, verb. glug.
gutter, noun. shuch.
gym shoes, noun. gutties, mutton-dummies, slippers.

H

haddock, noun. finnan-haddie.
hag, noun. cailleach, cyarl.
hair covering, noun. clouster, snood.
hair-parting, noun. shade.
half-and-half, adv. halfers/halvies.
halfpenny, noun. make.
half-wit, noun. eejit, gam, kitter, lig.
hallucination, noun. rath, vision.
halo (round moon), noun. brach, brath.
harlot, noun. hoor, streeler, strumpet, tail, trollop.
harp on, verb. mither, yap.
harridan, noun. barge, targe.
(make) haste, noun and verb. tear.
hatch, verb. clock.
haunch, noun. hinch.
haunches, noun. hunkers.
haunt, verb. hunt.
have, verb. hae.
hawk, verb. redd the throat.
hawker, noun. tickieman.
(amount of) hay, noun. bottle, cock, kile, rick.
head, noun. pow.
headache, noun. sore head.
headdress, noun. clouster, snood.
headlong, adv. ramstam.
headstrong, adj. stubborn, thickwitted.
healthy, adj. sancy.
hear about, verb. hear tell of.
(have excellent) hearing, verb. hear the grass growing.
hearth, noun. backstone.
hedge, noun. dyke.
hedge, verb. hum an' ha.

hedgehog, noun. porcupint.
helter skelter, adv. ramstam.
hen, noun. chookie, clocking-hen, fowl, patten-hen.
heron, noun. cran.
herring, noun. harn, pullin.
(amount of) herring, noun. cran.
hesitate, verb. hum an' ha, swither.
high (smell), noun. hogo, hum.
highlander, noun. chookther, kiltie.
hill, noun. brae, cleugh.
hip, noun. hinch.
hiss, noun and verb. bizz.
hit, verb. clock, clod, clout, hammer, lambaste, skelp, thump.
hoax, verb. cod.
hobble, verb. hirple.
hobstone, noun. backstone.
hod, noun. hud.
hold, noun. glam.
hollow, adj. boast.
homework, noun. exercise.
hood, noun. pixie, poke, slouster, snood.
hoof, noun. cloot.
hopscotch, noun. beddies.
horn, noun. dooter, tooter.
(sound one's) horn, verb. doot.
hornless, adj. moilly.
host, noun. trevally.
hotchpotch, noun. borgeegle, gallimuffry, hames, hodge-podge, prockus.
hound, noun. bagle, grew.
house-and-land, noun. sitting-down.
house of ill repute, noun. kip.
hovel, but-'n-ben, dunderin-in, huxther, shanty.
howl, verb. gowl, gulder, yowl.
huff, verb. strunt.
hum tune, verb. diddle, dowdle.
human, noun. body.
humdrum, adj. dreech.
humped, adj. humpy.

Humpty Dumpty, noun. Humpy Dumpy.
hungry, adj. chapfallen, hungersome.
husband, noun. man.
hush, verb. whisht.
hustle, verb. finnagle.
hut, noun. shanty.
hypocrite, noun. creeping-Jesus.

I

ice-cream cone, noun. poke.
idiot, noun. eejit.
idle, verb. mooch.
ill, adj. failed.
(become) ill, verb. take bad.
illegitimate child, noun. brat, by-blow, get.
ill-humoured, adj. crabbit, crooked, thrawin.
ill-mannered person, noun. bagle, brat.
image, noun. dead spit, natural draft.
impact, noun. dunt.
impeccable, adj. faultless.
impediment in speech, noun. stoppage, stutter.
impertinent, adj. bold, brazen, impident, uppity.
import, noun. owercome.
imprison, verb. lift.
indecisive, adj. swithering.
indifferent, adj. anaisy.
ineffectual, adj. useless.
infant, noun. bairn, child, wain.
infect, verb. smit.
inflammation near nail, noun. whittle.
inject(ion), noun and verb. jag/jeg.
innovative, adj. new-fangled.
insane, adj. not wise.
insignificant person, noun. atomy.
insincere, adj. sleekit.
insolence, noun. chick.
instant, noun. jiffy.
instruct, verb. learn.

intelligence, noun. gumption.
intelligent, adj. long-headed, smart.
intensely, adv. powerful.
interfere, verb. enterfere, entermeddle, put one's cuddy in among spoons.
interval, noun. spell.
intimate, adj. big, friends, great, thick.
into, prep. intil.
intoxicated, adj. blootered, half-cut/tore, footless, full, parlatic, stocious, have a drop taken.
invitation, noun. bidding, tinker's bidding.
iota, noun. hate.
irascible, adj. crabbit, crookit, cyarnaptious.
irritate, verb. pollute.
island, noun. inch.
isolated, adj. lonesome.
itinerant, noun. Gipsy, tinker, tramp.
ivy, noun. fog.

J

jabber, verb. yammer.
jacket, noun. bum-freezer.
jiggle, verb. joogle.
joke, noun and verb. crack, gag.
joker, noun. gag/geg.
jolt, noun and verb. dunder, dunt, junder.
jot, noun. hate.
jowls, noun. chullers.
jug, noun. joog.
jumble, noun and verb. jummle.
jump, noun. fidge, lep, lowp.
jump, verb. lep, lowp.
justice, noun. fair dos.

K

kiln, noun. kill.
kilt, noun. fillybeg.
kilted man, noun. chookther, kiltie.

kindling, noun. brosny, kibbens.
kitten, noun. kittlen.
(have) kittens, verb. kittle.
knack, noun. gamut.
knick-knacks, noun. nyiff-nyaffs.
knife, noun, gullyknife.
knock, noun and verb. chap, nap, rap, tap.
knot, noun. kinch.
knot (in hair), noun. tat.
know, verb. ken.
knowledge, noun. ken.
known, verb. acquent.

L

labourer, noun. spalpeen.
Labour Exchange, noun. beroo.
lack, noun and verb. want.
lad, noun. boy, child, cub, youngster.
ladder, noun. lather, lether.
lake, noun. lough.
lame, adj. backy, gammy, hip-at-the-clinch, nought-and-carry-one.
lament, verb. greet, keeny.
lamentation, noun. keenying.
(strip of) land, noun. clachan.
lane, noun. boreen, loanin.
(secret) language, noun. Shelta.
lapdog, noun. lepdog.
larder, noun. meatsafe, pantry.
large amount, noun. muckle.
large piece, noun. clipe, collop.
lass, noun. blade, child, colleen, wee girl.
last, noun. what the cobbler threw at the wife.
latch, noun and verb. hasp, sneck, snib.
late, adv. at tinker's time.
latter part, noun. back end.
laugh, noun and verb. kehee, kehoe, titter.

lay aside, verb. put by.
leak, verb. let in.
leap, noun and verb. lep, lowp.
leavings, noun. brock.
left-handed, clootie, corrie-fisted, fyuggy, kack-handed, kitter.
leg, noun. hough, huff, pin, shank.
length of thread, noun. bottom.
let-down, noun. gunk.
lie, noun and verb. lee.
life, noun. reed.
likeness, noun. image, natural draft, spit.
liking, noun. fondness, graw, notion.
light on one's foot, adj. lightsome.
limp, verb. hirple.
lineage, noun. breed, seed and generation.
linnet, noun. lintwhite.
linoleum, noun. oilcloth.
lithe, noun. soople.
little, adj. diddly, small, tiddly, tiny, totie, wee.
little amount, noun. colouring, pick, pickle, taste.
livelong, adj. leelang.
load, noun. rail.
loaf, noun. bannock, loafbread, panloaf.
loiter, verb. dander, doddle, dolly.
lonely, adj. lone, lonesome.
long, adj. drachy, longsome, like a Lurgan shovel/spade.
look, noun and verb. geek, keek.
look after, verb. mind.
look good in, verb. suit.
lose, verb. loss.
lose control of one's mind, verb. dote, go astray in the head/mind.
lot, noun. clatter, couple, lock.
lots (of), adj. galore.
louse, noun. baukie.
lovable, adj. luvesome.
love, noun. graw, mass.
lullaby, noun. hushaby.

lump, noun. blad, clod.
(packed) lunch, noun. piece.
lure, verb. while.

M

mad, adj. away in the head.
madness, noun. headstaggers.
magic, noun. freets, pishogues.
maize, noun. (Indian) male.
make fun of, verb. take a hand out of, teehee.
male, adj. buck.
malediction, noun. blink, heavy eye.
man, noun. bodach, body, dag.
malevolence, ill-will.
manure, noun. dung, muck.
marble, noun. marl; glassy, marley, taw.
market, noun. maggymore, mart.
marriage certificate, noun. marriage/wedding lines.
marsh, noun. bog, moss, munchees.
marshland, noun. inchland, munchees.
mashed potatoes, noun. brudgy, champ.
match, noun. fit.
(coarse) material, noun. ratten.
matter (in eyes), noun. blears.
maybe, adv. ablins, belike.
meal, noun. bite, bite and sup.
meal, noun. male.
meal-bin, noun. ark.
mean, adj. hard, mane, mingy, miserable, near, nearbe-gone, scrunty, stingy, tight; (wouldn't give you) daylight, (wouldn't give you the) skin of his skitter.
meander, verb. dander, doddle, dolly.
measure (of alcohol), noun. drop, half'n, neggin.
meat, noun. mate.
meddle, verb. enterfere, entermeddle, put your cuddy in among spoons.
medicine, noun and verb. physic.
meditate, verb. think long.

meek, adj. biddable, civil.
melt (of dripping), verb. render (down).
memory, noun. mind.
mendicant, noun. beggarman, gaberlunzie.
mental deficiency, noun. wee want.
merrymaking, noun. ceili, crack.
mesmerise, verb. dumbfounder.
mess, noun. borgeegle, boxty, gallimuffry, prockus, slouster.
message, noun. owercome.
meteor, noun. shooting star.
method, noun. road, road of hoking.
methylated spirits (for drinking), noun. blowhard.
midden, noun. duchill.
mighty, adj. powerful.
mildewed, adj. fusted, fusty.
mill pond, noun. dam.
milk, noun. bastins, bonnyclobber.
milk in tea, noun. colour, colouring.
mire, noun. clabber, clart, glar, muck.
mirror, noun. looking-glass.
mischief, noun. divilment.
mischievous, adj. mischievious.
miser, noun. nayger.
miserable. adj. dreech.
(fine) mist, noun. smoor.
misunderstanding, noun. trasby.
mixture, noun. borgeegle, boxty, prockus.
mob, noun. trevally.
mock, verb. take a hand out of.
moderate, adj. middling.
modern, adj. new-fangled.
money (returned to seal a bargain), noun. luckpenny.
monotonous, adj. dreech, longsome.
monster, noun. boggyman.
moon's halo, noun. brach, brath.
moonshine, noun. poteen, the crayther.
mop up, verb. redd up.
mope, verb. strunt, trail the wing.
morsel, noun. crumb, pick.

mortify, verb. break, cut, gunk.
mortified, adj. broke, cut, heartscalded.
moss, noun. fog.
mote, noun. stime.
mother, noun. mommy, the owl lass.
mottled, adj. marl(ey).
mould, noun. mowl.
mouldy, adj. fusted, fusty.
moult, verb. cast.
mourn, verb. fret, lament.
mouse-coloured, adj. gugglingrey.
mouth, noun. bake, gab, gob, gub, trap.
mouthful, noun. slog.
move house, verb. flit.
move (without clearing debts), noun. moonlight flit.
mucus (nose), snutters.
mucus (throat), clocher.
mud, noun. clabber, clart, clobber, glar, muck.
muddle, noun. borgeegle, prockus.
muddy, adj. guttery, mucky.
multitude, noun. big trevally.
mumble, verb. bubble, mummle.
must, verb. be to, maun, may.
musty, adj. fusty, kyoch.
mystify, verb. bumboozle, dumbfounder.

N

(have a) nap, verb. get one's eyes together.
nag, verb. mither, yammer.
naughty, adj. bold.
nausea, noun. scundher.
nearby, adv. nearhand.
neat, adj. nate, nate as a bee's toe, trig.
(bare) necessities , noun. daylight.
necessity, noun. call.
neigh, noun and verb. nyeeher.
nervous, adj. timorsome.
never, adv. nivir.

new, adj. branknew, sprank-new.
news, noun. schism.
New Year's Eve, noun. Old Year's Night.
nice, adj. quare.
niche, noun. nyook.
night, noun. nicht.
night attire, noun. dishabels.
nimble, adj. soople.
nitwit, noun. eejit, gam.
no, adv. nae.
noise, noun. brattle, dunder, glow, gowl, nyam, nyeeher, scringe.
none, pronoun. nane.
nonplus, noun and verb. amplush.
nonsense, noun. blether.
nook, noun. nyook.
nose, noun. neb, snipe.
nosy, adj. long-nebbed, pass remarkable.
not, adv. nae, nary.
notwithstanding, adv. still and all.
nourishment, noun. bite-'n-sup.
novelty, noun. newance.
number, noun. lock, wheen.
numbskull, dunderhead, gam, ganch.
nut without a kernel, noun. deaf nut.

O

oaf, noun. clift, pachal, slooter.
oatcake, noun. oatiecake.
oatmeal porridge, noun. stirabout.
obdurate, adj. thickwitted.
obedient, adj. biddable.
obstinate, adj. stubborn, thickwitted.
obstreperous, adj. opstrapolous.
odour (bad), noun. hogo, hum.
off, adv. and prep. aff.
offspring, noun. bairn, child, melt, wain.
oh yes, adv. och aye.

ointment, noun. embrocation, salve.
okay, adv. fair enough.
old, adj. owl.
old-fashioned, adj. owl-fangled.
omen, noun. freet.
only child, noun. cuckoo's lachter.
opening at front of trousers, noun. falls.
opinion, noun. cuddy.
opposing, adj. contrary.
ornament, noun. nyiffnyaff.
out, adv. and prep. oot.
outcome, noun. owercome.
outfit, noun. rigout.
outing, noun. jaunt.
outlive, verb. see somebody down.
out-of-doors, adv. abroad, outby.
outside, adv. abroad, outby.
outsider, noun. planter.
over, adv. and prep. ower.
over and above, adv. and prep. aboon.
overcoat, noun. topcoat.
overhead, adv. aboon.
overseas, adv. foreign.
overturn, verb. cowp.

P

pain, noun. eeroch, stoon.
pal, noun. chum, friend.
palaver, noun. prockus.
pale, adj. white in the face.
palm of hand, noun. heart of hand.
palpitating, adj. thumping.
palsy, noun. the trimmles.
pang of pain, noun. stoon.
pannier, noun. kish.
pantry, noun. armory.
paralysed, adj. parlatic.
paramour, noun. fancyman, fancywoman.

part hair, verb. shade.
particle, noun. crumb, hate, pick.
party, noun. ceili, do, get-together.
passageway between houses, noun. close, entry.
passion, noun. buzz.
pasture, noun. grass.
pat, noun. clap.
path, noun. boreen, loanin, pad.
pauper, noun. bedther, cotter, gaberlunzie.
pavement, noun. footpath, pad.
peace, noun. pace.
peat, noun. clamp o' torf, torf.
peat bog, noun. bog, moss, munchees.
peddler, noun. packieman, tickieman, tinker.
pedigree, noun. breed, seed and generation.
peep, noun and verb. geek, gleek, keek, juke.
peevish, adj. crooked, cyarnaptious.
pendulum clock, noun. wag o' the wall.
penis (bull), noun. peezle.
penniless person, noun. cotter.
people to be provided for, noun. care.
perfidious person, noun. hoodlum, renegade.
perhaps, adv. ablins, belike.
period of time, noun. spell.
pernickity, adj. finnickity.
persevere, verb. stick till.
person, noun. ashypot, body, chookther, cotter, crayther, culchie, cyarl, cyermudgeon, dilsy, dortboard, dunderhead, eejit, flibbertigibbet, fluter, footer, galoot, gam, ganch, gawp, gulpin, hag, hallion, harl o' bones, head-the-ball, herself, himself, hip-at-the-clinch, hobbledyhoy, hobnob, hoodlum, hoor, hoosler, humpy-dumpy, jessie, jinty, kiltie, kitter, kitterdy, lig, liggety, loughryman, nayger, nob, numbskull, pachal, pag, peeodler, picker, planter, plaster, playboy, puke, quilt, renegade, runagate, runt, scrunt, shooler, shower, skiboo, skinnymalink, slabber, slob, slooter, slouster, spalpeen, tail, taildraft, toerag, trollop, turncoat, wasp, yahoo, yoke.
person-in-charge, headbombadier, headbuckcat.
persuade, verb. insense.

pert, adj. forward, owl-fashioned.
perverse, adj. crooked, thrawin, twisting.
pet, noun. blue-eye, croodlin-doo, whitehead.
phantom, noun. bogle, boggyman, rath.
phlegm, noun. clocher.
piece, noun. hate, nip, pick, taste.
(young) pig, noun. turrey.
pigeon-toed, adj. hen-toed.
pig's trotter, noun. croobeen.
pigtails, noun. cowstails.
pile of stones, noun. cairn.
pincers, noun. pinchers.
pinch, noun and verb. nip.
pipe, noun. cuddy, didgeen.
pique, noun. huff.
pitchfork, noun. grape, pike.
plank, noun. boord.
plantation, noun. planting.
plash, noun and verb. jap, skite.
plate, noun. ashet, delph.
pleasant, adj. feasant, leesome.
(with) pleasure, adv. with a heart and a hand.
plead poverty, verb. make/plead a poor mouth.
plenty, noun. full and plenty, lashings and lavings.
plenty (of), adj. galore.
pliable, adj. soople.
pliers, adj. pinchers.
plucky, adj. game, spunky.
plump, adj. sancy.
poach, verb. nick, prog.
poke, verb. hoke.
poltergeist, noun. bogle.
poppyseed, noun. galseed.
porridge, noun. brachan, brochan, stirabout.
portend, verb. bode, freet, spay.
poseur, noun. playactor, playboy.
posterior, noun. ass, backside, bum, hind-end.
potato, noun. chat, cutling, marley, poureen, pretty, spa-chan, spud, tatie.
potato masher, noun. beetle.

potato-picking, noun. tatie-hoking.
poteen, noun. the crayther.
potluck, noun. luckybag.
poultry, noun. fowl.
poultrykeeper, noun. fowlman.
pour, verb. bucket down, teem.
pout, noun. puss.
prayer, noun. ejaculation.
precocious, adj. owl-fashioned.
predicament, noun. prockus.
predict, verb. spay.
pregnant, adj. away with it, in the pudding club.
premonition, noun. visions.
prepare flax, verb. scutch.
Presbyterian, adj. black.
present, noun and verb. hansel.
pretend, verb. let on.
pretty, adj. bonny, winsome.
prevaricate, verb. hum and ha, lee.
prick, noun and verb. jag/jeg.
private parts, noun. tiddleyhoy.
privation, noun. want.
process(ion), noun and verb. walk.
progress, verb. come speed.
(with) prominent teeth, adj. outmouthed.
prophetic vision, noun. second sight.
propose, verb. ask for.
prostitute, noun. hoor, streeler, strumpet, tail.
Protestant, adj. orange.
Protestant church, noun. chorch.
proud, adj. consaty.
proverb, noun. owl saying.
provide for, verb. squint for.
prudent, adj. canny.
prying, adj. long-nebbed.
puerile nonsense, noun. as-I-rode-out.
puff, noun and verb. pull.
pull, noun and verb. rug, thraw.
punch/punchbowl, noun. jorum.
puncture, noun and verb. pumpture.

punish, verb. kneecap.
puny, adj. shilpit.
puny child, noun. downy.
pus, noun. humour, matter.
purge, noun and verb. scour.
puzzle, verb. bumboozle, dumbfounder, riddle.

Q

quagmire, noun. bog, munchees.
quake with fear, verb. trimmle.
quandary, noun. swither.
quantity, noun. drop, pickle, smidgeon, taste.
quarrel, noun. trasby.
quarrel, verb. cyast the creels.
quaver in music, noun. twiddle, twiddly note.
querulous, adj. crabbit, crooked, cyarnaptious.
quibble, verb. cyarp.
quiet!, verb. whisht!
quickly, adv. like a blaze o' whins.

R

rabbit, noun, coney.
rag, noun. brachag, clout, slouster, snood.
rail, noun. paling.
rain, noun. drizzle, humidity, mizzle, plump, skiff, spit, teem.
rain, verb. bucket down, drizzle, mizzle, plash, plump, pour, spit, teem.
ramble, verb. rave.
(on the) rampage, noun. on the tear.
rampart, noun. ditch.
ramshackle, adj. down-and-out, dunderin-in.
rancid, adj. kyoch.
rankle, verb. fash, vex.
rant, verb. barge, rage, scowl.
rap, noun and verb. chap, knock, nap, tap.

rapacious, adj. grippy.
rascal, noun. playboy, peeodler, quilt, runagate.
rather, adv. a wee bit, a toty wee bit.
ravel, verb. fankle.
raw, adj. kyoch.
rear, verb. rare.
reason, noun. call.
rebuff, verb. break, cut.
recollect, verb. mind.
rectify, verb. rightify.
recuperate, verb. mend.
red, adj. red-headed.
red calf/cow, noun. roney.
reed, noun. rush.
reel (of thread), noun. bottom o' thread.
reel out, verb. screed.
refreshment, noun. drop o' tea.
refuse, noun. brock.
refuseman, noun. brockman.
refuse to move, verb. rust.
(high) regard, noun. mass.
region around a town, noun. townland.
relapse, noun. backset.
relative, noun. friend.
relieved, adj. shired.
relish, noun. kitchen.
remain, verb. bide, stay.
remember, verb. mind.
remote, adj. back o' beyond, not at home with ye, out-o'-the-way.
rent-collector, noun. bailiff.
repetition, noun. rhyme.
replete, adj. full as a shuch/trout, ploodacha.
reply, noun. backchat.
reprimand, verb. check, give someone the length of one's tongue, pull up, tell off.
resemble, verb. favour, take after.
residue, noun. lavings.
rested, adj. shired.
resuscitate, verb. bring round/till.

retch, verb. boke.
reticent, adj. backward.
retinue, noun. trevally.
retiring, adj. backward.
retriever, noun. coolie.
reveal, verb. let on.
reverie, noun. dwam.
revolve, verb. borl.
(get) rid, noun. get redd/shot of.
riddle, noun. puzzler, riddle-me-riddle-me-reech.
ride, noun. hurl, jaunt.
rigmarole, noun. come-all-ye.
rim, noun. selvedge.
ring, noun and verb. torl/turl.
ringing in the ears, noun. deadbell.
rinse, noun and verb. rensh.
river, noun. burn, dam.
roam, verb. stravague, wander.
roar, noun and verb. gulder.
robust, adj. hardy.
rock-candy, noun. yellaman.
roe, noun. melt.
roll, noun. bap.
rope, noun. spencel, suggin.
rosary, noun. beads.
rotten, adj. fusty, kyoch, mowly.
rough, adj. coorse.
route, noun. road.
rove, verb. gallivant, stravague.
row, noun. barney, trasby.
rowdy, adj. opstrapolous.
rude, adj. bold, cheeky, ignorant, uncivil.
ruin, verb. destroy.
rumour, noun. whisper, wind.
rung, noun. rong.
rustle, verb. fissle.

S

saliva, noun. spittle.
sallow, adj. darkavised.
sandwich lunch, noun. piece.
sauce, noun. kitchen.
sausage, noun. buddley, link, sausenger.
save up, verb. put by/past.
scallions, noun. saibies.
scanty, adj. skimpy.
scare, verb. scyar.
scarf, noun. snood.
scent, noun. whid.
school attendance officer, noun. cruelty man.
scold, noun. barge, targe.
scold, verb. barge, mither, scowl, tongue, yammer, yap.
scolding, noun. length of one's tongue.
scowl, noun and verb. girn.
scrap, noun. crumb, hate, pick, scantlins.
scrape, verb. scobe.
scratch, noun and verb. scrab, scrape.
scream, noun. mig, scrake.
screech, noun. scrake.
scrounge, verb. finnagle, mooch.
scum, noun. glit.
scurf, noun. scroof.
seat, noun. sate.
seaweed, noun. dullice.
(gifted with) second sight, noun. fey.
secret place, noun. hidey-hole.
sediment, noun. groundshels.
segment (of orange), noun. pig.
self, noun. barney.
self confidence, noun. gumption.
sense, noun. wit.
separate, verb. sinther.
(not) serious, adj. giddy.
settee, noun. sofy.
several, pronoun. lock, wheen.

shadow, noun. scad.
shaft of scythe, noun. sned.
shake, verb. joogle, wag, waggle.
shallot, noun. scallion, saibie.
share, noun. cuddy, divide, whack.
share, verb. go halfers/halvies.
shawl, noun. hug-me-tight.
shaving brush, noun. wobbler, wobbling brush.
sheaf, noun. stook.
shed, noun. shade.
shed, verb. cast.
shirk, verb. renegue.
shivery, adj. foundered, starving.
shock, noun. gunk.
shoes, noun. spags.
short (of person), adj. stumpy.
shortcut, noun. by-road.
shout, verb. gulder.
shove, verb. dunt, junder, jundey.
shower, noun. plump, skiff.
shrewd, adj. canny.
shrewdness, noun. gumption.
shrink, verb. weezen.
shrunken, adj. clapped in.
shuffle, verb. slooder.
shy, adj. backward.
sideboard, noun. armory.
sight, noun. light.
(no) sign, noun. (neither) hide nor hair.
silence, verb. howl your tongue/whisht.
silly, adj. daft, eejity, gormless, kitterdy.
(without) sin, noun. (no) harm in one.
sink, noun. jarbox.
(good) size, noun. lump.
skinflint, noun. gombeen, nayger.
skip, noun and verb. lowp.
slander, verb. miscall.
slap, noun and verb. bat, clout, skelp.
slattern, noun. hoor, slouster, trollop.
sleep, noun. Jack Nod.

sleeper, noun. blear.
slender, adj. trig.
slime, noun. glar, glit, muck.
slobber, noun and verb. slabber.
slow, adj. longsome, at tinker's time.
sly, adj. sleekit.
smack, noun and verb. lick, skelp.
small, adj. bunty, diddly, jinty, scrunty, shilpit, tiddly, toty, wee.
small man, noun. loughryman.
smallpox, noun. the pock disaise.
smart, adj. crafty.
(bad) smell, noun. hogo, hum.
(tisted) smile, noun. girn.
smithy, noun. smiddy.
smoke, noun. pull, shode, reek.
smudge, noun. smitch.
snarl, verb. fankle.
snatch, noun. glam.
snobbish, adj. uppity.
snot, noun and verb. snutter.
snout, noun. neb.
snowdrift, noun. sheebone.
soaked, adj. drenched, drookit, drowned, wringing.
sob, verb. greet.
socks, noun. markins.
sociable drink, noun. jar.
soft, adj. saft.
soiled, adj. clatty.
solitary, adj. lone.
sometimes, adv. betimes, whiles.
somewhere else, adv. ithergates.
soother, noun. dummy tit.
sorcery, noun. freets, pishogues.
sore, noun. hack.
sour, adj. tart.
space, noun. small bounds.
spade, noun. loy, slane, spalpeen.
spank, verb. give what Paddy gave the drum, lick, luder, skelp.

sparse, adj. skimpy.
spawn, noun. melt.
speck, noun. smitch, stime.
speckled, adj. bracky.
spectre, noun. banshee, boggyman, bogle, rath.
spend the winter, verb. winter.
spend time pleasantly, verb. while away the time.
spider, noun. feedogue.
spinning-top, noun. peerie.
spinster, noun. girl.
spirit, noun. banshee, bogle, kelpie, sheeoge.
spite, noun. illwill.
splash, noun and verb. jap, skite.
splinter, noun. skelf, skelp.
spool of thread, noun. bottom.
spoon, noun. cuddy.
spout, noun. stroup.
spree, noun. tear/tare.
sprightly, adj. soople.
spring onions, noun. saibies, scallions.
squat, verb. hunker down.
squeal, noun, mig.
squelchy, adj. guttery, plashy, slushy.
squint, noun. cyast, four o'clock eyes, eyes at tinker's time,
skelly, turn.
stale, adj. fusted, kyoch.
stammer, noun. stoppage, stutter.
stammerer, noun. bubbelizer.
stanza, noun. rann.
stare at, verb. gawk, gawp.
steal, verb. cadge, lift, nick, nim, prog.
steal away, verb. slope off.
stench, noun. hogo, hum.
stew, noun. labscouse.
stick, noun. brosny, kibben.
stick of rock, noun. Peggy's leg.
stickleback, noun. spricklybag.
stiffening in shoe, noun. yarkan.
stitch, verb. baste.
stomach, noun. bags.

story, noun. schism, shannach.
story-teller, noun. shannachie.
(small bit of) stone, noun. trawnyeen.
stool, noun. creepie.
stop, verb. cap.
strand (of hair), noun. rib.
strange, adj. eerie.
(amount of) straw, noun. bottle.
streak, noun and verb. strake.
stretch food, verb. kitchen.
stroll, noun and verb. dander, doddle, dolly.
stub one's toe, verb. clink, crig.
stubborn, adj. thickwitted, thrawin.
stuffing, noun. melt.
stupefy, verb. doit.
stupid, adj. fat in the forehead.
stupid person, noun. dunderhead, eejit, gam, gawk, gomeril.
stupor, noun. dwam, stoon.
success, noun. speed.
suffer, verb. stoon, thole.
(commit) suicide, verb. do away with oneself.
sulk, noun and verb. huff, strunt, trail the wing.
sunken, adj. clapped in.
superstition, noun. freets, pishogues.
supple, adj. soople.
suppurate, verb. bield, supturate.
surly, adj. crabbit, crooked, thrawin.
suspect, verb. doubt, jube.
sustain, verb. hold foot to.
sustenance, noun. bite-'n-sup.
swarthy, adj. darkavised.
(woollen) sweater, noun. gansey/gensey.
sustain (level of expense), verb. hold foot to.
sweet, noun. yellaman.

T

tack, verb. baste.
tale-bearer, noun. clash-bag.

talk, noun. crack, gab/geb, shannach.
talkative person, noun, blether(come)skite.
(idle) talk (idly), noun and verb. blether, gab/geb.
tangle, noun and verb. fankle, ravel.
tantrum, noun. strunt.
tardy, adj. longsome.
tea, noun. drop in your hand, drop o' scald.
tea leaves, noun. groundshels.
teach, verb. learn.
(unqualified) teacher, noun. jam.
tedious, adj. dreech.
(with prominent) teeth, adj. outmouthed.
teetotaller, noun. pioneer.
tell-tale, noun. clashbag.
tell tales, verb. clash.
temper, noun. anger, dander, rag.
tennis shoes, noun. gutties, mutton dummies, slippers.
terrible thing, noun. tarra.
terse, adj. cutting, short.
tether, noun. langle.
than, conj. nor.
that, adj. and pronoun. thon.
thereabouts, adv. thereaway.
thickset, adj. bunty, stumpy.
thin, adj. failed, like death upon wires, like hunger's mother, skinnymalink.
thin person, noun. gation, harl o' bones.
thirst, noun. druth.
thirsty, adj. dry.
thong, noun. twang, whang.
thoroughfare, noun. pad.
those, pronoun. them, they.
thrash, verb. bate, hammer, leather, luder.
threepence, noun. thruppence.
thrive, verb. come speed.
throat, noun. thrapple.
throng, noun. trevally.
throttle, verb. thrapple.
throw, verb. thow.
thud, noun and verb. dunt.

thump, noun and verb. dunt.
(rattle of) thunder, noun. brattle.
tidy, adj. hippity-tippity, nate, tidy of oneself, trig.
tidy up, verb. redd up.
tiff, noun. trasby, words.
(full) tilt, adv. full butt.
time, noun. weather.
timid, adj. cowardie, cyavvie, feardie, timorsome.
tinker, noun. Gipsy, tramp.
tiny, adj. bunty, diddly, tiddly, toty, wee.
tiny bit, noun. nyimf, nyimp.
tippler, noun. druth.
tipsy, adj. half-cut, have a drop taken.
tired, adj. deadbate.
tissue, noun. tishie.
titbit, noun. dainty.
to, adv. and prep. till, to.
toadstool, noun. dogstool
today, adv. and noun. the day.
toiled, verb. wrought.
tolerable, adj. middling.
tolerate, verb. thole.
tomorrow, adv. and noun. the morrow.
tonight, adv. and noun. the night.
topple, verb. cowp.
topsy-turvy, adv. ass about face, trummicky.
tottery, adj. doddery.
trance, noun. dwam.
travel about, verb. gallivant.
tremble, noun and verb. quake, trimmle.
tremendous, adj. powerful.
trench, noun. bruch, shuch.
trifle, noun. nyiffnyaff.
trimmings, noun. folderdol.
trivial, adj. footery, skittery.
trollop, noun. hoor, slouster, streeler.
trouble, noun. prockus.
(play) truant, verb. dob, mitch, skive.
trudge, verb. tramp.
trumpcard, noun. trumf.

tug, verb. rug.
turd, noun. tord.
turf, noun. fums, torf.
turfbog, noun. moss, munchees.
turfstack, noun. stook.
turncoat, noun. hoodlum, soup-taker.
turn round and round, verb. borl.
twaddle, noun. blether.
twice, adv. twict.
two-or-three, noun. couple, lock.

U

udder, noun. clash, elder.
ugly, adj. ill-favoured.
ugly person, noun. ugly plug.
umbilical cord, noun. navel string.
(take) umbrage, noun. (take the) huff.
umbrella, noun. umberstick.
unattractive person, noun. crow.
unbearable, adj. untholable.
unbelievable, adj. out of this world.
uncanny, adj. freetish, freety.
uncaring, adj. anaisy.
(be) uncertain, verb. haver, swither.
unchristian, adj. like a Tork (Turk).
uncompromising, adj. thickwitted.
undecided, adj. swithering.
undercooked, adj. kyoch.
underhand, adj. backhand.
undernourished, adj. half-starved.
undersized, adj. skimpy, terrible wee.
understand, verb. be up to, faddom, lift, twig.
undertaking, noun. handling.
undervest, noun. simmet.
undisciplined, adj. badly behaved.
(state of) undress, noun. dishabels.
uneasiness, noun. (have) a worry (on one).
unemployed, adj. at a loose end, on the dole/double.

unfit, adj. not able.
unfortunate, adj. misfortunate.
ungenerous, adj. tight.
unintelligent person, noun. clift.
unlatched, adj. on the latch/snib.
unless, conj. barring, without.
unlucky, adj. fortunate, misfortunate.
unmannerly, adj. ill-bred, uncivil.
unnoticed, adj. unbeknownst.
unpleasant (of taste), adj. falairy.
untidy, adj. houthern, slootery, throughother.
untrustworthy, adj. sleekit.
unskilful, adj. footery.
unsteady, adj. coggly.
upbraid, verb. barge, scowl.
uproar, noun. roaring-match, shouting-match, trevally.
uproot, verb. hoke up.
upset, verb. annoy, take a flinch out of, vex.
upset, adj. annoyed, heartscalded, vexed.
upside down, adv. trummicky.
upshot, noun. overcome.
upstart, noun. guttersnipe.
urge, verb. egg on.
urinate, verb. pee, pish.
urine, noun. pee, pish.
use, verb. take a trick out of.

V

vacate, verb. flit.
vacillate, verb. haver, swither.
vagabond, noun. shooler, tinker, tramp.
valiant, adj. game, spunky.
vase, noun. vause.
venture, verb. venter.
vertigo, noun. light-head.
very, adv., buck, brave and, daicent and, dead, gey,
mortal, odious, quare and, powerful, prime, quare and,
rattling, wild.

vest, noun. simmet.
vex, verb. anger, annoy, fash.
vexed, adj. heartscalded.
(hold a) vigil, noun and verb. wake.
villain, noun. gadderman.
violent times, noun. troubles.
virago, noun. barge, targe.
vision, noun. light, rath.
(evening) visit, noun. ceili.
visitor, noun. insleeper, planter.
vital parts, noun. reed.
vocabulary, noun. vocable.
vomit, verb. boke, th(r)ow up.

W

wade, noun and verb. paddle.
wail, verb. keeny.
wainscoting, noun. boxing.
wait for, verb. wait on.
wagtail, noun. willy wagtail.
walk, noun. dander, doddle, dolly, foot, trake.
walk, verb. dander, doddle, dolly, foot, hirple, hochle, shank, slooder, striddle, trake.
walker, noun. shooler.
wander, verb. gallivant, stravague.
wanderer, noun. runagate, shooler.
want, verb. look.
wary, adj. canny.
wash, noun. cat's lick.
wash, verb. clat.
wastrel, noun. body that'll neither work nor want.
water channel, noun. bruch, shuch.
water dog, noun. coolie.
waver, verb. haver, kiffle, swither.
way, noun. road.
wayward, adj. unbiddable.
weak, adj. croilly, downy, failed.
weakling, noun. chitterling, downy.

wealthy, adj. able.
weasel, noun. wheezle, whutherit.
weed, noun. canker, gortweed.
weep, verb. greet, keeny.
weight, noun. avoirdupois.
welcome, noun. folkie.
welcome, verb. make much of.
well, adj. bravely.
well-balanced, adj. steady.
well-dressed, adj. swotty, well put on.
well-endowed, adj. chancy.
well-to-do, adj. well-heeled.
wet, adj. drenched, drowned, soaked, soaking.
wheeze, verb. wheezle.
whelk, noun. willock.
when, conj. whenever.
whine, verb. whinge.
whinny, verb. nyeeher.
whirl, noun and verb. birl/borl.
whirring noise, noun. bore.
(home-brewed) whiskey, noun. the crayther, poteen.
whisper, verb. cugger.
whistle, noun. wheezle.
white bird, noun. whillocky.
whore, noun. hoor, streeler, strumpet, tail, trollop.
wickerwork basket, noun. kish.
widow, noun. widawoman.
widower, noun. widaman.
widow's peak, noun. cow's lick.
willow, noun. sally.
willow cane, noun. sally wattle.
wind, noun. wine.
window, noun. windy.
windowsill, noun. windystool.
windpipe, noun. thrapple.
wisdom, noun. wit.
wise, adj. longheaded.
wobbly, adj. coggly.
woman, noun. cailleach, cyarl, targe.
women, noun. weemen.

wooded area, noun. hagginblock, planting.
worked hard, verb. wrought.
worn, adj. scuffed.
worried, adj. astray in the head/mind.
worry, verb. fash, faze.
wraith, noun. banshee, boggyman, bogle, rath.
wrap, verb. lap.
wren, noun. jinty, jinty-wren.
write, noun and verb. scrape.
(be) wrong with, verb. ail.
wrong way, adv. ass-about-face, athra.

Y

yank, verb. rug.
yarn, noun. schism, shannach.
yellow, adj. yella.
yes, adv. aha, aye, aye surely, uh-huh.
yon, adj. thon.
yonder, adv. thonder.
you, pronoun. ye, yiz, you, youse.
young, adj. small, wee.
young girl, noun. wee blade, lassie.
youth, noun. cub, lad, laddie.

Z

zebra, noun. azebra.
zigzag, noun and verb. go wigglywaggly.
zip, noun and verb. azip
zoo, noun. azoo.

SECTION FOUR: SELECTED TEXTS

This section provides a short selection of written and spoken material from Northern Ireland. For ease of reference, it is subdivided as follows:

4.1 Printed Texts: Verse
4.2 Printed Texts: Prose
4.3 Spoken Texts

Each text is followed by a set of notes.

4.1 PRINTED TEXTS: VERSE

The first example is taken from Moira O'Neill's *Songs of the Glens of Antrim*, published in Edinburgh and London in 1900 by Blackwood and Sons. Antrim speakers have all been influenced by USc norms, but in the Glens Gaelic remained alive until the 1950s and exerted a strong influence on the English of the native Irish population. It is perhaps worth stressing that verse or 'poethry' has traditionally played an important role in social gatherings in Northern Ireland. People who could not sing frequently recited and many individuals had their own special 'poem', not always, or even often, identical with a written version. Poets such as Moira O'Neill were highly regarded throughout the community and could be described as follows:

> *At the other side of the bay is Rockport, formerly the home of Moira O'Neill, the most notable poet Ulster has produced since Sir Samuel Ferguson. Her Songs of the Glens of Antrim cannot fail to be a permanent contribution to Irish Literature.*
> (Hayward, 1946 (ed): 98)

'A Song of Glenann' (pp. 16–17)

Och, when we lived in ould Glenann
Meself could lift a song!
An' ne'er an hour by day or dark
Would I be thinkin' long.

The weary wind might take the roof,
The rain might lay the corn;
We'd up an' look for betther luck
About the morrow's morn.

But since we come away from there
An' far across the say,   **10**
I still have wrought, an' still have thought
The way I'm doin' the day.

An' now we're quarely betther fixed,
In troth! there's nothing wrong:
But me an' mine, by rain and shine
We do be thinkin' long.

NOTES

l.1   The use of *ould*, pronounced 'owl', can indicate affection:
th'owl house = our former home
th'owl lass = my mother.
l.2   Gaelic influence can be seen in the use of the reflexive 'meself' as the subject and in the use of 'lift a song', meaning 'carry a tune'.
l.4   To *think long* implies 'have sad thoughts'. It also suggests that the people had intelligence but had no way of using it.
l.7   Expressions using 'up and' were more common in English of the past and can still be found in comic verse:

He took pneumonia and he up and died.
He up and died. He up and died.
He took pneumonia and he up and died.
He up and died.

It is still current in the expression:
He's up and about now.
l.9   *Come* is often used as a past tense form in NIE:
When did he come? He come yestherday.
l.11   In many rural parts of NI, *wrought* is used as a past
tense form implying 'worked very hard indeed':

*Your father has wrought hard for yiz so it'd be to yiz to give him a
wee bit o' respect.*

The next sample comes from *Random Rhymes frae Cullybacky*
by Adam Lynn. The collection was published in Belfast in
1911, although the individual poems were written earlier.
Cullybacky is in Antrim and, even today, the English is
markedly USc.

'Coortin' (p.16, written 1901)

A wonder noo, 'tween me an' you,
Whut can A say that's richt;
A sort o' fear, there's some that's dear,
Wha' thinks A'm rether ticht.

A'm sure ye see, as well as me,
Young fellows wae their gal,
Either at nicht, or braid daylicht,
Afore that they ir twal.

An' oh, whut scenes whun in the teens,
Yin very aften sees;   **10**
A'll say nae mair, lest ye despair,
Or think A'm tellin' lees.

At twunty, boys and girls will toy,
Aye, try and dae whut's richt,
Whun one goes wrang, it's nae sae lang
Tae it comes tae the licht.

At twunty-yin young men will rin
The shaes richt aff their feet,
Tae get a crack, perhaps a smack,
Frae yin that's sma' an' neat.   **20**

An' sae on, freens, young men hae dreams
O' whar they'll yit arrive;
Until some day they're bound tae say,
We're nearly twunty-five.

Time rins awa', an' lees us a',
I say, young men, make haste,
Or if you don't, she'll say 'she won't,'
Whut joys ye'll niver taste.

An' sure we read, 'It is nae guid
Fur man tae lieve alane;'   **30**
Wha scorns this rule, is jist a fool
An' ten times waur than nane.

A think A should jist now conclude,
An' what A wish is this,
That coortin' shall be tae us al'
A source o' joy an' bliss.

NOTES

l.1 The orthographic conventions are inconsistent within this poem and throughout Lynn's verse. *Noo* occurs in l.1 but *now* in l.33 and *bound* (rather than 'boon') in l.23; *yin* in l.10 but *one* in l.15; *a'* in l.25 but *al'* in l.35; and *whut* in l.28 but *what* in l.34. Lynn was writing for an audience which was familiar with USc but less familiar with the written conventions of Scots.

The subject of 'courting', its pleasures and perils, is a common theme in NI verse.

'A' is the most widespread pronunciation of 'I' in casual speech in NI.

l.18 A reader of Lynn's verse, Robert Dunbar, told me that he had difficulty only with one word in the poem, *shaes*. As he put it:

I have never heard and never said 'shaes'. My mother uses most of the pronunciations given by Lynn but she would say 'shoes'.

We can therefore assume that *shaes* is either an inaccurate or an archaic representation.

l.25 In this line *lees* means 'leaves' and not 'lies' as in l.12.
l.32 *waur* = worse

The third poem is taken from *Ballads of Down* written by George Francis Savage-Armstrong (London: Longmans, Green and Co., 1901). According to the author, almost all of the dialect poems in the volume were written between 1892 and 1899. They show a strong influence from USc.

'Holy Bridget' (pp. 59–60)

The auld gaberlunzie sae reggit an' spare
That used tae gang leppin alang,
Wi' a skep, an' a twerl, an' a boon' in the air,
An' a 'whoop!', an' a bedlamite sang, -

'Holy Bridget' they ca'd him, acause as he went,
'Holy Bridget!' a' day wuz his cry,
As he shuck hissel' oot wi' a shiver, an' bent
Tae beg o' the stranger near-by.

Auld John o' Ralloo wuz sae braid i' the belt,
An' sae plump wi' guid leevin' he grew,   **10**
That 'Holy' wud sigh, 'Och, A wush A jist dwelt
In the belly o' John o' Ralloo!'

'Holy Bridget' haes vanish'd, an' nivver a frien'
Wull care in what hole he may dee;
But A won'er what doom in the Wurl'-Wi'oot-En'
Waits sic' an a craytur as he!

NOTES

Many of the vocabulary items and structures are similar to Scots and this poet makes a consistent use of Scots orthographic conventions.
l.1 Bridget is one of the three saints given special reverence in Ireland. She, St Patrick and St Colmcille (Dove of Church) are supposed to be buried in the one grave in Downpatrick:

In burgo Duno tumulo;
Tumulanter in uno,
Brigida, Patricius,
Atque Columba Pius.

St Bridget is often called 'the Mary of the Gael' and is closely associated with Mary's ability to intercede with her son.

l.1 'Gaberlunzie' is Scots for a 'beggar's wallet', with 'gaberlunzieman' being a 'licensed beggar'. The use of the object for the person associated with the object is well known. One can compare, for example how 'brat' changed from 'shawl' to 'child held in shawl'. 'Gaberlunzie' may well have influenced or been influenced by 'gobberlooney', a term for a fool, possibly deriving from Gaelic.

l.3 *boon'* = bound

l.5 In rural Ulster generally, the prefixes 'a-' and 'be-' are in free variation in words such as:

afore/before
ahind/behind
atween/between.

None of my informants could use *acause*.

l.9 The contrast between John and the beggarman is similar to the Gospel story of Dives and Lazarus.

l.15 *doom* = fate, judgement

l.16 The spelling of *craytur* possibly reflects an Irish influence, the preferred Scots form being 'cratur'.

Padraic Gregory was an architect who was born in Belfast and who travelled extensively in Ulster. He published eight well-known books of verse during the period 1912–1959. Our sample is taken from the *Complete Collected Ulster Ballads* (Belfast: William Mullan and Son Ltd., 1959). Gregory's verse owes much to the USc traditions but is not limited to this dialect. He himself, in words inspired by Yeats, associates himself with Irish writers in a poem 'The Poor Gleaner':

Let Moore, Mangan, Davis, an' Ferguson
Be honoured, both now an' in comin' times;
I only ax men for tae say o' me:
'His love o' the North folk filled all his rhymes.'

'The Bacach-Man'

I was walkin the dusty high-road
In undher the harvest moon,
When the twilight air bore to me
A fidil's silvery tune.

A hush-a-bye song 'twas playin',
Now risin', now fallin' low,
'Twas a song my mother sung me
In the ould days long ago.

So I listened a while, an' the music
Brought thoughts o' other years,   **10**
An' afore I knowed it my cheeks were
Asthremin' wi' scaldin' tears.

An' I breathed a wee prayer tae Heaven,
An' shouldered my heavy load,
An' happier - ay, far happier –
Wint wandherin' doon the road.

NOTES

'The Bacach-Man', meaning the Beggar-Man, is strongly influenced by AI and NHE poetic traditions which are more prone to sentimentality than samples of USc.
1.2 The doubling of prepositions is a widespread feature of Ulster English.
1.5 The use of *'twas* here and in l.7 is more reminiscent of NHE than of USc.
1.11 *afore* = before
1.12 The use of 'a-ing' is AI in force. In other words, it is a variant of 'streaming' rather than NHE 'being streamed'.
1.13ff The final verse has USc features in *wee, tae* and *doon*.

The example of verse which follows is from *Songs and Poems of Tyrone* by Felix Kearney (Omagh: Ulster Herald, n.d.). It represents NHE more clearly than any of the previous examples.

'Oul' Barney' (p. 13)

I was sittin' by the griosog;
Man, these Winter nights bes coul',
And I like to take things easy
For I'm getting brave an oul.
And a man bes quare an' lonesome
When his blood bes getting thin -
Troth, a was as pleased as Punch
When Barney More dropped in.

Now Barney was me neighbour
This forty years or more;   10
It would fill a book the knowledge
Our Barney has in store.
Of the men in Ireland's history
You ought to hear him tell,
Man, he has them on his fingers
From MacNessa to Parnell.

Now Barney got a Failte,
Of that you may be sure,
I riz and crushed an empty bag
Behind the kitchen door;   20
Then filled the pipe and lit it
And made sure it wouldn't choke,
Then I handed it to Barney
Saying, 'Sheod, Barney, smoke.'

There's a thing I always noticed
And I'll tell it now to you,
Our Barney chats far better
When he's had a reek or two.
So I let him smoke a minute,
He can pull, there's no mistake,   30
As tobacco's dear and money scarce
I thought 'twas time to speak.

Says I, I've got a paper
From my sister Mary Kate,
It says that England's winning,
They have Hitler nearly bate.

Oul Barney laughed and shook his head,
Says he: 'My decent chap,
If you nearly got to Heaven,
Do you know where you might stap?'   **40**

The two of us kept chatting
But we couldn't quite agree;
Our Barney's danged contrary
When it fits himself to be.
So says I, 'Will Davey give the Ports?'
Man dear, he let a shout:
'Will Davey give the Ports?' says he;
'No, not while I'm about.'

Says I, 'Hould on, be aisy,
I've a notion of my own   **50**
That Davey might do something
If we let the man alone.
Him and Churchill might fix up
A settlement of sorts -
If they gave us the Six Counties,
We might let them take the Ports.'

Be Japers, I was shaking,
And I'm not so aisy scared,
For he riz his fist above my head
And hit the table hard.   **60**
'Give them the Ports, and let them pay
With something that's our own?
You ought to be ashamed,' says he,
'And you come from Tyrone.'

I thought I'd try and soothe him
So I filled the pipe again.
I have my doubts Oul Barney
Would be more or less Sinn Fein;
And I'll have to watch my company,
The more Oul Barney's rale,   **70**
There's an empty cell in Belfast
And I'm oul for going to Jail.

NOTES

1.1 *griosog* = ashes (see *greeshy*)
1.2 In Tyrone, 'Man' is very frequently used as an introductory filler, as are 'Mans a boys', 'Boys a mans', 'Man dear'.
1.2 The verb 'be' is frequently inflected to indicate regularity:

It's cowl, the night.
It biz cowl, these nights.
It does be cowl from mornin ti' night, day in an day out.

1.16 Conchubar MacNessa was a legendary king of Ulster. Charles Stuart Parnell was a leader of the Irish Parliamentary Party in the House of Commons. He was cited in a divorce case in 1890 and his parliamentary career ruined.
1.17 *failte* = welcome. The traditional Gaelic welcome was:

"Céad míle fáilte" = A hundred thousand welcomes.
1.24 *Sheod* could be a reduction of 'Seo duit' = 'This is for you' or a variant of 'seodach' = 'smack one's lips with pleasure'. My informant from the Sperrins told me:

People used ti' say 'Sheod' when they give ye a pull at their pipe. It was like 'Here, you have a go.'
1.28 reek = smoke. The USc influence can be found even in communities which were, until recently, Gaelic-speaking.
1.30 *pull* = take deep draws of the pipe and so use up the tobacco
1.39 This line reinforces the proverb:

'Nearly' isn't all the way home.

1.47 The South of Ireland remained neutral during World War 2 and many English and NI people were angry when Churchill was denied access to Irish ports.
1.68 *Sinn Fein* = Ourselves Alone, a strongly republican political party.

The second verse example from Tyrone is from a Protestant writer, W.F. Marshall, whose collected poems were published by the Blackstaff Press, Belfast in 1983. The poems are much earlier, however, in that the Rev. Marshall was born in 1888 and died in 1959. It would be true to say that Marshall's ballads or variants on them (because Tyrone people made them their own) are among the most frequently recited poems in the county, being enjoyed equally by both communities. My version is from a recording made at a ceili in 1970. It was recited by a Tyrone woman, H.McR.

'Sarah Ann'

I'll change me way of goin
For me head is gettin grey,
I'm tormented washin dishes
An makin dhrops o tay;
The kitchen's like a midden,
An the parlour's like a sty,
There's half a foot of clabber
On the street outby:
I'll go down agane the morra
On me ceili to the Cross   **10**
For I'll have to get a woman
Or the place'll go to loss.

I fodther all the kettle
An there's nothin afther that
But clockin roun the ashes
Wi' an oul Tom cat;
Me very ears is bizzin
From the time I light the lamp,
An the place is like a graveyard,
Bar'n the mare 'd give a stamp,   **20**
So often I be thinkin
An conthrivin of a plan
Of how to make the match agane
With Robert's Sarah Ann.

I used to make wee Robert's
Of a Sunday afther prayers,
Ser' Ann wud fetch the taypot
To the parlour up the stairs.

An onct a week for sartin
I'd be chappin at the dure,   **30**
There wasn't wan would open it
But her, ye may be sure;
An then – for all was goin well –
I got a neighbour man
An took him down to spake for me,
An ax for Sarah Ann.

Did ye iver know wee Robert?
Well, he's nothin but a wart,
A nearbegone owl divil
With a wee black heart,   **40**
A crooked, crabbit crathur
That bees nether well nor sick,
Girnin in the chimley corner,
Or goin happin on a stick.
Sure ye mind the girl for hirin
That went shoutin through the fair,
'I winthered in wee Robert's,
I could summer anywhere.'

****

NOTES

l.5 *midden* = refuse dump. The word 'duchill', derived
from 'dunghill', is used for a dump that can subsequently
be used as manure. A 'midden' often implies dirt that can
be of no use.
l.7 *half a fut of clabber* = six inches of mud
outby = out beyond that
l.10 *ceili* = social visit
l.12 *go to loss* = go to waste
l.17 *bizzin* = ringing
l.20   bar'n = unless. The Blackstaff version gives "bar" but
the more usual expression is 'barring the mare...' and
'barring' is pronounced as one syllable, indistinguishable
from 'barn'.

l.21 The use of *be thinkin* as opposed to 'am thinkin' stresses the continuity of the action.

l.23 *match* = arranged marriage. Arranged marriages were the norm in rural areas of Tyrone until relatively recently. Care was taken to ensure that 'land married land' and a dowry was arranged with each daughter. The tradition was that the eldest daughter was married first and usually commanded the highest dowry. Additional benefits might accrue to a less good-looking daughter. The custom is described in the following narrative, recorded in 1982:

Well now, them was the days. Och they woren't bad days but a woman didn't have much say. I mind the time owl Pether X wanted a woman. He musta been fifty five if he was a day an the work was gettin too much for him. He come down till our house wi' a five neggin bottle:

'Henry,' says he, 'I want ye ti come up ti Paddy More's an tell him I'll tick the sisther.'

'Are ye not a wee bit hesky on it?' says me father.

'Divil the bit,' says Peter. 'The place is goin ti hell an desolation an Paddy More's sisther's brave an soople of herself. Long runs the fox but it's time this fox had a woman.'

Well him an me father went ti get Jemmy Kughes for ti go wi them an Jemmy was at his supper. Wi'out a word, the daughter set two more places an give them their fill.

'Bigod Jemmy,' says Pether, 'that's a brave wee blade o' yours. She can mick a right cup o' tay. Hear, what d'ye say? I have a farm o' lan an a bob or two behin' me. I'll tick your blade as she stands wi'out a stick or a stone.'

An that's what happened. Brigid couldn't a been sixteen at the time. By the day they got married she had the eyes cried out of her head but there was nahin for it. An she done rightly. Pether left her wi' a brave wee sittin' down...

l.28 In rural areas, it is still not uncommon to have the 'room' or the 'parlour' upstairs. This room is normally reserved for visiting dignitaries like a clergyman and is frequently used for waking a corpse in.

l.30 *chappin* = knocking lightly since the visit is expected

1.39 *nearbegone* = mean
1.42 *bees* = is habitually
1.43 *girnin* = making faces. It is etymologically the same word as 'grinning'.
1.45 In the past, young unmarried people often 'hired' themselves out for a seasonal wage. It might be for 'clampin turf' or 'potato pickin'. Traditionally, there was more food in summer and autumn than in winter and those who 'wintered out' often endured hardship.

4.2 PRINTED TEXTS: PROSE

The first text is from William Carleton's *Denis O'Shaughnessy Going to Maynooth*. William Carleton, (1794–1869) was born in Tyrone, into a bilingual Catholic family called O Carolan. He was originally destined for the priesthood but became a Protestant and went to live in Dublin. He is recognised as one of the father figures of Irish Literature in English and his recreation of dialect speech is particularly impressive.

The edition used was published by the Mercier Press, Cork and Dublin in 1973. *Denis O'Shaughnessy Going to Maynooth* is volume 2 in the 8-volume series *Traits and Stories of the Irish Peasantry*, originally published in two volumes in 1843–44.

'Why do I blush for your ignorance, is it? Why, thin, I'm sure I have sound rasons for it: only think of the gross persivarance wid which you call that larned work, the Lexicon in Greek, a Necksuggawn. Fadher, never attimpt to argue or display your ignorance wid me again. But, moreover, I can probate you to be an ungrammatical man, from your own modus of argument.'
'Go on, avourneen. Phadrick!' (p.4)

'Franky,' they would say, 'is no finished priest in the larnin'; he's but a *scondher*.'
Now a *scondher* is an oaten cake laid upon a pair of tongs placed over the *greeshaugh*, or embers, that are spread out

for the purpose of baking it. In a few minutes the first side laid down is scorched; it is then turned, and the other side is also scorched; so that it has the appearance of being baked, though it is actually quite raw within. It is a homely but an exceedingly apt illustration when applied to such men as Frank.

'Poor Frank,' they would observe, 'is but a *scondher*; the sign of the tongs – No. 11 – is upon him; so that it is asy known he never was laid to the *muddha arran* – that is to say, properly baked – or duly and thoroughly educated...' (pp. 31–2)

NOTES

1.1 The use of *is it* is again probably an influence from Gaelic. Frequently, in Gaelic, the tags 'an eadh' (Query BE) and 'nach eadh' (Query + not BE) are attached to the end of statements and imply 'Is that it?' and 'Isn't that so?'

1.3 English 'er' is frequently pronounced 'ar' in such words as *larn(ed)*, *sarvant* and *sarvice*. It is likely that such a pronunciation was formerly more widespread in many parts of the English-speaking world cf. US nonstandard *varmin(t)*.

1.4 The use of 'd' in *Fadher* and *wid* (1.3) is a feature of SHE rather than NHE today.

necksuggaun is an example of folk etymology.

1.8 *avourneen* = a mhuirnín = term of endearment. The 'a' is a vocative marker and it modifies the sound which follows, thus 'Padraig' is 'Patrick' but 'a Phadraig' where 'Ph' is pronounced 'f' is the address form. Carleton indicates this in his orthography. His use of 'd' in 'Phadrick' is also closer to the Gaelic form of the name.

1.10ff Carleton used italics to indicate Gaelic words. It is reasonable to assume that "scondher" is exactly what he describes. The only meaning of "scundher" in NI today is 'strong distaste', 'upset stomach':

I took a scundher agin cheese.
He has the scundher. He has ate something that has cruddled in his guts.

l.12 *gríosach* = burning embers, ashes
l.21 *maide* = stick and *arán* = bread. A *maide aráin* was a forked stick which could be placed on a stand close to a fire so as to allow a thin cake or loaf to bake slowly. A 'scund-her' is the equivalent of a person who is 'half-baked'.

The second prose text is from David Patterson's book *The Provincialisms of Belfast and the Surrounding Districts Pointed Out and Corrected*. This was published in Belfast in 1860 and provides the best account we have of the pronunciation of the period. One point that becomes clear when we compare Patterson's description with present-day usage is the con-servative nature of NI speech. A political motto is 'What we have, we hold'. It would appear that the sentiment applies to language as well. The extract comes from p. 23:

COMMON ERRORS IN THE USE OF VERBS.

A number of verbs in common use are incorrectly pro-nounced when used in the past tense – in some the past participle is improperly used instead of the past tense, thus, 'He *begun* to sing,' 'He *sung* well,' 'He *drunk* water,' 'He *rid* home,' should be, 'He *began* to sing,' 'He *sang* well,' 'He *drank* water,' 'He *rode* home.' 'He *ta'en* it away,' 'I *seen* him,' 'He *done* it himself,' should be, 'He *took* it away,' 'I *saw* him,' 'He *did* it himself.' In some a contraction of the past participle is improperly used for the past tense; thus *throve*, *drove*, *strove*, and *rose*, are improperly pronounced *thriv*, *driv*, *striv*, and *riz*. *Give*, *come*, and *run*, are improperly substituted for *gave*, *came*, and *ran*; thus, 'I *give* it to him an hour ago,' 'He *come* home this morning', 'He *run* down stairs,' should be, 'I *gave* it to him an hour ago,' 'He *came* home this morning,' 'He *ran* down stairs.' *Sat*, *spat*, and *let*, are improperly pronounced *sut*, *sput*, and *lot*, and *brought* is improperly pronounced *brung*.

WORDS NOT TO BE MET WITH IN OUR ORDINARY ENGLISH DICTIONARIES.

The following words, which are in everyday use in and around Belfast, are not to be met with in our ordinary English dictionaries. Generally speaking, they are in use among the low and vulgar only:-

Bing, a heap.
Boke, to retch; to vomit.
Brash, a short or sudden illness.
Clype, a large piece.
Coggle, to shake; to rock.
Cowp, to upset.
Curnaptious, crabbed; captious.
Dotther, to stagger.
Dunsh, to knock against; butt.
Dunt, a knock; a blow.
Dwine, to pine.
Farl, a cake of bread.
Floosther, to wheedle.
Foother, to bungle; a bungler.
Footy, mean; paltry.
Fozy, spongy.
Jeuk, to elude by shifting; to dodge.
Jubious, suspicious; mistrustful.
Jundy, to jostle.
Lappered, congealed; clotted.
Oxtther, the armpit.
Prod, to stab or thrust.
Ramp, rank; rancid.
Sapple, to soak; wet thoroughly.
Scam, to scorch.
Scringe, to creak.
Scrunty, a niggard; niggardly.
Scundther, to disgust.
Sevendible, thorough; sound.
Sheugh, a ditch.
Skelf, a small splinter.
Skelly, to squint.

Skelp, a slap; to slap.
Sleekit, sly.
Slocken, to allay thirst; to quench fire.
Smudge, to smirk.
Smush, refuse.
Speel, to climb.
Stoor, dust.
Stoon, a pang; to ache.
Stroop, a pipe or spout.
Thole, to endure or suffer pain or annoyance
Thraw, to twist.
Thud, a knock or thump.
Warsh, insipid.
Wheen, a quantity; a number.

NOTES

l.1ff The orthographic conventions of punctuation and italicisation are Patterson's. For ease of reference, I have put his wordlist into alphabetical order.
l.4ff The highlighted 'errors' are still widespread in une-ducated NI speech. As with the verb forms, most of the words listed are still in widespread use. The exceptions fall into three categories:

A those which no longer exist (*cleek, bing, sapple, footy, lappered, ramp*)
B those which occur mainly in the speech of the old (*fozy, scringe, smudge, sevendible, scrunty, brash, stoon, dwine*)
C those which now occur in a modified form (*smush > mush, jundy > junder, slocken > sleck*).

Virtually all the words listed by Patterson have Scots coun-terparts. The exceptions are: *thud* (onomatopoeic and standard), *smudge, jubious* (standard 'dubious'), *ramp* (the development of 'ramp' and 'rank' on analogy with 'damp' and 'dank'), *prod* (standard) and *floosther*.

The third text is taken from *Paddy McQuillan's Trip Tae Glesco*. It was written by an Ulster Scots speaker,

W.G. Lyttle (1844–1896) and printed by the author at his north Down printing works, Bangor in 1888. Lyttle was a prolific writer, keenly interested in the representation of dialect, in which he wrote his novel *Betsy Gray: or Hearts of Down: A Tale of Ninety-Eight* (1888). Our extract is from 'Part First' of Paddy's adventures.

Did I niver tell ye aboot my trip tae Glesco'? Man, that was the biggest spree iver I had in my life. It wuz a while efter that Christmas day I spent up in Belfast, an' I felt my courage risin in my breest at bein' able tae gang sae far frae hame, so I determined tae tak the shine oot o' the neibours by gaun whaur no yin o' them had iver set their fit. Weel, I kent my ma wud be agen my gaun, for there wuz a Scotchman jilted her whun she wuz a young lass, an' she hated the very name o' ocht that cum oot o' the country. Yin mornin' whun I was at my breakfast, I sez tae her, sez I –

"Ma, I'm thinkin' o' gaun frae hame a bit."

"It's no very far, I hope," sez she, "for there's a guid wheen o' the prittaes tae be riz yet, and ye cannae be weel spared awa. Whaur ye gaun?"

"I'm gaun ower the shough tae Glesco'," sez I.

"Ye're gaun tae the mischief!" sez she.

"Whaur's that?" sez I; "if its in ony pert o' Glesco' I'll be there, for I mean tae see a' that's tae be seen."

"Ye'll no gang yin fit," sez she, "an' if ye persist in it I'll lock up yer claes."

"Weel, if ye dae," sez I, "I'll gang an' list; I wull as sure as daith!"

I hadnae anither word tae say. Whuniver my ma refused me ocht, I jist threatened tae list, an' then I got whativer I wanted. Sez I, "Mebbe ye wud cum wae me. Ye micht get anither man there, an' its sae lang noo since my da dee'd that I wud like tae hae anither yin."

She gied me sich a luk that I thocht it best to say nae mair. Sez she, "Awa an' gie the pigs their drink, an' I'll see aboot it."

Puir buddy, she made as muckle preparations for me as if I had been gaun tae Americay. She bakit aboot three griddle fu's o' hard breed, an' a hale lot o' baith soda and pritta breed, an' then she put up a wee crock o' fresh butter. Sez I, "Ye dinnae mean me tae starve anyway."

"Oh," sez she, yer gaun to a gie cauld country, an' ye'll no fin' mony in it as kin' tae ye as yer auld ma."

"I'm very shair o' that," sez I, "an' I'll no forget ye whun I'm awa; hoo muckle money wull ye gie me wae me?"

"What'll pie yer passage, an' half-a-croon fur yer pocket," sez she.

"Ah, haud yer tongue!" sez I; "it'll take a cupple o' pun' at the least," sez I.

"Sorra cupple o' pun' ye'll tak there tae get rubbed o'," sez she; "ye wudnae be lang there till ye wud be releeved o' yer money."

"Yer far ower hard on the Scotch folk," sez I, "an' I dinnae beleeve they're half as bad as ye mak them appear. An' man, dear, I wuz richt whun I said that, fur I declare I met the nicest, kindest folk in Glesco that iver I saw in my life. They're jist like oursels, only they're a wee bit sherper, an' I think their hearts are twa inches farder doon than Irish yin's."

Weel, I got awa at last, but I didnae get very muckle money wae me. My ma made a bargain wae me that she wud gang intae the toon an' sen' me a money order. Puir buddy, whun I wuz startin' that day she roared like a waen.

"Paddy, dear," sez she, "I hope ye'll no be drooned, but I hae a forebodin' that sumthin'll happen ye. It's gaun tae be a coorse nicht, an' I'll no sleep a wink fur thinkin' aboot ye."

"Hoots, wuman!" sez I. "Cheer up, an' tell me what I'll bring ye frae Scotland."

"Oh, Paddy, jist bring me yersel' safe hame."

"I'll dae that," sez I, "an' noo guid-bye."

"Guid-bye and Guid bless ye; watch the Scotch folk, an' dinna be bringin' a wife wae ye, or I'll pit ye baith oot."

I got red o' her at last, got the lenth o' Belfast, made my way doon tae the quay, an' bocht my ticket. My guidness, but yon's big boats! I dinna ken how they make them ava. There maun be a gie lot o' timmer in them. I wasnae lang on the boat till they startit her, an' I declare they let her aff as easy as I wud oor auld meer an' cart. Whun I saw the folk an' hooses movin' past me, my heart begood tae quiver, an'

a lump got up in my throat. I went an' leaned ower the side
o' the boat, an' the great big tears drippit doon intae the
sea."

"Oh, ma dear," sez I, "I'll mebbe niver see ye mair."

Wae that I hears sumbuddy sayin',

"Yer no seek alreddy?"

Thinks I, "that's a Scotchman, but it'll no be me he's
speakin' tae," so I niver moved.

"Yer no seek alreddy?" sez he agen, an' this time he
tuched me on the shooder.

Wae that I birled roon an' luckit at him. He was a
Scotchman ivery inch o' him, an' had a thing on his heed as
big as oor griddle, wae a tossle on the tap o' it.

"Hoo de ye fin' yersel'?" sez he.

Sez I, "I didnae ken I wuz lost."

"Oh," sez he, I mean hoo dae ye feel?"

"Man," sez I, "I feel a' ower."

NOTES

l.1ff   The spelling and punctuation conventions used are
those of Lyttle. He is reasonably consistent in his use of
modified spellings but uses both 'Glesco'' (l.1) and 'Glesco'
(l.50) for 'Glasgow'; 'sae' (l.4) and 'so' (l.5) for 'so'; and 'oor'
(l.72) and 'oursels' (l.51) for 'our(selves)'. He also occasionally modifies the spelling of words which are not
pronounced differently in Ulster Scots, 'neibours' (l.5) for
'neighbours', 'cupple' (l.42) for 'couple' and 'tuched' (l.83)
for 'touched'. Generally, Lyttle uses 'in'' to represent the
pronunciation of 'ing' but we also find 'risin' (l.4) for 'rising'
and 'gaun' (l.6) for 'going'.

l.5   *tak the shine oot o'* = outdo, 'get one over on'

l.6   *no yin* = not one

l.7   *agen* = against

l.8   'Scotch' and not 'Scots' is the usual form in N. Ireland.

l.8   Standard English requires a relative pronoun as subject in such sentences as:

There was a Scotsman who jilted her.

The omission of this pronoun is not unusual in Northern Ireland speech. I have recorded:

She sent for me ma was hangin clothes out.
He gave it to the man was in first.
Similar structures occur in Scots ballads:

The king hath written a braw letter
An' sealed it wi' his hand,
An' sent it to Sir Patrick Spens
Was walkin' on the strand.

1.12–13   *good wheen o' the prittaes* = a lot of potatoes
1.13   *tae be riz* = to be picked. 'Riz' is occasionally used for 'raised':

Thon blade's temper's aisy riz = That woman's temper is easily raised.

1.15   *ower the shough* = over the Irish Sea. In jocular speech, we also find 'over the pond' for 'over the Atlantic' and 'over the water' for 'across the sea'.
1.20   *claes* = clothes
1.21   *list* = enlist
1.31   *muckle* = much, great
1.33   *breed* = bread
1.36   *cauld* = mean, ungenerous
1.40   *half-a-croon* = half a crown or 12.5 pence
1.44   *sorra* is an emphatic word, a polite equivalent of 'devil' or 'damn':

Have ye any torf?
Sorra the sod. (Not even one sod.)

1.52–3   *their hearts...yin's* = their hearts are not as easily reached as Irish ones
1.57   *roared like a waen* = cried like a child
1.59   In colloquial Ulster English:

What happened ye?
is more likely than 'What happened?' or 'What happened to you?'
1.65   'Good' and 'God' are not usually homophones.
1.67   *red* = rid

1.69 *ava* = at all
1.70 *gie* = big, great
1.73 *begood* = began. This form is unusual. None of my Down informants had ever heard it used.
1.79 Although Ulster Scots has much in common with Scots, Paddy knew after four words that his interlocutor was a Scot. The difference between the varieties is emphasised when Paddy misunderstands the question in 1.00.
1.83 *shooder* = shoulder
1.86 *tossle* = tassel

4.3 SPOKEN TEXTS

The spoken texts cover a range of ages, rural and urban speakers, both sexes and both communities. They include jokes, discussions and oral narrative. The first example is from a thirteen-year-old Belfast schoolboy, MM.

Hear about the wee boy, sittin on the bridge cryin – cryin his eyes out – an all the tears roll over the bridge – an this here man comes over – says: 'Scuse me, son, what are you cryin for? If you cry much longer you're gonna flood the bridge.' An the wee boy says: 'Well, I've dropped my mate – he's in the river.' An the man takes off his hat 'n coat – jumps in the water – comes back up 'n says: 'Scuse me, son, I can't find your wee friend.' The wee boy starts to laugh – he says: 'What are you laughin at?' He says: 'It's not my friend. I said it was my mate.' He says: 'Well, I can't find your mate.' He says: 'That's not my mate as in human,' he says, 'It's the mate out of my sandwich.'

NOTES

1.1 The terms 'wee boy' and 'wee girl' tend to denote affection or friendship rather than size or age:

Wasn't thon wee girl gettin married just lovely?
What do they call your last wee boy?

They can also be used as terms of address:

A say, wee boy, c'mere. Will ye run a message for me?

1.5 Children are often aware of the different pronunciations and grammatical patterns that occur. I tested this with a four-year-old girl whose parents spoke Standard English but whose grandmother spoke NHE:

LT *Now Mommy would say 'bull' /bul/ but Nana would say...?*
F *Bull /bʌl/.*
LT *And Mommy would say 'You should've gone.'*
F *An Nana would say 'Ye should a went.'*

The second is a County Down comedian, CF, in his mid-forties.

Hear, did ye hear the one about Mrs Murphy? She goes till the docthor an she says: 'Docthor,' says she, 'Will ye put me on the conthradictive pill?' Says he: 'The what?' 'The conthradictive pill,' says she. 'Begod, woman,' says he, 'you're ignorant.' 'Aye,' says she, 'Three months.'

Would yiz quit clappin – a haven't started crackin jokes yit. Some docthors has quare patients. O'Toole went intil his docthor an he says, 'Docthor,' says he, 'I'm in agony. I have a terrible cough an I was wondherin could ye give me somethin that would stop me coughing?' Well the docthor wrote out a prescription. 'That'll do the job,' says he. 'Take two tablespoons o syrp o figs before an afther meals.' O'Toole looks at your man an says he: 'An will syrp o figs stop me coughin?' 'By God an it will,' says the docthor. 'Afther a couple o doses o that, you'll be afraid ti cough.'

NOTES

1.1 There are some jokes that can be told by both Catholic and Protestant comedians but others are limited to one community. Jokes about contraception:

The Pope has just authorised a new birth control pill. It's three ton in weight. Ye prop it agin the bedroom door.

the IRA:

Did ye hear about the IRA man that got twelve years for shop liftin? Lifted Woolwuz (Woolworths) *two foot aff the groun.*

and people with names like 'Murphy' and 'O Reilly'.

Morphy went ti the biroo (dole) *one day last week. 'Is it work ye're signing on for?' asks yir man. 'Deed, begod it's not,' says Morphy. 'I'm signing on fir money.'*

are almost invariably told by Catholics. Jokes about Ian Paisley:

D'ye want to hear my impersomentation of Elvis Paisley?

or the Orange or Masonic Lodge:

Did ye hear about the man that went intil the Lawdge at Aghohill with his pet crocodile?
'Do yiz serve crocodiles here?' says he.
'Och aye,' says the barman. 'There's nahin in the rules agin crocodiles.'
'Well, serve me a beer an my crocodile a Cahlic.'

are the almost exclusive domain of Protestant comedians.

1.13 *Syrup* is nearly always realised as a monosyllabic word which rhymes with 'slurp'.

The third speaker, EB, is a Belfast housewife in her fifties.

Well my mommy stayed at home an kept the house lovely. She was very houseproud, ye know. We worked in the mill, like, making shirts an the work was hard, like. It wasn't like the kids of today. I was an only chile but Mommy still took me out of school at fourteen an put me in the mill. I wanted to be a teacher an I had the brains an all – but there was very little money for education. My father said there was no point like – educatin a girl for she'd ony marry – an mebbe he was right like for I did get married when I was eighteen. My man was lucky – he got a job as a postman – he was an ex-serviceman, so he was. Well anyway, he got artritis for he had to walk miles carryin a big heavy beg.

NOTES

1.1 'Mommy' tends to be used by all children and most women for their mother, irrespective of the mother's age.
1.2 The working-class streets of the Shankill area were renowned for their cleanliness. One eighty-year-old woman from Bristol Street told me:

Ye could've ate yir mate aff o anybody's stap. Houseproud now I suppose ye'd call it but if it was your last shallin ye'd a spant it on Cardinal Red (a red, lead-based polish used for steps and kitchen floors).

1.3 Fillers such as *like* are frequently used and there may be an age difference in the forms selected. 'So they are' and its variants seem to be used by all speakers:

You're not goin.
I am so I am.
whereas 'like' occurs in the speech of older people.

1.12 *Artritis* is a hypercorrect form.
1.12 *beg* = bag.

The fourth recording is of a male teacher, AS. He is in his mid forties, was born in Cushendall and spent most of his adult life in Limavady.

My best friend was trained as a teacher – and she was a young teacher – and she did her training in Belfast – and she was lectured to by a man who said that he wanted to pass on to them the best piece of advice he could remember – and he said:
  'What the first child you teach says to you in the first classroom on the first day will remain with you all your life – and it will set the tone for your teaching career.'
  And this young girl went into her first school on her first morning – and the headmistress took her along and introduced her to her fourth year class – and made a little speech and went out and left her alone with her class – and she came round to the front of the desk – and she talked to them for three or four minutes. – She said she wanted them to

regard her as their friend – that they had work to do together – hard work – but interesting work – that she looked forward to getting to know them and helping them – and she hoped they would get on well together and do good things together – and all the time she spoke to them, she was remembering what this lecturer had said, that the first thing said to her by a child would set the tone for her teaching career – and as she finished speaking she said:

'Now before we start our first lesson, which is going to be dictation, has anybody anything they'd like to tell me or say to me?'

And a wee girl in the back row stuck her hand up – and the teacher remembered what she had been told – she said:

'Yes, dear, what is it?'

And the wee girl said:

'Please, Miss, Veronica's vomitin.'

NOTES

l.24 The syllabus in many NI schools is traditional and even old-fashioned by English standards. Attention is still paid to handwriting in lessons called 'Transcription' and 'Dictation' is used to develop listening skills.
l.30 It is still usual for NI children to address teachers by 'Please, Miss/Ma'am/Sir'.

The fifth sample is an interview with two 16-year-old boys, Rodney and William. Both were born in Derry city and had left school without qualifications. Neither had found a job.

L. Mm. Would you ever think of leaving Londonderry?
R. No. The throubles aren't here – aren't really affectin Londonderry itself. S'not very often there's any real throuble – any, any – just maybe the minor riot or two like but no real throuble so 'ere's nohin really to be afraid of. I'll say I'll be stayin here the rest of me life.
L. What about you, William, would you ever leave Londonderry?

W.   Nah, no chance, cause you'd only be givin an ti the Cahlics, cause they'd just move on in straight ti your house as soon as you left.

L.   And is there any way that you can think of that the troubles will come to an end?

W.   No, th'won't.

L.   They'll just go on?

W.   Yes.

L.   How would you solve the problems? – No way?

W.   No.

L.   And what about you, Rodney? Can you think of any way to solve them?

R.   Well there's no real way out o it. Some was thinkin a united Ireland would solve them but I don't think it will though just because the Republic is different, y'know, no social health service an all that. An the Cahlics would jus be as bad off as we are if it's a united Ireland. That might stop the IRA an INLA, y'know, bombin an all but – then it'll probably be the Protestant groups that'll be doin all the bombin an shootin, if it's a united Ireland – so 'ere's no real way that you can stop the throubles 'at might keep both sides peaceful.

NOTES

l.1   I used 'Londonderry' because I knew that the use of 'Derry' would inhibit conversation with two boys from a Loyalist ghetto.

l.2ff   The tragedy is that Rodney accepted as normal a level of violence that would be considered intolerable in any other part of Europe.

l.5   Both boys often omitted the initial consonant in *there's*. They also tended to pronounce 'th' as 'h' in 'nothing' and 'Catholic', a word which was disyllabic for both.

l.9   William tends to pronounce 'in' as he does a stressed 'an'.

l.11   'As soon as' is telescoped to 'soon as' with extra stress on the initial 's'.

l.24   There is a widespread belief among uneducated

people in the North, both Catholic and Protestant, that there is no social security in the Republic. There is, but most poor people in NI would have a lower standard of living in Eire.

l.26 *IRA* = Irish Republican Army
INLA = Irish National Liberation Army

The sixth sample is a recording of a Derry woman, RM, in her early forties. She is explaining the intricacies of machine sewing to her eight-year-old daughter.

Mother: Well now, you see, first of all you make sure that the machine is threaded right. Look now, one, two, three, four, five and into the needle. You're in me light. – I can't get the thread in. Here you chile, you put it in. Your eyes are younger than mine. – Naw, naw not backroads. Would ye put it in the right road, chile.
Child: Well I don't know which road is the back road now, do I?
Mother: Don't you gimme any o' your owl backchat now or I'll put the machine away an there'll be no doll's clothes. Do you hear me?
Child: Aye.
Mother: Aye, what?
Child: Yes, Mommy.
Mother: That's bether. Well now, when you have the machine threaded, you put your cloth undher this wee foot, like that – Then you dhrop this wee snib an the foot sits tight on your cloth. Now you do it. – Och God chile, have ye no wit? What did ye pull all the thread out for? I ony meant ye to thry liftin the wee snib. God but ye'd need the patience of a saint to learn wains anything these days. They're that full o' television an nonsense they can't take their time to do nohin right.

NOTES

l.5 *Road* is often used where 'way' would occur in the standard language:
I don't know the road to do it.

1.6 *Child* is frequently used as a term of address and parallels its Gaelic equivalent 'a leanbh'. In NIE, terms of address are often obligatory, as in line 12, where the child omits the expected term and is corrected.

1.9 *Backchat* implies answering an adult back, usually rudely, although many parents would regard any reply from a child as rude. Children are encouraged to speak up and not *to let their bone go with a dog* but they are also instructed not *to turn their tongue* on an older person. It is not always easy to know which piece of advice to follow.

1.19 *wit* = intelligence

The seventh recording was made in Tyrone. The two women involved are Teresa (mid-forties) and Maureen (mid-thirties). The dash indicates a short, natural break in the conversation.

T.   Is that you, Maureen? How are you doin at all at all? I haven't seen ye fir a wheen o' Sundays – Are ye rightly?

M.   I am indeed, thank God, am bravely. – Ye know ye don't be able ti' -

T.   Och, ye seem ti have got a bit of a clogher with ye now . Is there somethin wrong with your chest? A well, wait ti' ye get yir breath back now.

M.   Aye, that hill was tarrible steep.

M.   Anyway -

T.   Och, you'll soon get it back wi a wee dhrop o' tay now if you'll come on up.

M.   Aye, well am in no hurry.

T.   A well take your time now till we get our breath back – the bray's pretty steep an we only live half way up – now take your time – there's no hurry at all at all.

M.   Och, am rightly now. – Sure what hurry would I be in? – There's no childher waitin ti' be fed an me work's all finished barrin a couple o' sheets that's ti' be step.

T.   A well now, the longer they steep the betther now. – If ye put in a wee bit o' soda in with it an lave them for a couple o' days an then just boil them when you finished boilin pitters for the pigs. – Put them on in.

M.   Aye that's right ye know – an ye know am tired o' sittin me lone up thondher in thon house.

T.   Aye, it must be lonely now.

M.   So a says ti' myself says I – Och I'll take a wee dandher out an mebbe a wee ceili – for ye know a body'd go daft if he nivir put his foot outside the dure. – But tell us, have ye heard any good schisms lately?

T.   A now, divil the wan. – But I'll make ye a wee dhrop o' tea first now. – It's no bo'er. – The place is a bit througho'er but that doesn't matther. – Anyway, we'll redd up afther us.

M.   Och now – now don't be puttin yirself – don't be puttin yourself about – A had a wee sup o' butthermilk.

T.   Och now – now howl yir whisht – sure butthermilk's the worse thing ye could take fir that loss o' wine now. – Ye need a mouthful o' tay an yere gonna get a mouthful now just in your hand – sure now don't be makin any fuss about it. – Ye'll be all right in a minute, Maureen.

M.   Well all right then – but just a dhrop in me han – I don't want anyhin ti' ate unless ye've got any o' them tatie farls. – Och your mother was the great han at makin them. – Thanks very much – That's grand – Lovely – But tell us, where's your mo'er the day?

T.   Och now – she's away ti' Ardboe – She's about borrowin a clockin hen. – We've a power of eggs an the owl hens just won't sit – Me ma says it's the we'er but I ast 'er if they couldn't have the same we'er in Ardboe sure – but she wouldn't have it. – She thinks she wanted the day out with 'er owl aunt Ally. – I wouldn't go wi' er. – I wouldn't take Britain an walk up them big loanins – sure ye'd be clabber ti' the eyebrows. – A well, ye've got the lenth o' yourself, hev'n ye?

[The conversation continues and Maureen tells a story of her last visit to Ardboe.]

Well hear, wait till a tell ye. It was the eighth o' September. – I'll nivir forget it. – They said somethin big was goin ti' happen so down I went an me only afther comin from school. – It was gettin quare'n dark by the time I got there – an when we reached the field they were there in their thousands. – Well, ye know me – I couldn't be like another body an stand me groun. – Aw naw – I had ti' get up neardther the place. – Well up I pushed. – Ye shoulda seen

the looks a got – But anyway on I went till I was standin
undher the three (tree).

T.   An did ye see anyhin when ye got there now?

M.   Och would ye have a titther o' wit. – See anyhin, how
are ye? I seen nahin – but a got a crick in me neck lookin up.
– Anyway a don't know how long it was afther that I
shouldhered me way out again. – They were shovin an
pushin like all that. – An when a got ti' the edge of the
crowd divil the know a knowed where a was. – It was that
dark. – It was pitch. – An there was a line o' buses no miss
all down the road. – Says I ti myself says I: 'I'll just walk past
them buses until I come till our own –'

NOTES

l.1   'Is that you?' and 'Och is it yourself?' are common
greetings.

l.1   The reduplicated form 'at all at all' is a widely used
intensive. See also line 15.

l.5   *to have got a bit of a clogher* = to be a bit chesty

l.14   T uses *brae* where M prefers *hill*. T originally came
from the north of the county where the influence from USc
is stronger.

l.18   *barrin* = with the exception of, except for

l.20   *soda* = sodium carbonate crystals used for getting
sheets white

l.22   *pitters* = potatoes. I have never heard 'pitthers', the
pronunciation one might expect.

l.26   *dandher* = walk for pleasure

l.29   *schisms* = good stories, interesting bits of news

l.31   *throughother* = untidy

l.35   *howl yir whisht* = say nothing. The expression is
friendly although the translation might appear rude.

l.36   *wine* = wind = breath

l.37   People in NI invariably offer guests some
refreshment which can vary from 'a mouthful o' tay'
(something very simple, perhaps only tea and a biscuit)
through 'a dhrop in your hand' (something simple, tea and
a sandwich or a piece of cake) to 'your tea' (a cooked meal).

The hospitality is often joked about. In one song, for example, a Belfast woman tells a soldier:

Here son, howl me bomb till a make ye a cup o tay.

1.41 *tatie farls* = type of bread made from potatoes
1.45 *Ardboe* is pronounced 'Are+bo' and means 'high cow'. Legend has it that the monks who were building the Celtic cross had no water for the cement. Each day a large cow appeared which the monks milked and so they used milk instead of water.
1.45–6 *she's about borrowing* = she has gone to borrow
1.46 *a power of eggs* = a large number of eggs
1.48–9 *she wouldn't have it* = she wouldn't listen to my objections
1.51 *loanins* = smalls lanes
1.51 *clabber* = mud
1.52 *the length of yourself* = a short distance. The expression is often used by someone complaining about not getting out:

It's a wee lifetime since I got the lenth o' meself.

1.56 September 8 is the birthday of the Blessed Virgin Mary. Maureen was telling about a series of apparitions in Ardboe in the mid-fifties.
1.62 *stand me ground* = stay where I was
1.65 The 'tree' refers to the one on which the Blessed Virgin Mary was said to appear.
1.66 Notice how Teresa prefaces her question with 'and'.
1.67 *a titther o' wit* – a tiny amount of common sense
1.72 *Divil the know I knowed* is an emphatic way of saying 'I hadn't a clue'.
1.73 *a line o buses no miss* = an extremely long line of buses.

The eighth passage is a recording made of a Fermanagh woman in her forties.

I was born just a couple o' miles out o' Lisnaskea – Like, we always called it 'Lisnaskay' but my childher tells me to pronounce it right. Well, as I was sayin, I have no time for the men of violence or the weemin either – an there's plenty

o' them involved. I believe in keepin myself ti' myself. Och I
don't mean that I go around like a dumb divil – not a bit of it!
But ye'd be well advised these days to be sayin nothin ti'
nobody – like nothin important anyway. I mind the days
well when we had good Prodisan neighbours, the best o'
people. They would come ti' yir house at the time of a wake
– they wouldn come in, ye know, for I think Prodisans are
not too fond of lookin at a corpse. They're not like us, bred
till it, ye might say. They'd come wi' panbread an butther
and two pound o' sugar an they'd say: 'Mebbe this'll help
ye wi' the visitors.' An ano'er thing about Prodisans that
I've always noticed. They nivir say 'God' or utter a wee
ejaculation, like. Like, as God is my judge, I'm nivir done
wi' ejaculations – It's 'Jesus, Mary an Joseph this' an 'Sacred
Heart o' Jesus that' an 'God and his holy mother preserve
us from all harm'. Like Prodisans don't understand. – I'm
not cursin but like they might think I have a dirty tongue.

NOTES

l.1   Many places which end in "-ea" have two pronunciations, the old one 'ay' and the modern one 'ee'.
l.3   Adjectives are frequently used as adverbs, thus 'right'
meaning 'correctly'.
l.4   *weemin* = women
l.7   The speaker probably selected 'to be sayin nothin'
rather than 'to say nothin' to indicate that one must be
constantly on one's guard.
l.9   Many speakers pronounce 'Protestant' as if it were
'Prodison'.
l.16ff   It is true that only Catholics use ejaculations or
short prayers. Many Protestants feel that Catholics are
'taking the name of the Lord in vain'.
l.21   *curse* = swear. The more usual expression for cursing
is 'blinking':

That'n would blink ye as quick as look at you.
l.21   *have a dirty tongue* = swear a lot.

BIBLIOGRAPHY

The following bibliography is not meant to be exhaustive. It will, however, provide further information on the references that occur in the book.

Brendan Adams et al. (eds), *Ulster Dialects: an Introductory Symposium* (Cultra, Co. Down: Ulster Folk Museum, 1964).
Useful background reading. Unsophisticated but of considerable linguistic and folkloristic value.

M.V. Barry (ed), *Aspects of English Dialects in Ireland* (Belfast: Institute of Irish Studies, 1981).
Accurate and scholarly information on a wide range of dialects including those still being influenced by Gaelic.

M.V. Barry and P. Tilling (eds), *G.B. Adams: The English Dialects of Ulster* (Cultra, Co.Down: Ulster Folk and Transport Museum, 1986).
A collection of Brendan Adams's articles written between 1950 and 1980. Adams was a true scholar of dialect. He knew Northern Ireland intimately and wrote about its language with simplicity and understanding.

A.J. Bliss, *Spoken English in Ireland 1600–1740* (Dublin: Dolmen, 1979).
Valuable collection of texts.

K. Boyle and T. Hadden, *Ireland: a Positive Proposal* (Harmondsworth: Penguin, 1985).
Realistic account of how Northern Ireland's problems could be solved by men who understand both Catholic and Protestant aspirations.

J. Braidwood, "Ulster and Elizabethan English", *Ulster Dialects*, ed B. Adams et al.
The most detailed and best researched article on the subject.

J.W. Byers, *Sayings, Proverbs and Humour of Ulster* (Belfast: W. Strain and Sons, 1904).

Extremely interesting and informative monograph. It
tends to be anecdotal but is never inaccurate.

W. Carleton, *Autobiography* (London: MacGibbon and Kee,
1968).

The novelist, Carleton, was born in Northern Ireland in
1794 and vividly recreates in his books the conditions
existing in the country in the nineteenth century. His
description of Northern Ireland in the 1800s is particularly interesting:

> *Merciful God! In what a frightful condition was the country
> at that time. I speak now of the North of Ireland. It was then,
> indeed, the seat of Orange ascendancy and irresponsible
> power. To find a justice of the peace not an Orangeman would
> have been an impossibility. The grand jury room was little
> less than an Orange lodge. There was then no law against an
> Orangeman, and no law for a Papist. I am now writing not
> only that which is well known to be historical truth, but that
> which I have witnessed with my own eyes. (p. 37)*

L.P. Curtis, *Apes and Angels: The Irishman in Victorian Carica-
ture* (Newton Abbot: David and Charles, 1971).

Early examples of prejudice. Interesting to see how similar
stereotypes were applied to the Irish and the Africans.

J.P. Darby, *Northern Ireland: The Background to the Conflict*
(Belfast: Appletree Press, 1983).

A simple account, providing information on the social
and economic background from the time of the Plantation.

I. De Bhaldraithe, *English-Irish Dictionary* (Dublin: 1959).

B. Devlin, *The Price of my Soul* (London: Pan).

The story of Bernadette Devlin's development and con-
tribution to the early Civil Rights Movement.

P. S. Dineen, *Foclóir Gaedhilge agus Béarla*, (Dublin: Irish
Texts Society, 1927).

S.G. Ellis, *Tudor Ireland* (London: Longman, 1985).

Detailed description of the 1470–1603 period.

M. Fraser, *Children in Conflict* (Harmondsworth: Penguin,
1974).

Description of the traumas suffered by children in the
early years of the Troubles.

W. Graham, *The Scots Word Book* (Edinburgh: The Ramsay Head Press, 1980).
  Provides not only a glossary of Scots to English and English to Scots but details on pronunciation, grammar, idiom and spelling.

David Greene, *The Irish Language* (Dublin: Cultural Relations Committee of Ireland, 1966).
  Simple, easy-to-read account of the structures of Gaelic.

R.J. Gregg, *The Scotch-Irish Dialect Boundaries in the Province of Ulster* (Ottawa: Social Science and Humanities Council of Canada, 1985).
  Extremely detailed, Ortonian dialect study of the phonology and vocabulary of the northeastern corner of Northern Ireland.

P. Gregory, *The Ulster Folk* (London: David Nutt, 1912).
— — *Ulster Songs and Ballads* (Dublin: Talbot Press, 1920).
— — *Complete Collected Ulster Ballads* (Belfast: William Mullan and Son, 1959).
  Many of the ballads are sentimental but Gregory has also recorded a number of traditional verses. He represents both Scottish- and Gaelic-influenced English in his dialect verse.

D. Hammond (ed), *Songs of Belfast*, (Dublin: Gilbert Dalton, 1978).
  A useful collection of songs, many illustrating urban attitudes.

J.F. Harbinson, *The Unionist Party 1882–1973* (Belfast: Blackstaff Press, 1973).
  Clear description of the aims and ideals of the Unionist Party before it split into the Unionist and the Democratic Unionist Parties.

John Harris, *Phonological Variation and Change: Studies in Hiberno-English* (Cambridge: University Press, 1985).
  Detailed and accurate description of the phonology of some Belfast speakers.

G. Hill, *Historical Account of the Plantation of Ulster 1608–1620* (Belfast: McCaw, Stevenson and Orr, 1873).
  Useful survey of a crucial period in the history of Northern Ireland.

J.J. Hogan, *The English Language in Ireland* (Dublin: Educational Company of Ireland, 1927).
  A book of considerable historical importance.
N.M. Holmer, *On Some Relics of the Irish Dialect Spoken in the Glens of Antrim* (Uppsala: Uppsala Universitets Arsskrift, 1940).
— — *The Irish Language in Rathlin Island, Co. Antrim* (Dublin: Hodges, Figgis and Co., 1942).
  Extremely useful accounts of areas where Gaelic survived until comparatively recently.
A. Hume, "Origin and Characteristics of the Population of Down and Antrim", *Ulster Journal of Archaeology*, Vol. 1, 1853, pp. 9–26.
— — "The Irish Dialect of the English Language", *Ulster Journal of Archaeology*, Vol. 6, 1858, pp. 47–56.
— — *Origin and Characteristics of the People of Down and Antrim* (Belfast: Newsletter, 1874).
  Stimulating papers. The third is a booklet and deals with very much the same information as the earlier article.
P.J. Joyce, *English as We Speak It in Ireland* (Dublin: Gill and Son, 1910).
  Full of interesting information, much of it anecdotal.
— — *The Origin and History of Irish Names and Places* (Dublin: Gill and Son, 1910).
  Useful, stimulating and always interesting.
F. Kearney, *Songs and Poems of Tyrone* (Omagh: Ulster Herald, no date).
  Thirty pages of verse, from the early twenties. Much of it is sentimental but it contains more Gaelic items than other contemporary dialect material.
A. Lynn, *Random Rhymes frae Cullybackey*, (Belfast: W. & G. Baird, 1911).
  Seems to provide an accurate representation of Ulster Scots at the turn of the century.
F.S.L. Lyons, *Ireland since the Famine* (London: Weidenfeld and Nicholson, 1971).
  Detailed study of the country over a period of 120 years.
W.G. Lyttle, *Betsy Gray; or Hearts of Down: A Tale of Ninety-Eight* (Bangor: W.G. Lyttle, 1888).

A well-written, if under-rated novel, in the Scott tradition. It contains long passages of dialect, most of it depicting Ulster Scots.

John Magee, *Northern Ireland: Crisis and Conflict* (London: Routledge and Kegan Paul, 1974).
Historical texts on Northern Ireland, drawn from a wide range of contemporary sources.

R.L. Marshall, *At Home in Tyrone* (Belfast: The Quota Press, 1944).
Marshall wrote under the pseudonym "Tullyneil" about rural matters in Tyrone. His dialect is excellent.

W.F. Marshall, *Ulster Speaks* (London: BBC, 1936).
Series of well-illustrated talks on Ulster English.

— — *Livin' in Drumlister: The Collected Ballads and Verses of W.F. Marshall* (Belfast: Blackstaff Press, 1983).
The dialect verse written by Marshall over fifty years ago is still regularly recited at ceilis, often in a slightly modified form.

E. McCann, *War and an Irish Town* (London: Pluto Press, 1980).
Evocative description of life in Derry's Bogside from the late 1940s until the recent past, together with socialist solutions to Northern Ireland's problems.

J. McGuffin, *Internment* (Tralee: Anvil, 1973).
On August 9, 1971, Brian Faulkner introduced imprisonment without trial for people suspected of "terrorist" associations. The Act was used almost exclusively against the Catholic population.

R. McIlroy, *A Concise History of the Stuart Period (English and Irish)* (Dublin and Belfast: The Educational Company of Ireland, no date).
Extremely significant book in the education of Catholics in the early 1920s.

I. McLeod, *The Pocket Guide to Scottish Words* (Glasgow: Richard Drew Publishing, 1986).
An excellent little glossary. Many of the items listed are also current in parts of Northern Ireland.

J. Milroy, *Regional Accents of English: Belfast* (Belfast: Blackstaff Press, 1981).
Clear, simple account of Belfast speech.

L. Milroy, *Language and Social Networks* (Oxford: Basil Blackwell, 1980).
Useful account of working-class speech in Belfast.

C. Mish et al., *Webster's Ninth New Collegiate Dictionary* (Springfield, Mass.: Merriam-Webster Inc., 1983).

F. Molloy, *No Mate for the Magpie* (London: Virago Press, 1985).

T.W. Moody, *The Ulster Question 1603–1973* (Dublin: Mercier Press, 1974).
A very readable survey of the period.

Dervla Murphy, *Changing the Problem: Post-Forum Reflections* (Mullingar: Lilliput Press, 1984).
Examines the options, including independence, for Northern Ireland.

M. Murphy, *Tyrone Folk Quest* (Belfast: Blackstaff Press, 1973).

— — *Now You're Talking...* (Belfast: Blackstaff Press, 1975).

— — *Mountainy Crack* (Belfast: Blackstaff Press, 1976).
Much of Murphy's work was done in the west of Northern Ireland and offers an interesting contrast to the work written or collected in the east.

New Ireland Forum Studies, *Report of the New Ireland Forum* (Dublin: Stationery Office, 1983).

— — *The Cost of Violence Arising from the Northern Ireland Crisis since 1969* (Dublin: Stationery Office, 1983).
Useful information on Northern Ireland mainly from the point of view of Eire and Northern Ireland Nationalists.

D. O Donnchada, *An Ráleabhar Gaeilge: The Irish Phrase Book* (Dublin: Mercier Press, 1986).

P. O'Malley, *The Uncivil War* (Belfast: Blackstaff Press, 1984).
Clear account of the current Troubles in Northern Ireland.

D. O'Muirithe, *The English Language in Ireland* (Cork: Mercier, 1977).
Relates mostly to southern Hiberno-English but allows useful comparisons to be made.

M. O'Neill, *Songs of the Glens of Antrim* (Edinburgh: Blackwood and Son, 1900).

Many of the items reveal a Gaelic, rather than a Lowland Scots influence.

C.T. Onions, *The Oxford Dictionary of English Etymology* (Oxford: Oxford University Press, 1966).

H. Orton et al., *Linguistic Atlas of England* (London: Croom Helm, 1977).

R.D. Osborne, *Religion and Educational Qualifications in Northern Ireland*, Research Paper 8 (Belfast: Fair Employment Agency, 1985).
This non-sectarian publication indicates a strong correlation between one's religion and one's prospects for employment.

D. Patterson, *The Provincialisms of Belfast and Surrounding Districts Pointed Out and Corrected* (Belfast: Mayne, 1860).
Interesting to see how many of these "provincialisms" are still current.

T.G. Patterson, *Country Cracks* (Dundalk: Dundalgan Press, 1939).
Excellent collection of short stories from Co. Armagh in a good approximation to the dialect.

W.H. Patterson, *A Glossary of Words in Use in the Counties of Antrim and Down* (London: English Dialect Society, 1880).
Many of the items listed can be found in the verse of the same period.

R. Rowley, *Ballads of Mourne* (Dundalk: W. Tempest, 1940).
Many of the items enclosed reflect the dialect of the 1920s.

R. Swift and S. Gilley (eds), *The Irish in the Victorian City* (London: Croom Helm, 1986).
Very interesting set of essays on the Irish immigrants in the cities of mainland Britain.

Loreto Todd, *Base-form and Substratum: Two Case Studies of English in Contact* (Leeds: Unpublished Ph.D. thesis, 1975).
Provides recorded data from Northern Ireland and compares and contrasts a dialect and a pidgin.

— — *The Language of Irish Literature* (London: Macmillan, 1989.)

Attempts to show how one's appreciation of Irish Literature can be deepened by a knowledge of the varieties of
English employed in Ireland.

H. Wagner and C. O Boyle, *Linguistic Atlas and Survey of
Irish Dialects* (Dublin: Institute for Advanced Studies,
1969).

A. Warrack, *A Scots Dialect Dictionary* (Edinburgh: W. and
R. Chambers, 1911).

D. Watt (ed), *The Constitution of Northern Ireland: Problems
and Prospects* (London: Heinemann, 1981).

A lucid but not very optimistic survey.

J. Wright, *The English Dialect Dictionary* (London: Henry
Froude, 1896–1905).

The most detailed data still available on British dialects
generally.